Best of Bridge

Weekday Suppers

All-New Easy Everyday Recipes

Robert
ROSE

Best of Bridge Weekday Suppers

Text copyright © 2018 Sylvia Kong and Emily Richards
Photographs copyright © 2018 Robert Rose Inc.
Cover and text design copyright © 2018 Robert Rose Inc.

For complete cataloguing information, see page 288.

Disclaimer
The recipes in this book have been carefully tested by our kitchen and our tasters. To the best of our knowledge, they are safe and nutritious for ordinary use and users. For those people with food or other allergies, or who have special food requirements or health issues, please read the suggested contents of each recipe carefully and determine whether or not they may create a problem for you. All recipes are used at the risk of the consumer.

We cannot be responsible for any hazards, loss or damage that may occur as a result of any recipe use.

For those with special needs, allergies, requirements or health problems, in the event of any doubt, please contact your medical adviser prior to the use of any recipe.

Design and production: Kevin Cockburn/PageWave Graphics Inc.
Editor: Sue Sumeraj
Recipe editor: Jennifer MacKenzie
Proofreader: Kelly Jones
Indexer: Gillian Watts
Photographer: Matt Johannsson, Reflector Inc.
Food stylist: Michael Elliott
Prop stylist: Charlene Erricson

Cover image: Curried Turkey Pot Pies (page 192)

The publisher gratefully acknowledges the financial support of our publishing program by the Government of Canada through the Canada Book Fund.

Canadä

Published by Robert Rose Inc.
120 Eglinton Avenue East, Suite 800, Toronto, Ontario, Canada M4P 1E2
Tel: (416) 322-6552 Fax: (416) 322-6936
www.robertrose.ca

Printed and bound in China

1 2 3 4 5 6 7 8 9 PPLS 26 25 24 23 22 21 20 19 18

CONTENTS

INTRODUCTION

THE IDEA OF PREPARING WEEKNIGHT SUPPERS CAN BE DAUNTING — WHO HASN'T ARRIVED HOME WITH GLAZED EYES TO FIND A HOUSE FULL OF STARVING PEOPLE WAITING TO BE FED? THIS COOKBOOK PROVIDES YOU WITH SIMPLE, DELICIOUS RECIPES THAT WILL KEEP YOU FROM HAVING CEREAL FOR DINNER OR OPTING FOR TAKEOUT (AGAIN!). YOU'LL FIND A VARIETY OF QUICK-TO-PREPARE MEAL OPTIONS USING INTERNATIONAL FLAVORS, ALONG WITH FAMILIAR CLASSICS THAT ARE SURE TO SATISFY YOUR BUSY FAMILY. YOU PROBABLY ALREADY HAVE MANY OF THE INGREDIENTS IN YOUR CUPBOARD AND CAN FIND THE REST AT YOUR LOCAL SUPERMARKET. THESE MEALS WILL CARRY YOU THROUGH ALL THE SEASONS, AND IT'S EASY TO INCORPORATE LOCAL MEAT AND PRODUCE INTO THEM, WHETHER YOU SHOP AT A FARMERS' MARKET OR GROCERY STORE.

WE'VE PROVIDED SIMPLIFIED METHODS TO SPEED UP COOKING, USING SHEET PAN, PRESSURE COOKER AND ONE-POT RECIPES TO HELP STREAMLINE WEEKDAY MEAL PREPARATION. WE RECOGNIZE THAT YOU HAVE A HECTIC SCHEDULE AND DON'T ALWAYS HAVE TIME TO MAKE EVERYTHING FROM SCRATCH, SO TO HELP JUMP-START YOUR MEALS, WE'VE INCLUDED A NUMBER OF FOOLPROOF RECIPES THAT TAKE ADVANTAGE OF CONVENIENT STORE-BOUGHT COOKED CHICKEN, BOTTLED PASTES AND SAUCES, AND FROZEN FILLED PASTAS. MANY OF THE RECIPES MAKE ENOUGH TO GIVE YOU LEFTOVERS TO TUCK IN TO AT LUNCHTIME THE NEXT DAY. BE SURE TO INCLUDE FAMILY MEMBERS (ESPECIALLY THOSE KIDS) IN MEAL PREPARATION; YOU'LL BE SPENDING QUALITY TIME TOGETHER AND SHARING VALUABLE LIFE SKILLS AT THE SAME TIME.

WEEKDAY SUPPERS INCLUDES THE TRADITIONAL FULL MEALS YOU EXPECT, BUT ALSO PROVIDES CHAPTERS FULL OF RECIPES FOR HEARTY SALADS, SOUPS, SANDWICHES AND MEATLESS OPTIONS THAT ARE SATISFYING AND SUBSTANTIAL ENOUGH FOR DINNER. IF YOUR FAMILY HAS LARGER APPETITES, SIMPLY ADD YOUR FAVORITE COOKED VEGETABLES OR A SIDE SALAD TO ROUND OUT THE MEAL. AND OF COURSE, WE KNOW YOU LIKE THE OCCASIONAL TREAT TO END YOUR MEAL ON A SWEET NOTE, SO WE'VE GOT YOU COVERED THERE, TOO.

AS HOME ECONOMISTS AND THE NEWEST MEMBERS OF THE BEST OF BRIDGE FAMILY, WE HOPE TO INSPIRE YOU WITH OUR TASTY GO-TO RECIPES TO HELP GET YOU THROUGH THE SUPPERTIME CRUNCH. BE SURE TO DOG-EAR YOUR FAVORITES AND KEEP THE INGREDIENTS ON HAND TO MAKE OVER AND OVER AGAIN. VISIT OUR WEBSITE AT BESTOFBRIDGE.COM AND LET US KNOW WHAT YOU'RE COOKING AT HOME, TOO — WE CAN ALWAYS USE MORE WEEKNIGHT SUPPER IDEAS!

ENJOY!

— SYLVIA AND EMILY

MEASURING TIPS

HERE ARE SOME TIPS AND HELPFUL HINTS ON MEASURING INGREDIENTS FOR YOUR BEST OF BRIDGE RECIPES:

* THERE ARE DRY AND LIQUID MEASURING CUPS. NESTING DRY MEASURING CUPS COME IN METAL OR PLASTIC AND ARE USED TO MEASURE DRY INGREDIENTS LIKE FLOUR, SUGAR, OATMEAL AND BREAD CRUMBS. BUT THEY ARE ALSO SUPER-HELPFUL FOR MEASURING OTHER INGREDIENTS, SUCH AS SALSA, SOUR CREAM AND YOGURT! WHY, YOU ASK? BECAUSE YOU CAN LEVEL THEM OFF AT THE TOP TO GET AN ACCURATE MEASURE. SO KEEP THOSE GLASS OR PLASTIC SPOUTED MEASURING CUPS FOR LIQUIDS LIKE MILK, OIL, BROTH AND WATER.

* MEASURING FLOUR ACCURATELY IS THE KEY TO SUCCESS FOR MANY DISHES, ESPECIALLY BAKED GOODS. SIMPLY SPOON THE FLOUR INTO THE DRY MEASURING CUP WITHOUT TAPPING IT DOWN. USE THE BACK OF A KNIFE (OR SOMETHING STRAIGHT) TO LEVEL OFF THE FLOUR, AND THERE YOU HAVE IT: AN ACCURATE AMOUNT OF FLOUR, READY FOR USE.

* MEASURING SPOONS CAN BE MADE OF EITHER METAL OR PLASTIC AND ARE USED FOR BOTH DRY AND LIQUID INGREDIENTS.

KEEP AN EYE OUT FOR MORE TIPS ONLINE AND IN UPCOMING COOKBOOKS!

SUPPER SOUPS

PRESSURE COOKER
BEEF AND BARLEY SOUP

*HEARTY AND FILLING, THIS SOUP COOKS UP FASTER
THAN THE STOVETOP METHOD.*

1 1/2 LBS	BONELESS BEEF BLADE OR CHUCK, CUT INTO 1-INCH (2.5 CM) CUBES	750 G
1/2 TSP	SALT (APPROX.)	2 ML
1/2 TSP	BLACK PEPPER (APPROX.)	2 ML
2 TBSP	CANOLA OIL, DIVIDED	30 ML
3	LARGE CARROTS, DICED	3
3	CELERY STALKS, CHOPPED	3
1	LARGE ONION, DICED	1
2 CUPS	SLICED MUSHROOMS	500 ML
2 TBSP	TOMATO PASTE	30 ML
3	GARLIC CLOVES, MINCED	3
3/4 CUP	PEARL OR POT BARLEY	175 ML
1	BAY LEAF	1
2 TSP	DRIED THYME	10 ML
1/2 TSP	CRUSHED DRIED ROSEMARY	2 ML
6 CUPS	READY-TO-USE REDUCED-SODIUM BEEF BROTH	1.5 L
1 TSP	SOY SAUCE	5 ML
1 CUP	FROZEN PEAS, THAWED	250 ML

SPRINKLE BEEF WITH SALT AND PEPPER. IN PRESSURE
COOKER, HEAT 1 TBSP (15 ML) OIL OVER MEDIUM-HIGH
HEAT. WORKING IN BATCHES, BROWN BEEF ALL OVER AND
TRANSFER TO A BOWL. WITHOUT CLEANING COOKER, ADD
REMAINING OIL, CARROTS, CELERY, ONION, MUSHROOMS
AND TOMATO PASTE. COOK, STIRRING, FOR 5 MINUTES.
SCRAPE UP ANY BROWNED BITS ON BOTTOM OF POT.

ADD GARLIC AND COOK, STIRRING, FOR 30 SECONDS. STIR IN BEEF AND ANY ACCUMULATED JUICES, BARLEY, BAY LEAF, THYME, ROSEMARY, BROTH AND SOY SAUCE. LOCK LID AND BRING COOKER UP TO FULL PRESSURE OVER HIGH HEAT. REDUCE HEAT TO MEDIUM-LOW, JUST TO MAINTAIN EVEN PRESSURE, AND COOK FOR 25 MINUTES. REMOVE FROM HEAT AND LET PRESSURE DROP NATURALLY. DISCARD BAY LEAF. STIR IN PEAS. SEASON TO TASTE WITH SALT AND PEPPER. SERVES 6 TO 8.

TIP: HULLED BARLEY IS THE WHOLE-GRAIN FORM. POT BARLEY HAS SOME OF THE OUTER HUSK AND BRAN LAYER REMOVED, WHICH MAKES IT SOFTER IN TEXTURE AND SPEEDS UP COOKING TIME. PEARL BARLEY IS MORE PROCESSED AND IS POLISHED TO REMOVE ALL OF THE HULL AND THE BRAN; LIKE POT BARLEY, IT COOKS FASTER THAN HULLED.

TIP: THIS SOUP CAN BE STORED IN AIRTIGHT CONTAINERS IN THE REFRIGERATOR FOR UP TO 4 DAYS.

AN APRON IS JUST A CAPE WORN BACKWARDS.

VIETNAMESE BEEF NOODLE SOUP

THIS SHORTCUT VERSION OF PHO, VIETNAM'S BELOVED COMFORT FOOD, COMES TOGETHER QUICKLY FOR A SATISFYING BOWL OF GOODNESS. USE THAI BASIL, IF IT IS AVAILABLE, FOR A MORE AUTHENTIC FLAVOR.

1 TBSP	CANOLA OIL	15 ML
3	GARLIC CLOVES, MINCED	3
1	ONION, THINLY SLICED	1
1 TBSP	GRATED FRESH GINGER	15 ML
1/2 TSP	CHINESE FIVE-SPICE POWDER	2 ML
8 CUPS	READY-TO-USE BEEF BROTH	2 L
2 TBSP	HOISIN SAUCE	30 ML
2 TBSP	FISH SAUCE	30 ML
8 OZ	DRIED FLAT RICE NOODLES	250 G
1 LB	BONELESS BEEF SIRLOIN STEAK, CUT INTO VERY THIN SLICES	500 G
2	GREEN ONIONS, THINLY SLICED	2
2 CUPS	BEAN SPROUTS	500 ML
1 CUP	CHOPPED FRESH CILANTRO	250 ML
1/2 CUP	CHOPPED FRESH MINT OR BASIL	125 ML
2	LIMES, QUARTERED	2
1	JALAPEÑO PEPPER, THINLY SLICED (OPTIONAL)	1
	SRIRACHA	

IN A LARGE POT, HEAT OIL OVER MEDIUM HEAT. SAUTÉ GARLIC, ONION AND GINGER FOR 5 MINUTES. ADD FIVE-SPICE POWDER, BROTH, HOISIN SAUCE AND FISH SAUCE; BRING TO A BOIL. BOIL FOR 5 MINUTES. ADD NOODLES AND BOIL FOR 5 MINUTES. STIR IN BEEF AND BOIL UNTIL

NOODLES ARE TENDER AND BEEF IS HOT. (BE CAREFUL NOT TO OVERCOOK NOODLES OR THEY WILL BECOME MUSHY.) LADLE SOUP INTO LARGE BOWLS AND SPRINKLE WITH GREEN ONIONS, BEAN SPROUTS, CILANTRO AND MINT. SERVE WITH LIME QUARTERS, JALAPEÑO SLICES (IF USING) AND SRIRACHA. SERVES 4 TO 6.

TIP: PLACE BEEF IN FREEZER FOR 15 MINUTES BEFORE SLICING; THIS MAKES IT EASIER TO SLICE THE MEAT VERY THINLY.

I DON'T NEED AN INSPIRATIONAL QUOTE, I NEED COFFEE.

MARIA'S MEATBALL CABBAGE SOUP

WHEN EMILY'S COUSIN MARIA FIRST MADE THIS SOUP, SHE WASN'T QUITE SURE WHAT TO EXPECT. BUT TO QUOTE HER, "IT WAS SURPRISINGLY DELICIOUS!" CAN'T MESS WITH THOSE WORDS.

1 LB	GROUND TURKEY	500 G
1/4 CUP	SEASONED DRY BREAD CRUMBS	60 ML
1/4 CUP	GRATED PARMESAN CHEESE	60 ML
1/4 TSP	SALT	1 ML
1/4 TSP	BLACK PEPPER	1 ML
1 TBSP	CANOLA OIL	15 ML
2	GARLIC CLOVES, MINCED	2
1	ONION, SLICED	1
1	RED BELL PEPPER, SLICED	1
1	BAG (12 OZ/340 G) CABBAGE COLESLAW MIX	1
1/2 TSP	FENNEL SEEDS, CRUSHED	2 ML
4 CUPS	READY-TO-USE VEGETABLE OR CHICKEN BROTH OR TURKEY STOCK	1 L

IN A BOWL, USING YOUR HANDS, COMBINE TURKEY, BREAD CRUMBS, CHEESE, SALT AND PEPPER. FORM INTO 16 MEATBALLS; SET ASIDE ON A PLATE. IN A MEDIUM POT, HEAT OIL OVER MEDIUM HEAT. SAUTÉ GARLIC, ONION AND RED PEPPER FOR 2 MINUTES OR UNTIL STARTING TO SOFTEN. STIR IN COLESLAW MIX AND FENNEL SEEDS AND SAUTÉ FOR ABOUT 3 MINUTES OR UNTIL VEGETABLES ARE SOFTENED. STIR IN BROTH AND BRING TO A BOIL. REDUCE HEAT TO A SIMMER AND, USING A SLOTTED SPOON, SLOWLY ADD MEATBALLS. STIR GENTLY AND

SIMMER FOR ABOUT 15 MINUTES OR UNTIL MEATBALLS ARE NO LONGER PINK INSIDE AND VEGETABLES ARE TENDER. SERVES 4.

TIP: SUBSTITUTE OTHER GROUND MEATS, SUCH AS CHICKEN, PORK OR BEEF, FOR THE TURKEY. FOR A ZIPPY ALTERNATIVE, TRY HOT ITALIAN SAUSAGE (BULK OR CASINGS REMOVED).

SLOW COOKER VARIATION: OMIT THE OIL AND SKIP SAUTÉING THE GARLIC, ONION AND RED PEPPER. IN A 4- TO 6-QUART SLOW COOKER, COMBINE GARLIC, ONION, RED PEPPER, COLESLAW MIX AND FENNEL SEEDS. LAY MEATBALLS ON TOP AND POUR IN BROTH. COVER AND COOK ON LOW FOR 4 HOURS.

THE MOST DANGEROUS ANIMAL IN THE WORLD IS A SILENT SMILING WOMAN.

SAUSAGE, RED LENTIL AND KALE SOUP

A HEARTY, RICH SOUP THAT'S PERFECT FOR A CHILLY DAY. ADDING THE GREENS JUST BEFORE SERVING KEEPS THE COLOR VIBRANT. SERVE GARNISHED WITH PARMESAN CHEESE, AND WITH CRUSTY BUNS ON THE SIDE.

1 TBSP	CANOLA OIL	15 ML
8 OZ	ITALIAN SAUSAGE (BULK OR CASINGS REMOVED)	250 G
2	CELERY STALKS, DICED	2
2	CARROTS, DICED	2
1	ONION, DICED	1
1	GARLIC CLOVE, MINCED	1
1/4 TSP	HOT PEPPER FLAKES	1 ML
1 CUP	DRIED RED LENTILS, SORTED AND RINSED	250 ML
2	BAY LEAVES	2
1	CAN (28 OZ/796 ML) DICED TOMATOES, WITH JUICE	1
5 CUPS	WATER	1.25 L
2 CUPS	SHREDDED TRIMMED KALE LEAVES	500 ML

IN A LARGE POT, HEAT OIL OVER MEDIUM HEAT. ADD SAUSAGE AND COOK, BREAKING IT UP WITH A SPOON, UNTIL BROWNED. ADD CELERY, CARROTS, ONION, GARLIC AND HOT PEPPER FLAKES; COOK, STIRRING, FOR 5 MINUTES. ADD LENTILS, BAY LEAVES, TOMATOES WITH JUICE AND WATER; BRING TO A BOIL. REDUCE HEAT, COVER AND SIMMER FOR ABOUT 25 MINUTES OR UNTIL LENTILS AND VEGETABLES ARE TENDER. DISCARD BAY LEAVES. STIR IN KALE AND COOK FOR ABOUT 5 MINUTES OR UNTIL TENDER. SERVES 8.

CREAMY CELERY SOUP WITH HAM

NOTHING BEATS A BOWL OF COMFORTING CREAMY SOUP. THIS ONE IS A FAVORITE OF SYLVIA'S BROTHER.

1/4 CUP	CANOLA OIL	60 ML
8	CELERY STALKS, CHOPPED	8
1	GARLIC CLOVE, MINCED	1
1	POTATO, PEELED AND DICED	1
1 CUP	CHOPPED ONION	250 ML
1 TSP	DRIED THYME	5 ML
1/2 TSP	BLACK PEPPER	2 ML
2 TBSP	ALL-PURPOSE FLOUR	30 ML
4 CUPS	READY-TO-USE CHICKEN BROTH	1 L
1 CUP	CHOPPED COOKED HAM	250 ML
1 CUP	MILK OR HALF-AND-HALF (10%) CREAM	250 ML

IN A MEDIUM POT, HEAT OIL OVER MEDIUM-HIGH HEAT. SAUTÉ CELERY, GARLIC, POTATO, ONION, THYME AND PEPPER FOR 8 MINUTES. ADD FLOUR AND STIR UNTIL ABSORBED, ABOUT 1 MINUTE. GRADUALLY STIR IN BROTH AND BRING TO A BOIL. REDUCE HEAT TO MEDIUM, COVER AND COOK FOR ABOUT 15 MINUTES OR UNTIL VEGETABLES ARE TENDER. STIR IN HAM AND MILK; COVER AND COOK UNTIL HEATED THROUGH. SERVES 4 TO 6.

TIP: THIS RECIPE IS A GREAT WAY TO USE UP CELERY THAT'S BEGINNING TO FADE IN THE REFRIGERATOR.

TIP: THE REFRIGERATED SOUP KEEPS WELL FOR UP TO 4 DAYS.

BROCCOLI AND BACON CHOWDER

THIS SIMPLE SUPPER SOUP IS AN EASY ONE TO PUT TOGETHER AND GET SOME VEGGIES INTO YOUR FAMILY. WHEN BROCCOLI IS ON SALE, STOCK UP AND MAKE THE SOUP. FREEZE IT AND ENJOY LATER, WHEN YOU DON'T WANT TO DO MUCH PREP WORK FOR DINNER.

6	SLICES BACON, CHOPPED	6
1	ONION, CHOPPED	1
1	CELERY STALK, CHOPPED	1
1	HEAD BROCCOLI, CHOPPED (ABOUT 6 CUPS/1.5 L FLORETS AND TRIMMED STALKS)	1
1	BAKING POTATO, PEELED AND CHOPPED	1
1/2 TSP	DRIED THYME	2 ML
1/2 TSP	BLACK PEPPER	2 ML
1/4 TSP	SALT	1 ML
3 CUPS	READY-TO-USE VEGETABLE OR CHICKEN BROTH	750 ML
1 CUP	LIGHT (5%) CREAM OR WHOLE MILK	250 ML
3/4 CUP	SHREDDED SHARP (OLD) CHEDDAR CHEESE	175 ML

IN A MEDIUM POT, FRY BACON OVER MEDIUM-HIGH HEAT UNTIL CRISP. USING A SLOTTED SPOON, REMOVE BACON TO A PLATE LINED WITH PAPER TOWEL; SET ASIDE. IN THE SAME POT, OVER MEDIUM HEAT, ADD ONION, CELERY AND BROCCOLI, STIRRING TO COAT WITH BACON FAT. SAUTÉ FOR 3 MINUTES. STIR IN POTATO, THYME, PEPPER, SALT, BROTH AND CREAM; BRING TO A SIMMER. REDUCE HEAT, COVER AND SIMMER GENTLY FOR 20 MINUTES OR UNTIL

VEGETABLES ARE VERY TENDER. USING AN IMMERSION BLENDER, PURÉE SOUP (OR PURÉE IN BATCHES IN A BLENDER AND RETURN TO POT). STIR IN BACON AND COOK FOR ABOUT 5 MINUTES TO BLEND THE FLAVORS. SERVE SPRINKLED WITH CHEESE, OR STIR IT RIGHT INTO THE SOUP. SERVES 4 TO 6.

TIP: IF YOU WANT TO COOK UP A LITTLE EXTRA BACON, IT ADDS A NICE CRUNCH ON TOP OF THE SOUP.

VARIATION: SUBSTITUTE CAULIFLOWER FOR THE BROCCOLI, OR MIX THEM TOGETHER.

DON'T GO BACON MY HEART.

HEARTY MUSHROOM, BACON AND QUINOA SOUP

QUINOA HELPS THICKEN THIS RICH, FLAVORFUL SOUP.

8	SLICES BACON, CHOPPED	8
I TSP	CANOLA OIL	5 ML
I CUP	FINELY CHOPPED ONION	250 ML
2	GARLIC CLOVES, MINCED	2
2	CELERY STALKS, CHOPPED	2
6 CUPS	READY-TO-USE CHICKEN BROTH	1.5 L
5 CUPS	SLICED MUSHROOMS (ABOUT 10 OZ/300 G)	1.25 L
$2/3$ CUP	QUINOA, RINSED AND DRAINED	150 ML
$1\frac{1}{2}$ TSP	DRIED THYME	7 ML
$\frac{1}{2}$ TSP	SALT	2 ML
$\frac{1}{2}$ TSP	BLACK PEPPER	2 ML
$1\frac{1}{2}$ CUPS	MILK	375 ML

IN A LARGE POT, FRY BACON OVER MEDIUM-HIGH HEAT UNTIL CRISP. USING A SLOTTED SPOON, REMOVE BACON TO A PLATE LINED WITH PAPER TOWEL; SET ASIDE. IN THE SAME POT, OVER MEDIUM HEAT, ADD OIL, ONION, GARLIC AND CELERY; SAUTÉ FOR 7 MINUTES. ADD BROTH AND BRING TO A BOIL. STIR IN MUSHROOMS, QUINOA, THYME, SALT AND PEPPER. REDUCE HEAT, COVER AND SIMMER FOR 15 MINUTES OR UNTIL VEGETABLES AND QUINOA ARE TENDER. STIR IN MILK AND SIMMER UNTIL HEATED THROUGH. SERVE TOPPED WITH BACON. SERVES 6.

TIP: THE MILK CAN BE REPLACED WITH ANY NONDAIRY MILK.

Vietnamese Beef Noodle Soup (page 10)

Chicken Orzo Soup (page 19)

Grilled Steak and Potato Salad (page 34)

Grilled Chicken, Barley and Corn Salad Bowl (page 40)

CHICKEN ORZO SOUP

THE LEMON ADDS A ZESTY FRESHNESS TO THIS
VERSION OF COMFORTING CHICKEN NOODLE SOUP.

2 TBSP	CANOLA OIL	30 ML
I LB	BONELESS SKINLESS CHICKEN THIGHS, CUT INTO SMALL CUBES	500 G
I CUP	FINELY DICED ONION	250 ML
3	GARLIC CLOVES, MINCED	3
2 CUPS	DICED CARROTS	500 ML
2 CUPS	DICED CELERY STALKS	500 ML
1/2 TSP	DRIED THYME	2 ML
1/2 TSP	BLACK PEPPER (APPROX.)	2 ML
1/2 TSP	CRUMBLED DRIED ROSEMARY	2 ML
2	BAY LEAVES	2
6 CUPS	READY-TO-USE CHICKEN BROTH	1.5 L
I CUP	DRIED ORZO PASTA	250 ML
3 TBSP	CHOPPED FRESH PARSLEY	45 ML
I TSP	GRATED LEMON ZEST	5 ML
3 TBSP	LEMON JUICE	45 ML
	SALT TO TASTE	

IN A LARGE POT, HEAT OIL OVER MEDIUM-HIGH HEAT.
COOK CHICKEN AND ONION, STIRRING OCCASIONALLY,
FOR 7 TO 10 MINUTES OR UNTIL CHICKEN IS BROWNED
ON ALL SIDES. STIR IN GARLIC, CARROTS, CELERY, THYME,
PEPPER, ROSEMARY AND BAY LEAVES; COOK, STIRRING, FOR
5 MINUTES. ADD BROTH AND BRING TO A BOIL. ADD ORZO,
REDUCE HEAT AND SIMMER FOR 10 MINUTES OR UNTIL
ORZO IS TENDER. DISCARD BAY LEAVES. STIR IN PARSLEY,
LEMON ZEST AND LEMON JUICE. SEASON WITH SALT AND
PEPPER. SERVES 6.

CHICKEN TORTILLA SOUP

EMILY'S FRIEND KATE CREATED THIS VERSION OF A RESTAURANT CLASSIC. IT HAS A SPICY KICK AND EASY GARNISHES THAT YOUR FAMILY WILL LOVE.

1 TBSP	CANOLA OIL	15 ML
3	GARLIC CLOVES, MINCED	3
2	TOMATOES, CHOPPED	2
1	ONION, CHOPPED	1
2 TSP	ANCHO CHILE POWDER	10 ML
1/3 CUP	CHOPPED FRESH CILANTRO, DIVIDED	75 ML
2 CUPS	SHREDDED COOKED CHICKEN	500 ML
4 CUPS	READY-TO-USE CHICKEN BROTH	1 L
1/2 TSP	GRATED LIME ZEST	2 ML
1	LARGE WHOLE WHEAT TORTILLA	1
	NONSTICK COOKING SPRAY	
1	AVOCADO, CUBED	1
	FETA CHEESE AND LIME WEDGES (OPTIONAL)	

IN A MEDIUM POT, HEAT OIL OVER MEDIUM HEAT. SAUTÉ GARLIC, TOMATOES, ONION AND CHILE POWDER FOR ABOUT 5 MINUTES OR UNTIL ONION IS SOFTENED. STIR IN HALF THE CILANTRO UNTIL COATED. STIR IN CHICKEN AND BROTH; REDUCE HEAT AND SIMMER FOR 10 MINUTES. STIR IN LIME ZEST AND REMAINING CILANTRO.

MEANWHILE, PREHEAT OVEN TO 400°F (200°C). CUT TORTILLA INTO LONG 1/2-INCH (1 CM) THICK STRIPS AND PLACE ON A PARCHMENT-LINED BAKING SHEET. SPRAY LIGHTLY WITH COOKING SPRAY, TOSS TO COAT EVENLY AND SPREAD IN A SINGLE LAYER. TOAST IN OVEN FOR ABOUT 8 MINUTES OR UNTIL GOLDEN.

LADLE SOUP INTO BOWLS AND TOP WITH TORTILLA STRIPS AND AVOCADO. IF DESIRED, GARNISH WITH CHEESE AND LIME WEDGES. SERVES 4.

TIP: IF YOUR FAMILY WOULD ENJOY A MILDER VERSION, SIMPLY REDUCE THE CHILE POWDER TO 1 TSP (5 ML).

TIP: THIS SOUP MAKES GREAT PICNIC FARE. JUST PACK THE GARNISHES SEPARATELY FOR A FUN GET-TOGETHER WITH FRIENDS.

WHAT'S THE MOST MUSICAL PART OF A CHICKEN?
THE DRUMSTICK!

CHUNKY CHICKEN AND BUTTERNUT SQUASH SOUP

WITH HINTS OF SPICES AND HERBS, THIS SOUP IS MILD ENOUGH FOR YOUNG PALATES AND TASTY ENOUGH FOR ADULTS. FOR AN ADDED KICK OF FLAVOR, ADD A SPLASH OF HOT PEPPER SAUCE.

1	SMALL BUTTERNUT SQUASH (ABOUT 2 LBS/1 KG)	1
1 TBSP	CANOLA OIL	15 ML
4	GARLIC CLOVES, MINCED	4
1	LARGE ONION, CHOPPED	1
2	BONELESS SKINLESS CHICKEN BREASTS (ABOUT 1 LB/500 G TOTAL), CHOPPED	2
2 TSP	DRIED OREGANO	10 ML
1 TSP	SMOKED OR SPANISH PAPRIKA	5 ML
1/4 TSP	SALT	1 ML
1/4 TSP	BLACK PEPPER	1 ML
1/4 TSP	GROUND CINNAMON	1 ML
5 CUPS	READY-TO-USE CHICKEN OR VEGETABLE BROTH	1.25 L
2 TBSP	CHOPPED FRESH CILANTRO	30 ML

CUT SQUASH IN HALF CROSSWISE AND PEEL. REMOVE SEEDS AND CHOP SQUASH TO GET ABOUT 5 CUPS (1.25 L). IN A MEDIUM POT, HEAT OIL OVER MEDIUM HEAT. SAUTÉ GARLIC AND ONION FOR 3 MINUTES. ADD CHICKEN AND STIR TO COAT. ADD SQUASH, OREGANO, PAPRIKA, SALT, PEPPER AND CINNAMON; COOK, STIRRING, FOR 2 MINUTES. STIR IN BROTH AND BRING TO A BOIL. REDUCE HEAT, COVER AND SIMMER FOR ABOUT 20 MINUTES OR UNTIL SQUASH IS TENDER AND CHICKEN IS NO LONGER PINK INSIDE. STIR IN CILANTRO. SERVES 6 TO 8.

SMOKED TURKEY LENTIL SOUP

WE'RE ALWAYS LOOKING FOR A RELIABLE GO-TO RECIPE, AND THIS ONE FITS THE BILL. QUICK-COOKING RED LENTILS ARE PERFECT FOR A SIMPLE, COMFORTING SOUP FOR ANY WEEKNIGHT. SERVE WITH SOME CRUSTY BREAD AND A SALAD.

2 TBSP	CANOLA OIL	30 ML
3	CELERY STALKS, DICED	3
2	CARROTS, DICED	2
1	SMALL ONION, DICED	1
1	GARLIC CLOVE, MINCED	1
1	BAY LEAF	1
1 CUP	DRIED RED LENTILS, SORTED AND RINSED	250 ML
1 TSP	DRIED ITALIAN SEASONING	5 ML
5 CUPS	READY-TO-USE CHICKEN BROTH	1.25 L
1½ CUPS	CUBED DELI SMOKED TURKEY	375 ML

IN A MEDIUM POT, HEAT OIL OVER MEDIUM-HIGH HEAT. SAUTÉ CELERY, CARROTS AND ONION FOR 8 MINUTES. STIR IN GARLIC, BAY LEAF, LENTILS, ITALIAN SEASONING AND BROTH; BRING TO A BOIL. REDUCE HEAT, COVER AND SIMMER FOR 15 MINUTES. ADD TURKEY, COVER AND SIMMER FOR 10 MINUTES OR UNTIL LENTILS ARE TENDER. DISCARD BAY LEAF. SERVES 4 TO 5.

TIP: HAM CAN BE SUBSTITUTED FOR THE TURKEY.

TURKEY CHILI SOUP

CHILI IS A FAVORITE IN MANY HOUSEHOLDS AND A GREAT EVERYDAY SUPPER. SO TAKE THAT CHILI AND MAKE IT A SOUP! EMILY'S KIDS LOVE THEIR BOWLS WITH A HEAVY SPRINKLE OF AGED CHEDDAR.

1 TBSP	CANOLA OIL	15 ML
4	GARLIC CLOVES, MINCED	4
1	LARGE ONION, CHOPPED	1
1 TBSP	CHILI POWDER	15 ML
1 TSP	GROUND CUMIN	5 ML
1 TSP	DRIED OREGANO	5 ML
1 LB	GROUND TURKEY	500 G
2 TBSP	TOMATO PASTE	30 ML
1	YELLOW OR GREEN BELL PEPPER, CHOPPED	1
1/4 TSP	SALT	1 ML
1/4 TSP	BLACK PEPPER	1 ML
1	CAN (19 OZ/540 ML) STEWED TOMATOES	1
3 CUPS	TURKEY STOCK OR READY-TO-USE CHICKEN OR VEGETABLE BROTH	750 ML

IN A MEDIUM POT, HEAT OIL OVER MEDIUM HEAT. SAUTÉ GARLIC, ONION, CHILI POWDER, CUMIN AND OREGANO FOR 3 MINUTES OR UNTIL SOFTENED. ADD TURKEY AND COOK, BREAKING IT UP WITH A SPOON, FOR ABOUT 5 MINUTES OR UNTIL NO LONGER PINK. STIR IN TOMATO PASTE TO COAT. STIR IN YELLOW PEPPER, SALT, PEPPER, TOMATOES AND STOCK; BRING TO A SIMMER. REDUCE HEAT, COVER AND SIMMER FOR ABOUT 15 MINUTES TO BLEND THE FLAVORS. SERVES 4.

TIP: ADD A SPLASH OF TABASCO FOR SOME HEAT.

QUICK SEAFOOD CHOWDER

LIGHTER THAN A TRADITIONAL CREAM VERSION,
THIS CHOWDER IS QUICK ENOUGH TO MAKE FOR
A WEEKNIGHT MEAL. TARRAGON,
A LICORICE-FLAVORED HERB, SHINES HERE.

2 TBSP	CANOLA OIL	30 ML
3	GARLIC CLOVES, MINCED	3
2	CELERY STALKS, THINLY SLICED	2
1	SHALLOT, CHOPPED	1
1	RED BELL PEPPER, DICED	1
8 OZ	MUSHROOMS, THINLY SLICED	250 G
1 TBSP	CHOPPED FRESH TARRAGON	15 ML
1/2 TSP	SALT	2 ML
2 CUPS	FISH STOCK, READY-TO-USE CHICKEN BROTH OR CLAM JUICE	500 ML
2 CUPS	WHOLE MILK OR HALF-AND-HALF (10%) CREAM	500 ML
2	CANS (EACH 3.7 OZ/106 G) BABY SHRIMP, DRAINED	2
1	CAN (4 OZ/120 G) CRABMEAT, DRAINED	1
1	CAN (5 OZ/142 G) BABY CLAMS, RINSED AND DRAINED	1

IN A MEDIUM POT, HEAT OIL OVER MEDIUM-HIGH HEAT. SAUTÉ GARLIC, CELERY, SHALLOT, RED PEPPER, MUSHROOMS, TARRAGON AND SALT FOR 10 MINUTES OR UNTIL NO LIQUID REMAINS. STIR IN STOCK AND MILK; BRING TO A GENTLE BOIL. STIR IN SHRIMP, CRAB AND CLAMS; REDUCE HEAT AND SIMMER FOR ABOUT 5 MINUTES OR UNTIL SEAFOOD IS HEATED THROUGH. SERVES 4.

TIP: IF TARRAGON ISN'T AVAILABLE, YOU CAN USE FRESH FLAT-LEAF (ITALIAN) PARSLEY FOR A MILDER FLAVOR.

ROASTED TOMATO AND SHRIMP SOUP

EMILY'S NEIGHBOR PAM SHARES THIS SOUP WITH FRIENDS ALL THE TIME BECAUSE GRAPE TOMATOES ARE SWEET YEAR-ROUND. THEY ARE THE PERFECT CHOICE FOR TOMATO SOUP IN COLDER MONTHS WHEN FRESH FIELD TOMATOES ARE NOT IN SEASON.

2 LBS	GRAPE TOMATOES	1 KG
1	HEAD GARLIC, CLOVES PEELED	1
4 TBSP	CHOPPED FRESH FLAT-LEAF (ITALIAN) PARSLEY, DIVIDED	60 ML
2 TSP	CHOPPED FRESH ROSEMARY	10 ML
1/4 TSP	SALT	1 ML
1/4 TSP	BLACK PEPPER	1 ML
3 TBSP	EXTRA VIRGIN OLIVE OIL	45 ML
3 CUPS	READY-TO-USE VEGETABLE OR CHICKEN BROTH	750 ML
3/4 CUP	HEAVY OR WHIPPING (35%) CREAM	175 ML
2 TBSP	BUTTER	30 ML
1 LB	LARGE SHRIMP (THAWED IF FROZEN), PEELED AND DEVEINED	500 G
1	LARGE GARLIC CLOVE, MINCED	1

PREHEAT OVEN TO 400°F (200°C). IN A BOWL, COMBINE TOMATOES, GARLIC CLOVES, 2 TBSP (30 ML) PARSLEY, ROSEMARY, SALT, PEPPER AND OIL. SPREAD ON A PARCHMENT-LINED BAKING SHEET AND ROAST FOR ABOUT 20 MINUTES OR UNTIL TOMATOES ARE GOLDEN BROWN AND STARTING TO BURST. SCRAPE INTO A SAUCEPAN AND ADD BROTH. USING AN IMMERSION BLENDER, BLEND UNTIL SMOOTH. (OR PURÉE IN A BLENDER, THEN TRANSFER TO

SAUCEPAN.) STIR IN CREAM AND BRING TO A SIMMER OVER MEDIUM-LOW HEAT. SIMMER, STIRRING OCCASIONALLY, FOR 10 MINUTES TO BLEND THE FLAVORS.

MEANWHILE, IN A SMALL NONSTICK SKILLET, MELT BUTTER OVER MEDIUM-HIGH HEAT. SAUTÉ SHRIMP, MINCED GARLIC AND REMAINING PARSLEY FOR 3 MINUTES OR UNTIL SHRIMP ARE PINK, FIRM AND OPAQUE. STIR INTO SOUP. SERVES 4.

TIP: THIS SOUP FREEZES WELL; SIMPLY OMIT THE SHRIMP. WHEN YOU ARE READY TO SERVE THE SOUP, THAW IT AND HEAT IT THROUGH, AND COOK THE SHRIMP AS DIRECTED.

TIP: FOR A FUN WAY TO PLATE THIS SOUP, LADLE IT INTO SHALLOW SOUP BOWLS AND SPOON THE SHRIMP IN THE CENTER OF EACH BOWL. YOUR GUESTS WILL LOVE IT.

VARIATION: YOU CAN SUBSTITUTE SCALLOPS FOR THE SHRIMP.

IF YOU'VE LOST YOUR APPETITE TODAY, I THINK I HAVE IT.

EGG-TOPPED NOODLE SOUP

WITH ITS FRESH VEGETABLE FLAVORS ENHANCED BY SOY BEAN PASTE (MISO) AND THE ADDITION OF PROTEIN-RICH EGGS OVER TOP, THIS BOWL IS A PERFECT MEAL.

1 TBSP	CANOLA OIL	15 ML
2	GARLIC CLOVES, MINCED	2
6	GREEN ONIONS, CHOPPED	6
2 TSP	MINCED FRESH GINGER	10 ML
8 OZ	MUSHROOMS, SLICED	250 G
1	RED BELL PEPPER, CHOPPED	1
1	CARROT, CHOPPED	1
5 CUPS	READY-TO-USE VEGETABLE OR CHICKEN BROTH	1.25 L
1 TBSP	WHITE MISO PASTE	15 ML
2/3 CUP	DRIED MEDIUM EGG NOODLES	150 ML
1 CUP	CHOPPED COOKED CHICKEN OR TOFU (OPTIONAL)	250 ML
	NONSTICK COOKING SPRAY	
4	LARGE EGGS	4
PINCH	SALT	PINCH
PINCH	BLACK PEPPER	PINCH

IN A MEDIUM POT, HEAT OIL OVER MEDIUM HEAT. SAUTÉ GARLIC, GREEN ONIONS AND GINGER FOR 2 MINUTES. ADD MUSHROOMS, RED PEPPER AND CARROT; INCREASE HEAT TO MEDIUM-HIGH AND SAUTÉ FOR ABOUT 8 MINUTES OR UNTIL VEGETABLES ARE SOFTENED. STIR IN BROTH AND MISO PASTE; BRING TO A SIMMER. STIR IN NOODLES AND SIMMER FOR ABOUT 5 MINUTES OR UNTIL NOODLES ARE SOFTENED. IF USING CHICKEN OR TOFU, STIR IT IN AND SIMMER UNTIL HEATED THROUGH.

MEANWHILE, SPRAY A NONSTICK SKILLET WITH COOKING SPRAY AND FRY EGGS, IN BATCHES AS NECESSARY, UNTIL WHITES ARE SET. FLIP EGGS AND FRY UNTIL YOLK IS JUST SLIGHTLY RUNNY. SPRINKLE WITH SALT AND PEPPER.

LADLE SOUP INTO BOWLS AND TOP EACH WITH AN EGG. SERVES 4.

TIP: IF DESIRED, SAVE SOME OF THE RAW GREEN ONIONS TO SPRINKLE OVER THE SOUP BEFORE SERVING.

TIP: YOU CAN FIND MISO PASTE IN ASIAN GROCERY STORES, HEALTH FOOD STORES AND GROCERY STORES WHERE SUSHI PRODUCTS ARE AVAILABLE.

HOW DO YOU MAKE A GOLD SOUP? PUT 24 CARROTS IN IT!

FRENCH ONION AND MUSHROOM SOUP

MUSHROOMS ADD SOME BULK AND TEXTURE IN THIS TWIST ON ONION SOUP. WITH SUCH A VARIETY AVAILABLE, YOU CAN USE YOUR FAVORITE ONES.

2 TBSP	BUTTER	30 ML
1	LARGE SPANISH ONION, THINLY SLICED	1
4	GARLIC CLOVES, MINCED	4
1 LB	CREMINI MUSHROOMS, THINLY SLICED	500 G
1/4 CUP	DRIED SLICED MUSHROOMS (SUCH AS PORCINI OR SHIITAKE)	60 ML
1 TBSP	CHOPPED FRESH THYME	15 ML
1/3 CUP	DRY WHITE WINE	75 ML
5 CUPS	READY-TO-USE VEGETABLE OR CHICKEN BROTH	1.25 L
4 to 6	SLICES VIENNA BREAD OR BAGUETTE	4 to 6
4 to 6	SLICES CHEESE (SUCH AS BRIE, GRUYÈRE OR CHEDDAR)	4 to 6

IN A MEDIUM POT, MELT BUTTER OVER MEDIUM-HIGH HEAT. SAUTÉ ONION FOR 10 MINUTES OR UNTIL STARTING TO BECOME GOLDEN AND SOFT. ADD GARLIC, FRESH MUSHROOMS, DRIED MUSHROOMS AND THYME; SAUTÉ FOR 10 MINUTES OR UNTIL NO LIQUID REMAINS. STIR IN WINE UNTIL EVAPORATED. STIR IN BROTH AND BRING TO A SIMMER. REDUCE HEAT AND SIMMER FOR 10 MINUTES.

MEANWHILE, PREHEAT OVEN TO 400°F (200°C). PLACE BREAD SLICES ON A BAKING SHEET AND TOP EACH WITH A SLICE OF CHEESE. TOAST IN OVEN FOR ABOUT 5 MINUTES OR UNTIL CHEESE IS MELTED. LADLE SOUP INTO BOWLS AND TOP EACH WITH A CHEESY BREAD SLICE. SERVES 4 TO 6.

PRESSURE COOKER FRENCH CANADIAN PEA SOUP

YELLOW AND GREEN SPLIT PEAS WORK EQUALLY WELL IN THIS RECIPE, THOUGH YELLOW PEAS TEND TO BE SLIGHTLY MILDER AND SWEETER IN FLAVOR.

2 TBSP	CANOLA OIL	30 ML
3	CARROTS, DICED	3
3	CELERY STALKS, DICED	3
1	LARGE ONION, DICED	1
2	GARLIC CLOVES, MINCED	2
2 CUPS	DRIED YELLOW OR GREEN SPLIT PEAS, SORTED AND RINSED	500 ML
2 CUPS	CHOPPED SMOKED HAM	500 ML
2	BAY LEAVES	2
1 TSP	DRIED THYME	5 ML
1/2 TSP	DRIED SAVORY OR MARJORAM	2 ML
8 CUPS	READY-TO-USE CHICKEN BROTH	2 L
1 TSP	SALT	5 ML
1/2 TSP	BLACK PEPPER	2 ML

IN A PRESSURE COOKER, HEAT OIL OVER MEDIUM-HIGH HEAT. SAUTÉ CARROTS, CELERY AND ONION FOR 5 MINUTES OR UNTIL ONION IS SOFTENED. ADD GARLIC AND SAUTÉ FOR 1 MINUTE. ADD PEAS, HAM, BAY LEAVES, THYME, SAVORY AND BROTH. LOCK LID AND BRING COOKER UP TO FULL PRESSURE OVER HIGH HEAT. REDUCE HEAT TO MEDIUM-LOW, JUST TO MAINTAIN EVEN PRESSURE, AND COOK FOR 20 MINUTES. REMOVE FROM HEAT AND LET PRESSURE DROP NATURALLY. DISCARD BAY LEAVES. SEASON WITH SALT AND PEPPER. ADD A LITTLE WATER IF SOUP IS TOO THICK. SERVES 6 TO 8.

SPEEDY VEGGIE PASTA SOUP

*THIS RECIPE USES A FOOD PROCESSOR
TO SPEED UP THE PREPARATION.*

2	CARROTS	2
2	CELERY STALKS	2
1	ONION	1
1	SMALL ZUCCHINI	1
2 TBSP	CANOLA OIL	30 ML
1 TSP	DRIED ITALIAN SEASONING	5 ML
1 TSP	SALT	5 ML
1 TSP	BLACK PEPPER	5 ML
1/2 TSP	GARLIC POWDER	2 ML
1	CAN (28 OZ/796 ML) DICED TOMATOES, WITH JUICE	1
2 CUPS	READY-TO-USE CHICKEN BROTH	500 ML
1 1/2 CUPS	CORN KERNELS (THAWED IF FROZEN)	375 ML
1 CUP	DRIED SMALL PASTA (SUCH AS MACARONI OR DITALINI)	250 ML
	GRATED PARMESAN CHEESE (OPTIONAL)	

USING A FOOD PROCESSOR WITH THE LARGE SHREDDER ATTACHMENT, GRATE CARROTS, CELERY, ONION AND ZUCCHINI. IN A LARGE POT, HEAT OIL OVER MEDIUM-HIGH HEAT. SAUTÉ GRATED VEGETABLES FOR 5 MINUTES. STIR IN ITALIAN SEASONING, SALT, PEPPER AND GARLIC POWDER. STIR IN TOMATOES WITH JUICE, BROTH, CORN AND PASTA; BRING TO A BOIL. REDUCE HEAT, COVER AND SIMMER, STIRRING OCCASIONALLY, FOR 15 MINUTES OR UNTIL PASTA IS TENDER. SERVE SPRINKLED WITH CHEESE, IF DESIRED. SERVES 6.

SUPPER SALADS

GRILLED STEAK AND POTATO SALAD

MEAT AND POTATOES ARE A SPECTACULAR COMBINATION
ON THE SAME PLATE; NOW JAM THEM TOGETHER
IN A BOWL, FOR A SUPER-DELICIOUS SALAD,
AND DINNER IS SERVED.

2 LBS	YELLOW-FLESH POTATOES, PEELED AND QUARTERED	1 KG
1/2 CUP	THINLY SLICED RED ONION	125 ML
1/2	ORANGE BELL PEPPER, THINLY SLICED	1/2
2	BEEF STRIP LOIN STEAKS (EACH ABOUT 8 OZ/250 G)	2
3 TBSP	CANOLA OIL, DIVIDED	45 ML
1	LARGE GARLIC CLOVE, MINCED	1
1 TSP	DRIED THYME	5 ML
1/2 TSP	SALT, DIVIDED	2 ML
1/2 TSP	BLACK PEPPER, DIVIDED	2 ML
3 TBSP	APPLE CIDER VINEGAR	45 ML
1 TBSP	PREPARED HORSERADISH	15 ML
1/4 CUP	CHOPPED FRESH BASIL OR PARSLEY	60 ML
3 CUPS	LIGHTLY PACKED BABY ARUGULA OR SPINACH	750 ML

PLACE POTATOES IN A POT, COVER WITH COLD SALTED WATER AND BRING TO A BOIL. BOIL FOR 8 TO 10 MINUTES OR UNTIL TENDER BUT FIRM. DRAIN WELL AND PLACE IN A LARGE BOWL. ADD ONION AND ORANGE PEPPER.

MEANWHILE, PREHEAT BARBECUE GRILL TO MEDIUM-HIGH. PLACE STEAKS IN A SHALLOW DISH AND DRIZZLE WITH 1 TBSP (15 ML) OIL. SPRINKLE WITH GARLIC, THYME AND HALF OF EACH OF THE SALT AND PEPPER. TURN TO

COAT BOTH SIDES. GRILL STEAK, TURNING ONCE, FOR ABOUT 5 MINUTES FOR MEDIUM-RARE OR TO DESIRED DONENESS. TRANSFER TO A CUTTING BOARD AND LET STAND FOR 2 MINUTES, THEN THINLY SLICE. ADD TO POTATO MIXTURE.

IN A SMALL BOWL, WHISK TOGETHER VINEGAR, HORSERADISH AND REMAINING OIL, SALT AND PEPPER. DRIZZLE OVER POTATO MIXTURE. ADD BASIL AND TOSS GENTLY TO COMBINE. SPREAD ARUGULA ON A SERVING PLATTER AND SPOON SALAD OVER TOP. SERVES 4.

TIP: THIS SALAD CAN BE SERVED WARM OR AT ROOM TEMPERATURE. THE BED OF ARUGULA ABSORBS THE FLAVOR OF THE SALAD AS IT SITS.

I DON'T LIKE TO COMPLAIN. (I LOVE IT!)

GRILLED PORK SKEWERS ON RICE NOODLE SALAD

SERVE THIS COLORFUL FRESH SALAD EITHER FAMILY-STYLE ON A PLATTER OR IN INDIVIDUAL BOWLS.

RICE NOODLE SALAD

1	GARLIC CLOVE, MINCED	1
2 TBSP	PACKED BROWN SUGAR	30 ML
1/2 TSP	HOT PEPPER FLAKES	2 ML
1/4 CUP	FISH SAUCE	60 ML
3 TBSP	LIME JUICE	45 ML
2 TBSP	CANOLA OIL	30 ML
1 LB	WIDE RICE NOODLES	500 G
3	ROMAINE LETTUCE LEAVES, SHREDDED	3
2	GREEN ONIONS, SLICED	2
1	ENGLISH CUCUMBER, GRATED	1
1	CARROT, GRATED	1
1/2 CUP	LIGHTLY PACKED BASIL LEAVES, SLICED	125 ML
1/4 CUP	LIGHTLY PACKED CILANTRO OR MINT LEAVES, SLICED	60 ML

PORK SKEWERS

	METAL SKEWERS OR SOAKED BAMBOO SKEWERS (SEE TIP)	
2	GARLIC CLOVES, MINCED	2
2 TSP	PACKED BROWN SUGAR	10 ML
2 TBSP	CANOLA OIL	30 ML
2 TSP	FISH SAUCE	10 ML
1 TSP	THAI RED CURRY PASTE	5 ML
1 LB	BONELESS PORK LOIN, CUT INTO THIN 4- BY 1-INCH (10 BY 2.5 CM) STRIPS	500 G

SALAD: IN A SMALL BOWL, COMBINE GARLIC, BROWN SUGAR, HOT PEPPER FLAKES, FISH SAUCE, LIME JUICE AND OIL; SET ASIDE. IN A LARGE POT OF BOILING WATER, COOK NOODLES FOR 3 TO 4 MINUTES OR UNTIL JUST TENDER. DRAIN, RINSE WITH COLD WATER, THEN DRAIN WELL. TRANSFER NOODLES TO A LARGE BOWL AND ADD ROMAINE, GREEN ONIONS, CUCUMBER, CARROT, BASIL AND CILANTRO; SET ASIDE.

SKEWERS: PREHEAT BARBECUE GRILL TO HIGH. IN A MEDIUM BOWL, STIR TOGETHER GARLIC, BROWN SUGAR, OIL, FISH SAUCE AND CURRY PASTE. ADD PORK AND TOSS TO COAT. THREAD PORK ONTO SKEWERS; DISCARD ANY EXCESS OIL MIXTURE. REDUCE HEAT TO MEDIUM-HIGH AND GRILL SKEWERS, TURNING ONCE, FOR 4 TO 6 MINUTES OR UNTIL JUST A HINT OF PINK REMAINS INSIDE PORK.

STIR DRESSING, POUR OVER SALAD AND TOSS TO COAT. SERVE WITH GRILLED PORK. SERVES 5.

TIP: IF USING BAMBOO SKEWERS, SOAK THEM IN WATER FOR 30 MINUTES BEFORE STARTING THE RECIPE. KEEP A CLOSE WATCH ON THEM WHILE ON THE GRILL, AS THEY CAN BURN VERY EASILY.

TIP: THE PORK SKEWERS CAN ALSO BE BROILED. PREHEAT BROILER, WITH RACK ABOUT 6 INCHES (15 CM) FROM THE HEAT. PLACE SKEWERS ON A FOIL-LINED BAKING SHEET AND BROIL FOR 2 TO 3 MINUTES PER SIDE.

ROASTED PARMESAN CHICKEN AND TOMATO BREAD SALAD

YOUR TASTE BUDS WILL LOVE THE FLAVOR OF THIS SATISFYING BREAD SALAD!

PARMESAN CHICKEN

2	BONELESS SKINLESS CHICKEN BREASTS (ABOUT 1 1/4 LBS/625 G TOTAL)		2
1/4 CUP	MAYONNAISE	60 ML	
1/2 CUP	PANKO	125 ML	
1/2 CUP	GRATED PARMESAN CHEESE	125 ML	
1/2 TSP	BLACK PEPPER	2 ML	
1/2 TSP	DRIED ITALIAN SEASONING	2 ML	
1/2 TSP	PAPRIKA	2 ML	
1/4 TSP	GARLIC POWDER	1 ML	

TOMATO BREAD SALAD

1	GARLIC CLOVE, MINCED		1
1/2 TSP	SALT	2 ML	
1/2 TSP	BLACK PEPPER	2 ML	
1/4 CUP	EXTRA VIRGIN OLIVE OIL	60 ML	
2 TBSP	RED WINE VINEGAR	30 ML	
1/2 TSP	DIJON MUSTARD	2 ML	
1	DAY-OLD BAGUETTE (ABOUT 10 OZ/300 G), TORN INTO 1-INCH (2.5 CM) CUBES		1
3	TOMATOES, CUT INTO 1-INCH (2.5 CM) PIECES		3
1	YELLOW BELL PEPPER, CHOPPED		1
1/2	ENGLISH CUCUMBER, CHOPPED		1/2
1/2	RED ONION, THINLY SLICED		1/2
1 CUP	LIGHTLY PACKED ARUGULA	250 ML	
1/2 CUP	LIGHTLY PACKED FRESH BASIL, THINLY SLICED	125 ML	

CHICKEN: PREHEAT OVEN TO 400°F (200°C). CUT EACH CHICKEN BREAST DIAGONALLY INTO 5 LARGE STRIPS. IN A BOWL, COMBINE CHICKEN AND MAYONNAISE. IN A SHALLOW BOWL, COMBINE PANKO, CHEESE, PEPPER, ITALIAN SEASONING, PAPRIKA AND GARLIC POWDER. DREDGE CHICKEN IN CRUMB MIXTURE, PRESSING LIGHTLY TO COAT. DISCARD ANY EXCESS MAYONNAISE AND CRUMB MIXTURE. PLACE CHICKEN ON A LIGHTLY GREASED FOIL- OR PARCHMENT-LINED BAKING SHEET. BAKE FOR 13 TO 15 MINUTES OR UNTIL NO LONGER PINK INSIDE.

SALAD: IN A SMALL BOWL, COMBINE GARLIC, SALT, PEPPER, OIL, VINEGAR AND MUSTARD. IN A LARGE BOWL, COMBINE BAGUETTE, TOMATOES, YELLOW PEPPER, CUCUMBER AND ONION. DRIZZLE WITH DRESSING AND TOSS TO COAT; LET STAND FOR AT LEAST 5 MINUTES OR UP TO 30 MINUTES, UNTIL BREAD HAS ABSORBED DRESSING. ADD ARUGULA AND BASIL, TOSSING TO COAT. SERVE WITH PARMESAN CHICKEN. SERVES 4 TO 6.

TIP: THIS SALAD IS BEST EATEN THE DAY IT'S MADE.

GRILLED CHICKEN, BARLEY AND CORN SALAD BOWL

THE POPULAR "BUDDHA BOWL," WHICH MAKES AN APPEARANCE IN MANY HOMES AND RESTAURANTS, IS FULL OF COLOR, FLAVOR AND NUTRITION, AND THIS EASY MIX OF GRAINS, VEGETABLES AND PROTEIN MAKES FOR A WONDERFUL DINNER.

1/2 CUP	PEARL OR POT BARLEY	125 ML
2 CUPS	PACKED BABY ARUGULA	500 ML
1 CUP	CORN KERNELS (THAWED IF FROZEN)	250 ML
1/2 TSP	SALT	2 ML
1/2 TSP	BLACK PEPPER	2 ML
4	CARROTS, SLICED LENGTHWISE INTO THIRDS	4
2	RED BELL PEPPERS, QUARTERED	2
	NONSTICK COOKING SPRAY	
2	BONELESS SKINLESS CHICKEN BREASTS (ABOUT 1 LB/500 G TOTAL)	2
1 TSP	CHILI POWDER	5 ML
3 TSP	CANOLA OIL, DIVIDED	15 ML
1 TBSP	BALSAMIC VINEGAR (PREFERABLY WHITE)	15 ML

IN A SMALL SAUCEPAN, COVER BARLEY WITH WATER; BRING TO A BOIL. REDUCE HEAT AND SIMMER FOR ABOUT 20 MINUTES OR UNTIL BARLEY IS TENDER BUT STILL CHEWY. DRAIN WELL AND LET COOL SLIGHTLY, THEN TOSS WITH ARUGULA, CORN, SALT AND PEPPER.

PREHEAT BARBECUE GRILL TO MEDIUM-HIGH. SPRAY CARROTS AND RED PEPPERS WITH COOKING SPRAY. TOSS CHICKEN BREASTS WITH CHILI POWDER AND 1 TSP (5 ML) OIL TO COAT. GRILL CHICKEN FOR ABOUT 12 MINUTES,

TURNING OCCASIONALLY, UNTIL NO LONGER PINK INSIDE. AT THE SAME TIME, GRILL CARROTS AND RED PEPPERS FOR ABOUT 10 MINUTES, TURNING OCCASIONALLY, UNTIL TENDER. REMOVE CHICKEN AND VEGETABLES TO A CUTTING BOARD. CHOP CARROTS AND PEPPERS; TOSS WITH VINEGAR AND REMAINING OIL. SLICE CHICKEN. DIVIDE BARLEY MIXTURE AMONG BOWLS AND TOP WITH VEGETABLES AND CHICKEN. SERVES 4.

TIP: IF YOU HAVE LEFTOVER GRILLED CHICKEN, STEAK OR PORK, FEEL FREE TO USE IT IN THIS SALAD AND SKIP THE STEP OF GRILLING THE CHICKEN.

I PUT THE "PRO" IN PROCRASTINATE.

SOUTHWESTERN CHICKEN SALAD WITH QUINOA

*IF YOU'RE A FAN OF SOUTHWESTERN-STYLE SALADS,
YOU'LL ENJOY THIS VARIATION WITH ADDED QUINOA.*

I CUP	QUINOA, RINSED	250 ML
I 3/4 CUPS	WATER	425 ML
2	GARLIC CLOVES, MINCED	2
2 TSP	GROUND CUMIN	10 ML
2 TSP	SMOKED PAPRIKA	10 ML
I TSP	SALT	5 ML
1/4 CUP	EXTRA VIRGIN OLIVE OIL	60 ML
3 TBSP	LIME JUICE	45 ML
2 TSP	LIQUID HONEY	10 ML
2	GREEN ONIONS, SLICED	2
I	RED BELL PEPPER, DICED	I
I	AVOCADO, CUBED	I
3 CUPS	LIGHTLY PACKED MIXED SALAD GREENS	750 ML
3 CUPS	SHREDDED COOKED CHICKEN	750 ML
I CUP	CORN KERNELS (THAWED IF FROZEN)	250 ML
I CUP	COOKED OR DRAINED RINSED CANNED BLACK BEANS	250 ML
1/2 CUP	CHOPPED FRESH CILANTRO	125 ML
I 1/2 CUPS	CRUMBLED TORTILLA CHIPS	375 ML
	HOT PEPPER SAUCE (OPTIONAL)	

IN A MEDIUM SAUCEPAN, COMBINE QUINOA AND WATER;
BRING TO A BOIL. REDUCE HEAT, COVER AND SIMMER FOR
10 MINUTES. TURN OFF HEAT AND LET STAND, COVERED,
FOR 5 MINUTES. TRANSFER QUINOA TO A LARGE BOWL
TO COOL. IN A SMALL BOWL, COMBINE GARLIC, CUMIN,
PAPRIKA, SALT, OIL, LIME JUICE AND HONEY. TO COOLED

QUINOA, ADD GREEN ONIONS, RED PEPPER, AVOCADO, SALAD GREENS, CHICKEN, CORN, BEANS AND CILANTRO. DRIZZLE WITH DRESSING AND TOSS GENTLY TO COAT. SPRINKLE TORTILLA CHIPS ON TOP. SERVE WITH HOT PEPPER SAUCE, IF DESIRED. SERVES 6.

TIP: WHEN A RECIPE SAYS TO RINSE QUINOA, IT'S TO REMOVE A NATURAL PROTECTIVE COATING CALLED SAPONIN, WHICH CAN TASTE BITTER. MOST COMMERCIAL QUINOA IS RINSED DURING PROCESSING, BUT IT'S WORTH RINSING IT YOURSELF ANYWAY, JUST IN CASE.

TIP: THIS SALAD CAN BE MADE A DAY AHEAD. COVER AND REFRIGERATE; ADD AVOCADO AND TORTILLA CHIPS JUST BEFORE SERVING.

*THE BEST THING ABOUT THE GOOD OLD DAYS IS,
I WASN'T GOOD AND I WASN'T OLD.*

TURKEY COBB SALAD

THIS RESTAURANT CLASSIC IS EASY TO MAKE
AT HOME AND IS A FILLING SALAD THAT HAS
LOTS OF COLOR, CRUNCH AND FLAVOR.

2	ROMAINE HEARTS, CHOPPED	2
3 CUPS	LIGHTLY PACKED BABY SPINACH	750 ML
4	HARD-COOKED EGGS, PEELED AND CUT INTO 4 WEDGES EACH	4
8 OZ	SLICED DELI OVEN-ROASTED TURKEY, CHOPPED	250 G
2	AVOCADOS, CHOPPED	2
2 CUPS	GRAPE TOMATOES, HALVED	500 ML
1 CUP	COARSELY CHOPPED CRISPLY COOKED BACON	250 ML
1 CUP	SHREDDED SHARP (OLD) CHEDDAR OR BLUE CHEESE	250 ML
1/3 CUP	CANOLA OIL	75 ML
1/3 CUP	WHITE WINE VINEGAR	75 ML
1 TBSP	DIJON MUSTARD	15 ML
1/2 TSP	SALT	2 ML
1/2 TSP	BLACK PEPPER	2 ML
1	GREEN ONION, MINCED	1

COMBINE ROMAINE AND SPINACH; DIVIDE AMONG FOUR
PLATES. PLACE EGGS ON ONE SIDE OF THE SALAD, THEN
LINE UP TURKEY, AVOCADOS, TOMATOES, BACON AND
CHEESE ON EACH SALAD. IN A SMALL BOWL, WHISK
TOGETHER OIL, VINEGAR, MUSTARD, SALT AND PEPPER.
STIR IN GREEN ONION. SERVE DRESSING IN A SMALL
PITCHER SO EVERYONE CAN DRIZZLE THEIR OWN ON THEIR
SALAD (REFRIGERATE ANY LEFTOVERS). SERVES 4.

SEARED SALMON AND BEET SALAD

HERE'S A UNIQUE SALAD YOUR FAMILY WILL LOVE.

4	SMALL YELLOW OR RED BEETS, PEELED	4
1/3 CUP	WATER	75 ML
1 TBSP	CHOPPED FRESH PARSLEY	15 ML
3 TBSP	EXTRA VIRGIN OLIVE OIL, DIVIDED	45 ML
2 TBSP	WHITE WINE VINEGAR	30 ML
1/2 TSP	SALT, DIVIDED	2 ML
1/2 TSP	BLACK PEPPER, DIVIDED	2 ML
4	SKIN-ON SALMON FILLETS (EACH ABOUT 5 OZ/150 G)	4
1 TSP	DRIED THYME	5 ML
4 CUPS	LIGHTLY PACKED BABY ARUGULA OR SPINACH	1 L

PLACE BEETS AND WATER IN A MICROWAVE-SAFE BOWL. COVER WITH PLASTIC WRAP AND MICROWAVE ON HIGH FOR 8 MINUTES OR UNTIL TENDER. DRAIN AND LET COOL SLIGHTLY, THEN CUT INTO WEDGES. IN A BOWL, TOSS BEETS WITH PARSLEY, 2 TBSP (30 ML) OIL, VINEGAR AND HALF EACH OF THE SALT AND PEPPER; SET ASIDE.

SPRINKLE SALMON WITH THYME AND REMAINING SALT AND PEPPER. IN A LARGE NONSTICK SKILLET, HEAT REMAINING OIL OVER MEDIUM-HIGH HEAT. PLACE SALMON, SKIN SIDE DOWN, IN PAN AND SEAR FOR ABOUT 4 MINUTES OR UNTIL VERY GOLDEN BROWN. TURN OVER AND COOK FOR 5 MINUTES OR UNTIL FISH FLAKES EASILY WHEN TESTED WITH A FORK. DIVIDE ARUGULA AMONG DINNER PLATES AND SPOON BEET SALAD OVER TOP. PLACE SALMON ON TOP. SERVES 4.

WARM ASPARAGUS AND SALMON COUSCOUS SALAD

SALMON IS A PERFECT PROTEIN-RICH ADDITION TO SALADS, AND IT ALSO HAPPENS TO PAIR PERFECTLY WITH ASPARAGUS. A ZIPPY LEMON DRESSING BRINGS IT ALL TOGETHER.

1	GARLIC CLOVE, MINCED	1
1 CUP	COUSCOUS	250 ML
1¼ CUPS	READY-TO-USE VEGETABLE OR CHICKEN BROTH	300 ML
2 CUPS	CHOPPED ASPARAGUS	500 ML
1 CUP	JULIENNED CARROTS (CUT INTO MATCHSTICKS)	250 ML
½ TSP	SALT	2 ML
½ TSP	BLACK PEPPER	2 ML
½ TSP	GRATED LEMON ZEST	2 ML
1	CAN (7½ OZ/213 G) SALMON, DRAINED	1
2 TBSP	CHOPPED FRESH PARSLEY	30 ML
2 TBSP	LEMON JUICE	30 ML

IN A SAUCEPAN, COMBINE GARLIC, COUSCOUS AND BROTH; BRING TO A BOIL. STIR IN ASPARAGUS, CARROTS, SALT, PEPPER AND LEMON ZEST. COVER, REMOVE FROM HEAT AND LET STAND FOR 5 MINUTES.

USING A FORK, MASH SALMON, INCLUDING BONES. FLUFF COUSCOUS WITH FORK AND STIR IN SALMON, PARSLEY AND LEMON JUICE. SERVES 2.

TUNA TABBOULEH

*THIS MEDITERRANEAN SALAD GETS A BOOST OF
PROTEIN FROM TUNA — IT'S NOT JUST FOR LUNCH!*

2	LARGE GARLIC CLOVES, MINCED	2
I CUP	COUSCOUS	250 ML
1½ CUPS	READY-TO-USE VEGETABLE OR CHICKEN BROTH	375 ML
3	GREEN ONIONS, CHOPPED	3
2 CUPS	GRAPE TOMATOES, HALVED	500 ML
½ CUP	MINCED FRESH FLAT-LEAF (ITALIAN) PARSLEY	125 ML
2 TBSP	CHOPPED FRESH MINT	30 ML
2	CANS (EACH 6 OZ/170 G) CHUNK TUNA OR SALMON IN WATER, DRAINED	2
2 TBSP	CHOPPED FRESH OREGANO (OR 2 TSP/10 ML DRIED)	30 ML
¼ TSP	EACH SALT AND BLACK PEPPER	I ML
¼ CUP	RED OR WHITE WINE VINEGAR	60 ML
¼ CUP	EXTRA VIRGIN OLIVE OIL	60 ML

IN A SAUCEPAN, COMBINE GARLIC, COUSCOUS AND BROTH;
BRING TO A BOIL. COVER, REMOVE FROM HEAT AND LET
STAND FOR 5 MINUTES. FLUFF INTO A LARGE BOWL AND
STIR IN GREEN ONIONS, TOMATOES, PARSLEY AND MINT.
SPRINKLE TUNA OVER TOP. IN A SMALL BOWL, WHISK
TOGETHER OREGANO, SALT, PEPPER, VINEGAR AND OIL.
POUR DRESSING OVER SALAD AND STIR GENTLY TO
COMBINE. SERVES 4.

BEAN VARIATION: STIR IN A 19-OZ (540 ML) CAN OF YOUR
FAVORITE BEANS, RINSED AND DRAINED (2 CUPS/500 ML)
IN PLACE OF THE TUNA.

NIÇOISE SALAD

WE LOVE DINNERS LIKE THIS: FRESH AND SUMMERY AT ANY TIME OF YEAR! FOR EVEN MORE CRUNCH AND COLOR, USE A FEW BUTTERY BOSTON LETTUCE LEAVES AS A BED AND ADD A SPRINKLE OF KALAMATA OLIVES.

8 OZ	MINI RED-SKINNED POTATOES	250 G
6 OZ	GREEN BEANS, TRIMMED	175 G
2	HARD-COOKED EGGS, PEELED AND QUARTERED	2
1	TOMATO, CUT INTO WEDGES	1
2	CANS (EACH 6 OZ/170 G) CHUNK TUNA IN WATER, DRAINED	2
1 TBSP	CHOPPED FRESH MINT (OPTIONAL)	15 ML
2 TSP	CHOPPED FRESH PARSLEY	10 ML
1/2 TSP	SALT	2 ML
1/2 TSP	BLACK PEPPER	2 ML
3 TBSP	WHITE WINE VINEGAR	45 ML
2 TBSP	CANOLA OIL	30 ML
2 TSP	DIJON MUSTARD	10 ML

IN A POT OF BOILING SALTED WATER, BOIL POTATOES FOR 12 MINUTES OR UNTIL TENDER. REMOVE POTATOES WITH A SLOTTED SPOON AND LET COOL. ADD GREEN BEANS TO WATER AND BOIL FOR ABOUT 5 MINUTES OR UNTIL BRIGHT GREEN AND TENDER-CRISP. DRAIN AND RINSE WITH COLD WATER. CUT POTATOES INTO QUARTERS AND BEANS IN HALF; PLACE DECORATIVELY ON PLATTER ALONG WITH EGGS AND TOMATO. PLACE TUNA ON PLATTER AND SPRINKLE WITH MINT, IF USING. IN A SMALL BOWL, WHISK TOGETHER PARSLEY, SALT, PEPPER, VINEGAR, OIL AND MUSTARD. DRIZZLE OVER SALAD. SERVES 4.

SHRIMP CAESAR SALAD

KIDS LOVE CAESAR SALAD, AND CHICKEN IS USUALLY THE GO-TO PROTEIN. THIS SHRIMP VERSION WILL BECOME A NEW STAPLE, WITH ITS EASY DRESSING THAT IS LIGHT AND FRESH, PERFECT ANYTIME.

6 CUPS	CHOPPED ROMAINE LETTUCE	1.5 L
2 CUPS	GRAPE TOMATOES, HALVED	500 ML
12 OZ	COOKED PEELED LARGE SHRIMP (THAWED IF FROZEN), DRAINED	375 G
2	GARLIC CLOVES, MINCED	2
2	ANCHOVY FILLETS, FINELY MINCED	2
1 TBSP	DIJON MUSTARD	15 ML
1/4 CUP	CANOLA OIL	60 ML
2 TBSP	LEMON JUICE	30 ML
1/4 TSP	SALT	1 ML
1/4 TSP	BLACK PEPPER	1 ML
1 CUP	CROUTONS	250 ML

IN A LARGE SERVING BOWL, COMBINE ROMAINE, TOMATOES AND SHRIMP. IN A SMALL BOWL, USING A FORK, MASH TOGETHER GARLIC, ANCHOVIES AND MUSTARD. WHISK IN OIL, LEMON JUICE, SALT AND PEPPER. POUR OVER SALAD AND TOSS TO COAT. SPRINKLE WITH CROUTONS. SERVES 4.

TIP: YOU CAN USE 2 TSP (10 ML) ANCHOVY PASTE IN PLACE OF THE ANCHOVY FILLETS.

TIP: IF YOU LOVE YOUR FAMILY AND FRIENDS, BE SURE TO REMOVE THOSE PESKY TAILS FROM THE SHRIMP BEFORE TOSSING THE SALAD. THEY LOOK GREAT, BUT ARE TOO CRUNCHY FOR MOST TO ENJOY!

SPICY SHRIMP SALAD

SHOW UP TO A PARTY WITH THIS SALAD AND EVERYONE WILL BE ASKING FOR THE RECIPE. SYLVIA SAYS IT'S A POTLUCK WINNER. FEEL FREE TO USE A COMBINATION OF DIFFERENT LETTUCE GREENS.

CILANTRO LIME DRESSING

1	GARLIC CLOVE	1
1/2 CUP	LIGHTLY PACKED FRESH CILANTRO LEAVES AND STEMS	125 ML
1/4 TSP	SALT	1 ML
1/3 CUP	MAYONNAISE	75 ML
1 TBSP	FRESH LIME JUICE	15 ML
1/2 TSP	LIQUID HONEY	2 ML

SALAD

1 LB	MEDIUM SHRIMP (41/50 COUNT), PEELED AND DEVEINED	500 G
3	GARLIC CLOVES, MINCED	3
1 TSP	CHIPOTLE CHILE POWDER	5 ML
1/2 TSP	GROUND CUMIN	2 ML
1/2 TSP	SALT	2 ML
1/2 TSP	BLACK PEPPER	2 ML
1 TBSP	CANOLA OIL	15 ML
2	PLUM (ROMA) TOMATOES, SEEDED AND CHOPPED	2
8 CUPS	CHOPPED ROMAINE LETTUCE	2 L
1 CUP	CORN KERNELS (THAWED IF FROZEN)	250 ML
1 CUP	SHREDDED MONTEREY JACK CHEESE	250 ML
2 CUPS	COARSELY CRUSHED TORTILLA CHIPS	500 ML
	LIME WEDGES	

DRESSING: IN A BLENDER OR FOOD PROCESSOR, PROCESS ALL INGREDIENTS UNTIL SMOOTH. TRANSFER TO A BOWL, COVER AND REFRIGERATE UNTIL READY TO USE.

SALAD: PAT SHRIMP DRY WITH PAPER TOWELS. IN A MEDIUM BOWL, COMBINE SHRIMP, GARLIC, CHILE POWDER, CUMIN, SALT, PEPPER AND OIL. COVER AND REFRIGERATE FOR AT LEAST 10 MINUTES OR UP TO 24 HOURS.

IN A LARGE BOWL, COMBINE TOMATOES, ROMAINE, CORN AND CHEESE. DRIZZLE WITH DRESSING AND TOSS TO COAT. HEAT A LARGE SKILLET OVER HIGH HEAT FOR $1\frac{1}{2}$ MINUTES. ADD SHRIMP AND COOK, STIRRING OFTEN, FOR ABOUT 3 MINUTES OR UNTIL PINK, FIRM AND OPAQUE. DIVIDE SALAD ONTO PLATES AND TOP WITH SHRIMP AND TORTILLA CHIPS. SERVE WITH LIME WEDGES. SERVES 4.

TIP: DOUBLE THE RECIPE IF YOU'RE FEEDING A CROWD.

MARRIAGE MEANS COMMITMENT.
OF COURSE, SO DOES INSANITY.

PASTA AND GRILLED VEGGIE SALAD

SOMETIMES YOU JUST WANT SOMETHING SIMPLE AND FRESH, AND THIS SALAD COVERS BOTH. USE UP YOUR VEGGIES FROM THE CRISPER OR WHATEVER YOU PICKED UP AT THE MARKET TO CHANGE THINGS UP.

2	CARROTS, SLICED LENGTHWISE INTO THIRDS	2
2	RED BELL PEPPERS, QUARTERED	2
1	ZUCCHINI, SLICED LENGTHWISE INTO QUARTERS	1
1	ASIAN EGGPLANT, CUT LENGTHWISE INTO 1/2-INCH (1 CM) THICK SLICES	1
1/4 CUP	EXTRA VIRGIN OLIVE OIL, DIVIDED	60 ML
1/2 TSP	SALT, DIVIDED	2 ML
1/4 TSP	BLACK PEPPER, DIVIDED	1 ML
4 CUPS	DRIED BOWTIE (FARFALLE) PASTA (ABOUT 12 OZ/375 G)	1 L
3 TBSP	GRATED PARMESAN CHEESE	45 ML
2 TBSP	CHOPPED FRESH PARSLEY	30 ML
2 TBSP	CHOPPED FRESH BASIL	30 ML
1/4 CUP	AGED BALSAMIC VINEGAR	60 ML
2 TBSP	BASIL PESTO	30 ML

PREHEAT BARBECUE GRILL TO MEDIUM-HIGH. TOSS CARROTS, RED PEPPERS, ZUCCHINI AND EGGPLANT WITH HALF EACH OF THE OIL, SALT AND PEPPER. GRILL VEGETABLES, TURNING OCCASIONALLY, FOR ABOUT 10 MINUTES OR UNTIL GOLDEN BROWN. TRANSFER TO A CUTTING BOARD AND COARSELY CHOP.

MEANWHILE, IN A POT OF BOILING SALTED WATER, COOK PASTA FOR ABOUT 10 MINUTES OR UNTIL AL DENTE. RINSE WITH COLD WATER. DRAIN WELL.

IN A LARGE BOWL, COMBINE PASTA AND VEGETABLES. SPRINKLE WITH CHEESE, PARSLEY AND BASIL. IN A SMALL BOWL, WHISK TOGETHER VINEGAR, PESTO AND REMAINING OIL, SALT AND PEPPER. ADD TO PASTA MIXTURE AND TOSS TO COAT. SERVES 4 TO 6.

TIP: CHOP UP LEFTOVER GRILLED CHICKEN, STEAK OR FISH AND STIR INTO THE SALAD FOR A PROTEIN HIT.

MY WEIGHT IS PERFECT FOR MY HEIGHT ... WHICH VARIES.

PESTO TORTELLINI SALAD WITH BOCCONCINI AND WHITE BEANS

WE LOVE USING OUR FAVORITE INGREDIENTS, ESPECIALLY WHEN THEY COME TOGETHER QUICKLY. SERVE THIS HEARTY SALAD AS AN ALTERNATIVE TO A TRADITIONAL LEAFY GREEN ONE.

1	PACKAGE (26 OZ/750 G) FRESH CHEESE TORTELLINI	1
1	CAN (19 OZ/540 ML) WHITE BEANS, RINSED AND DRAINED (2 CUPS/500 ML)	1
1	RED OR YELLOW BELL PEPPER, CHOPPED	1
3 CUPS	LIGHTLY PACKED BABY SPINACH OR ARUGULA	750 ML
1 1/2 CUPS	CHERRY TOMATOES, HALVED	375 ML
1 1/2 CUPS	DRAINED SMALL BOCCONCINI CHEESE	375 ML
1/2 CUP	CHOPPED DRY SALAMI	125 ML
1/2 CUP	BASIL PESTO	125 ML
1/2 TSP	BLACK PEPPER	2 ML

IN A LARGE POT OF BOILING SALTED WATER, COOK TORTELLINI ACCORDING TO PACKAGE INSTRUCTIONS. DRAIN AND RINSE UNDER COLD WATER, THEN TRANSFER TO A LARGE BOWL. ADD BEANS, RED PEPPER, SPINACH, TOMATOES, BOCCONCINI, SALAMI, PESTO AND PEPPER; TOSS TO COMBINE. SERVES 6.

TIP: THIS SALAD CAN BE MADE 1 DAY IN ADVANCE. COVER AND REFRIGERATE UNTIL READY TO SERVE.

Spicy Shrimp Salad (page 50)

Pasta and Grilled Veggie Salad (page 52)

Mediterranean Beef Kebab Wraps (page 60)

Hot Tuna Melts with Chickpeas (page 75)

BROCCOLI, FETA AND CHICKPEA SALAD

HERE'S A REFRESHINGLY ZESTY SALAD THAT'S PACKED WITH FLAVOR.

5 CUPS	CHOPPED BROCCOLI	1.25 L
1	GARLIC CLOVE, MINCED	1
1/2 TSP	SALT	2 ML
1/2 TSP	BLACK PEPPER	2 ML
1/4 CUP	EXTRA VIRGIN OLIVE OIL	60 ML
1 TSP	GRATED LEMON ZEST	5 ML
2 TBSP	LEMON JUICE	30 ML
1	CAN (19 OZ/540 ML) CHICKPEAS, RINSED AND DRAINED (2 CUPS/500 ML)	1
1 CUP	FROZEN GREEN PEAS, THAWED	250 ML
1/2 CUP	LIGHTLY PACKED FRESH PARSLEY, CHOPPED	125 ML
1/3 CUP	SLICED PITTED DRAINED OLIVES	75 ML
3/4 CUP	CRUMBLED FETA CHEESE	175 ML

IN A POT OF BOILING WATER, COOK BROCCOLI FOR 1 MINUTE, THEN DRAIN WELL. IN A LARGE BOWL, COMBINE GARLIC, SALT, PEPPER, OIL, LEMON ZEST AND LEMON JUICE. ADD BROCCOLI, CHICKPEAS, GREEN PEAS, PARSLEY AND OLIVES, STIRRING TO COAT. SPRINKLE WITH FETA. SERVES 5.

TIP: REMEMBER TO ZEST THE LEMON BEFORE JUICING IT.

TIP: USE THE TINES OF A FORK TO BREAK LARGE PIECES OF FETA INTO SMALLER CHUNKS.

SHAVED BRUSSELS SPROUT, BACON AND EGG SALAD

THIS FILLING SALAD IS PERFECT FOR A SUMMER MEAL. BACON MAKES EVERYTHING TASTE BETTER!

1	SHALLOT, FINELY CHOPPED	1
1/2 TSP	SALT	2 ML
1/2 TSP	BLACK PEPPER	2 ML
1/4 CUP	EXTRA VIRGIN OLIVE OIL	60 ML
3 TBSP	LEMON JUICE	45 ML
1 TBSP	LIQUID HONEY	15 ML
1 TSP	GRAINY MUSTARD	5 ML
6	SLICES BACON, CRISPLY COOKED AND CHOPPED	6
1 LB	BRUSSELS SPROUTS, SHREDDED	500 G
1/2 CUP	TOASTED WALNUT HALVES, COARSELY CHOPPED	125 ML
1/2 CUP	GRATED PARMESAN CHEESE	125 ML
8	HARD-COOKED EGGS, CUT IN HALF	8

IN A SMALL BOWL, WHISK TOGETHER SHALLOT, SALT, PEPPER, OIL, LEMON JUICE, HONEY AND MUSTARD. IN A LARGE BOWL, COMBINE BACON, BRUSSELS SPROUTS, WALNUTS AND CHEESE. DRIZZLE WITH DRESSING AND TOSS GENTLY TO COAT. DIVIDE SALAD AND EGGS ONTO PLATES. SERVES 4.

TIP: YOU CAN SHRED THE BRUSSELS SPROUTS BY HAND OR REALLY SPEED THINGS UP BY USING A FOOD PROCESSOR WITH A SLICING BLADE OR A MANDOLINE.

TIP: THE DRESSING AND THE SALAD INGREDIENTS CAN BE PREPPED THE NIGHT BEFORE AND REFRIGERATED.

SUPPER SANDWICHES

GARLIC HERB STEAK SANDWICHES

*OUR FAMILIES LOVE STEAK AND MUSHROOMS
PAIRED TOGETHER. A SIMPLE MARINADE
ADDS WONDERFUL FLAVOR TO THE STEAK.
BEEF STRIP LOIN STEAKS ARE TENDER, SO
A LONG MARINATING TIME IS NOT NECESSARY.*

ROSEMARY GARLIC MARINADE

2	GARLIC CLOVES, MINCED	2
2 TSP	CHOPPED FRESH ROSEMARY OR THYME	10 ML
PINCH	SALT	PINCH
PINCH	BLACK PEPPER	PINCH
3 TBSP	RED WINE OR SHERRY VINEGAR	45 ML
1 TBSP	CANOLA OIL	15 ML
2 TSP	DIJON MUSTARD	10 ML

SANDWICHES

6	THIN BEEF STRIP LOIN STEAKS (ABOUT 1½ LBS/750 G), EXCESS FAT TRIMMED	6
1 TBSP	CANOLA OIL	15 ML
1 LB	MUSHROOMS, SLICED	500 G
1	ONION, THINLY SLICED	1
1 TSP	CHOPPED FRESH ROSEMARY OR THYME	5 ML
½ CUP	READY-TO-USE BEEF BROTH OR DRY RED WINE	125 ML
	SALT AND BLACK PEPPER	
6	SMALL SUBMARINE BUNS (OR 2 BAGUETTES, CUT INTO THIRDS)	6

MARINADE: IN A SHALLOW DISH, COMBINE GARLIC, ROSEMARY, SALT, PEPPER, VINEGAR, OIL AND MUSTARD.

SANDWICHES: ADD STEAKS TO MARINADE AND TURN TO COAT EVENLY. LET STAND AT ROOM TEMPERATURE FOR 10 MINUTES.

MEANWHILE, PREHEAT BARBECUE GRILL TO MEDIUM-HIGH. IN A LARGE SKILLET, HEAT OIL OVER MEDIUM-HIGH HEAT. SAUTÉ MUSHROOMS, ONION AND ROSEMARY FOR ABOUT 10 MINUTES OR UNTIL SOFTENED AND STARTING TO TURN GOLDEN. STIR IN BROTH TO DEGLAZE THE PAN. SEASON TO TASTE WITH SALT AND PEPPER. SET ASIDE.

GRILL STEAKS, TURNING A FEW TIMES, FOR ABOUT 5 MINUTES FOR MEDIUM OR UNTIL DESIRED DONENESS. SLICE BUNS IN HALF LENGTHWISE AND TOAST ON GRILL, IF DESIRED. PLACE A STEAK ON THE BOTTOM HALF OF EACH BUN AND TOP WITH MUSHROOM MIXTURE. COVER WITH TOP HALVES OF BUNS. SERVES 6.

TIP: LOOK FOR THINLY SLICED STRIP LOIN OR OTHER GRILLING STEAKS AT YOUR GROCERY STORE OR ASK THE BUTCHER FOR SOME FAST-FRY GRILLING STEAKS.

MEDITERRANEAN BEEF KEBAB WRAPS

THESE KEBOBS COOK FASTER THAN WAITING FOR TAKEOUT. YOU CAN PREPARE THE SAUCE AND THE KEBABS AHEAD AND GRILL WHEN YOU'RE READY TO EAT.

CUCUMBER YOGURT SAUCE

1	GARLIC CLOVE, MINCED	1
1/2	ENGLISH CUCUMBER, FINELY DICED	1/2
2 TSP	DRIED DILL	10 ML
1/2 TSP	SUGAR	2 ML
1/2 TSP	SALT	2 ML
1/2 TSP	BLACK PEPPER	2 ML
1 CUP	PLAIN GREEK YOGURT	250 ML
1 TBSP	LEMON JUICE	15 ML

KEBAB WRAPS

1 1/2 LBS	BEEF TOP SIRLOIN OR FLANK STEAK, CUT INTO 1-INCH (2.5 CM) CUBES	750 G
1	SMALL ONION, CUT INTO 1-INCH (2.5 CM) PIECES	1
1	GREEN OR RED BELL PEPPER, CUT INTO 1-INCH (2.5 CM) PIECES	1
3	GARLIC CLOVES, MINCED	3
2 TSP	DRIED ITALIAN SEASONING	10 ML
1/2 TSP	SALT	2 ML
1/4 CUP	CANOLA OIL	60 ML
2 TBSP	LEMON JUICE	30 ML
6	GREEK-STYLE PITAS	6
6	ROMAINE LETTUCE LEAVES	6
1	TOMATO, CHOPPED	1
1/3 CUP	CRUMBLED FETA CHEESE	75 ML
1/3 CUP	SLICED PITTED DRAINED OLIVES	75 ML

SAUCE: IN A MEDIUM BOWL, COMBINE ALL INGREDIENTS. COVER AND REFRIGERATE UNTIL READY TO SERVE.

WRAPS: IN A LARGE BOWL, COMBINE BEEF, ONION, GREEN PEPPER, GARLIC, ITALIAN SEASONING, SALT, OIL AND LEMON JUICE. COVER AND REFRIGERATE FOR 45 MINUTES.

PREHEAT BARBECUE GRILL TO HIGH. REMOVE MEAT AND VEGETABLES FROM MARINADE, DISCARDING MARINADE. THREAD MEAT AND VEGETABLES ONTO METAL SKEWERS, ALTERNATING MEAT, ONIONS AND PEPPERS. GRILL FOR 2 TO 3 MINUTES PER SIDE OR UNTIL MEAT IS COOKED TO DESIRED DONENESS. SERVE SKEWERS WITH PITAS, ROMAINE, TOMATO, FETA, OLIVES AND CUCUMBER YOGURT SAUCE. SERVES 6.

TIP: PITA BREAD WILL CRACK IF IT IS TOO DRY. TO MAKE IT PLIABLE, SPRITZ IT WITH A LITTLE WATER, THEN MICROWAVE, ONE AT A TIME, FOR A FEW SECONDS. OR PREHEAT OVEN TO 350°F (180°C). WET PARCHMENT PAPER AND SHAKE OFF EXCESS WATER. WRAP STACK OF PITAS WITH PARCHMENT, PLACE ON A BAKING SHEET AND HEAT IN OVEN FOR ABOUT 10 MINUTES.

MICHELLE'S DELI BEEF HERBED CHEESE WRAPS

WHEN TIME IS TIGHT AND YOU NEED SOMETHING TO BRING WITH YOU, A WRAP MIGHT DO THE TRICK. EMILY'S FRIEND MICHELLE LIKES SUPER-EASY, FAST RECIPES, AND THIS QUICK DINNER HAS SAVED HER ON MANY OCCASIONS.

1/2	SMALL RED BELL PEPPER, DICED	1/2
1/2 CUP	HERB-AND-GARLIC-FLAVORED CREAM CHEESE	125 ML
2 TSP	CREAMY HORSERADISH	10 ML
4	10-INCH (25 CM) WHOLE WHEAT TORTILLAS	4
8 OZ	THINLY SLICED DELI RARE ROAST BEEF	250 G
1/2 CUP	SHREDDED CARROT	125 ML
1/2 CUP	SHREDDED LETTUCE	125 ML

IN A BOWL, STIR TOGETHER RED PEPPER, CREAM CHEESE AND HORSERADISH. SPREAD EVENLY OVER TORTILLAS. TOP WITH ROAST BEEF. SPRINKLE CARROT AND LETTUCE ALONG CENTER OF EACH TORTILLA. FOLD IN TWO EDGES OF EACH TORTILLA AND ROLL UP. CUT IN HALF TO SERVE. SERVES 4.

TIP: WRAP THESE INDIVIDUALLY AND LEAVE THEM IN THE FRIDGE FOR DINNER ON THE RUN. MAKE A FEW EXTRA FOR LUNCH THE NEXT DAY TOO; YOUR FAMILY WILL THANK YOU.

TIP: IF YOU LOVE HORSERADISH, BUMP UP THE AMOUNT TO 1 TBSP (15 ML).

CUBANO SANDWICHES

THIS FLORIDIAN-INSPIRED SANDWICH IS PERFECT
TO PACK UP AND TAKE FOR A PICNIC SUPPER OR DINNER
ON THE GO WHEN TIME IS OF THE ESSENCE.

1	SOFT-CRUSTED OVAL BREAD LOAF		1
1/3 CUP	MAYONNAISE	75 ML	
1 TSP	SMOKED PAPRIKA	5 ML	
2 TSP	DIJON MUSTARD	10 ML	
8	SLICES SWISS CHEESE		8
8 OZ	SLICED DELI OR LEFTOVER PORK ROAST	250 G	
8 OZ	SLICED DELI BLACK FOREST HAM	250 G	
8	SLICES DILL PICKLE		8

SLICE BREAD IN HALF HORIZONTALLY. STIR TOGETHER
MAYONNAISE, PAPRIKA AND MUSTARD; SPREAD ALL OVER
CUT SIDES OF BREAD. PLACE 4 CHEESE SLICES ON
BOTTOM HALF OF LOAF. TOP WITH PORK ROAST, HAM,
PICKLES AND REMAINING CHEESE SLICES. COVER WITH
TOP HALF OF LOAF. CUT INTO 4 PIECES AND ENJOY AS IS
OR, FOR A HOT SANDWICH, WRAP LOAF IN FOIL AND PLACE
IN A 350°F (180°C) OVEN FOR ABOUT 10 MINUTES TO HEAT
THROUGH, THEN CUT INTO 4 PIECES. SERVES 4.

TIP: YOU CAN WARM UP THE SANDWICH ON A GRILL OVER
MEDIUM-LOW HEAT IF YOU ARE TAKING IT ON A PICNIC OR
TO A FRIEND'S HOUSE FOR DINNER.

PINEAPPLE PULLED PORK BUNS

THE PRESSURE COOKER MAKES SPEEDY WORK OF THIS TENDER AND DELICIOUS SANDWICH FILLING. THE RECIPE IS INTENDED TO MAKE A LARGE AMOUNT OF PULLED PORK, FOR PLANNED LEFTOVERS. SERVE IT IN BUNS ON DAY ONE, THEN TRANSFORM LEFTOVERS INTO QUESADILLAS, PIZZA OR A CASSEROLE, OR SERVE OVER RICE.

1 TBSP	CANOLA OIL	15 ML
3 LBS	BONELESS PORK SHOULDER BLADE ROAST, CUT INTO 8 PIECES	1.5 KG
2	ONIONS, DICED	2
6	GARLIC CLOVES, MINCED	6
2 TBSP	PACKED BROWN SUGAR	30 ML
1½ TBSP	SMOKED PAPRIKA	22 ML
2 TSP	HOT PEPPER FLAKES	10 ML
1 TSP	SALT	5 ML
1	CAN (14 OZ/398 ML) PINEAPPLE TIDBITS, WITH JUICE	1
3/4 CUP	KETCHUP	175 ML
1/4 CUP	APPLE CIDER VINEGAR	60 ML
3 TBSP	WORCESTERSHIRE SAUCE	45 ML
	BUNS, SPLIT	
	COLESLAW	
	HOT PEPPER SAUCE	

IN A PRESSURE COOKER, HEAT OIL OVER MEDIUM-HIGH HEAT. WORKING IN BATCHES, BROWN PORK ALL OVER AND TRANSFER TO A BOWL. WITHOUT CLEANING COOKER, ADD ONIONS AND SAUTÉ FOR 5 MINUTES. STIR IN GARLIC, BROWN SUGAR, PAPRIKA, HOT PEPPER

FLAKES, SALT, PINEAPPLE WITH JUICE, KETCHUP, VINEGAR AND WORCESTERSHIRE SAUCE. RETURN PORK AND ANY ACCUMULATED JUICES TO COOKER, LOCK LID AND BRING COOKER UP TO FULL PRESSURE OVER HIGH HEAT. REDUCE HEAT TO MEDIUM-LOW, JUST TO MAINTAIN EVEN PRESSURE, AND COOK FOR 70 MINUTES. REMOVE FROM HEAT AND LET PRESSURE DROP NATURALLY. TRANSFER MEAT TO A CUTTING BOARD AND LET COOL FOR A FEW MINUTES. USING TWO FORKS, SHRED MEAT.

MEANWHILE, SKIM FAT FROM SAUCE. BRING SAUCE TO A BOIL OVER MEDIUM-HIGH HEAT AND BOIL UNTIL REDUCED BY HALF (TO ABOUT 3 CUPS/750 ML), ABOUT 15 MINUTES. RETURN PORK TO POT, STIRRING TO COAT. PILE PORK ONTO BUNS AND SERVE WITH COLESLAW AND HOT SAUCE. SERVES 12.

TIP: LEFTOVERS CAN BE STORED IN THE FRIDGE FOR UP TO 4 DAYS OR FROZEN FOR 2 MONTHS. YOU CAN FREEZE THE PORK IN 1-CUP (250 ML) PORTIONS AND THAW ONLY THE AMOUNT YOU NEED.

BAKED SAUSAGE AND PEPPERS ON FOCACCIA WITH GOAT CHEESE AND AVOCADO

THE GOAT CHEESE ADDS A TANGY AND CREAMY RICHNESS TO THE SANDWICH.

4	HOT ITALIAN SAUSAGES (ABOUT 1 LB/500 G TOTAL)	4
2	RED OR YELLOW BELL PEPPERS, SLICED	2
1	SMALL ONION, THINLY SLICED	1
2 TSP	CANOLA OIL	10 ML
1 TSP	DRIED ROSEMARY	5 ML
1/2 TSP	DRIED OREGANO	2 ML
1/2 TSP	SALT	2 ML
1/2 TSP	BLACK PEPPER	2 ML
1/2 TSP	GARLIC POWDER	2 ML
1	FOCACCIA LOAF (8 TO 10 INCHES/ 20 TO 25 CM LONG)	1
1 CUP	SOFT GOAT CHEESE (8 OZ/250 G)	250 ML
1	AVOCADO, SLICED	1

PREHEAT OVEN TO 450°F (230°C). ARRANGE SAUSAGES, RED PEPPERS AND ONION IN A SINGLE LAYER ON A RIMMED BAKING SHEET. DRIZZLE WITH OIL AND SPRINKLE WITH ROSEMARY, OREGANO, SALT, PEPPER AND GARLIC POWDER. BAKE FOR 30 MINUTES OR UNTIL SAUSAGES ARE COOKED THROUGH.

MEANWHILE, CUT FOCACCIA INTO 4 PIECES, THEN CUT EACH PIECE IN HALF HORIZONTALLY. PLACE FOCACCIA PIECES, CUT SIDE UP, ON ANOTHER RIMMED BAKING SHEET. ADD TO OVEN FOR THE LAST 5 MINUTES OF BAKING, TO

LIGHTLY TOAST. SPREAD GOAT CHEESE ON CUT SIDES OF FOCACCIA. EVENLY DIVIDE AVOCADO, SAUSAGES AND ROASTED VEGETABLES OVER BOTTOM HALVES OF BREAD PIECES, THEN COVER WITH TOP HALVES. SERVES 4.

TIP: IF HOT ITALIAN SAUSAGES ARE TOO SPICY FOR YOUR FAMILY, FEEL FREE TO SUBSTITUTE MILD ITALIAN SAUSAGES.

TIP: PREPARE THE SAUSAGES AND VEGETABLES ON THE BAKING SHEET, COVER AND REFRIGERATE OVERNIGHT TO SPEED UP MEAL PREP FOR THE NEXT DAY.

FOOD IS THE INGREDIENT THAT BINDS US TOGETHER.

PIZZA PANINI

SOME FAVORITE PIZZA INGREDIENTS MAKE THEIR WAY INTO THESE DELICIOUSLY EASY SANDWICHES. WHETHER YOU USE A PANINI PRESS OR PAN-FRY THEM LIKE TRADITIONAL GRILLED CHEESE, THIS IS A GREAT WAY TO CHANGE UP A SUPPERTIME FAVORITE.

1/2 CUP	TOMATO PIZZA OR PASTA SAUCE	125 ML
2 TBSP	SUN-DRIED TOMATO OR BASIL PESTO	30 ML
1/2 TSP	DRIED OREGANO	2 ML
4	CIABATTA BUNS, SPLIT	4
4	SLICES SMOKED MOZZARELLA OR PROVOLONE CHEESE	4
4 OZ	THINLY SLICED SERRANO HAM OR PROSCIUTTO	125 G
1	SMALL RED BELL PEPPER, THINLY SLICED (OPTIONAL)	1
8	LARGE FRESH BASIL LEAVES	8
2 TBSP	EXTRA VIRGIN OLIVE OIL	30 ML

STIR TOGETHER PIZZA SAUCE, PESTO AND OREGANO. SPREAD OVER CUT SIDES OF BUNS. LAYER CHEESE, HAM, RED PEPPER (IF USING) AND BASIL ON BOTTOM HALVES OF BUNS. COVER WITH TOP HALVES. BRUSH OUTSIDE OF BUNS WITH OIL. PLACE IN A PANINI PRESS OR A NONSTICK SKILLET SET OVER MEDIUM-HIGH HEAT. COOK, TURNING ONCE IF USING SKILLET, FOR ABOUT 6 MINUTES OR UNTIL BOTH SIDES ARE GOLDEN AND CRISP. SERVES 4.

CLASSIC CHICKEN SALAD SANDWICHES

EMILY'S FRIEND RANI HAS THREE KIDS WHO LOVE FOOD! BUT THEY HAD NEVER TRIED THIS CLASSIC SANDWICH, SO SHE WAS WORRIED THEY WOULDN'T LIKE IT. THANKFULLY, THEY ALL LOVED IT AND WANTED HER TO MAKE IT AGAIN. WHEW, ANOTHER DINNER DISASTER AVERTED.

3 CUPS	CHOPPED COOKED CHICKEN	750 ML
2	CELERY STALKS, DICED	2
1	GREEN ONION, FINELY SLICED	1
1/4 TSP	SALT	1 ML
1/4 TSP	BLACK PEPPER	1 ML
1/3 CUP	MAYONNAISE	75 ML
2 TBSP	APPLE CIDER VINEGAR	30 ML
8	SLICES WHOLE WHEAT OR MULTIGRAIN BREAD	8
	SMOKED PAPRIKA	
4	LETTUCE LEAVES (OPTIONAL)	4

IN A LARGE BOWL, STIR TOGETHER CHICKEN, CELERY, GREEN ONION, SALT, PEPPER, MAYONNAISE AND VINEGAR UNTIL WELL COMBINED. SPREAD CHICKEN MIXTURE OVER 4 SLICES OF BREAD AND SPRINKLE EACH WITH A PINCH OF PAPRIKA. TOP WITH LETTUCE, IF USING, AND REMAINING BREAD. SERVES 4.

TIP: IF YOU ARE A MAYONNAISE LOVER, FEEL FREE TO SPREAD SOME OVER THE BREAD BEFORE ADDING THE FILLING. LOOK FOR FUN MAYO FLAVORS LIKE ROASTED GARLIC, CHIPOTLE OR SRIRACHA TO JAZZ UP THIS CLASSIC.

HEATHER'S SPICY CHICKEN MELTS

WHEN EMILY'S FRIEND HEATHER'S SON ASKED HIS MOM TO MAKE MORE OF THESE SANDWICHES, SHE KNEW THEY WERE A WINNER. NOW THEY MAKE A RECURRING APPEARANCE IN LUNCH BAGS AND ON THE DINNER TABLE.

2 TBSP	CHOPPED FRESH CILANTRO OR BASIL	30 ML
1/4 CUP	MAYONNAISE	60 ML
1 TBSP	SRIRACHA	15 ML
2 CUPS	SHREDDED COOKED CHICKEN	500 ML
4	SLICES MULTIGRAIN OR CHEESE BREAD, TOASTED	4
4	SLICES JALAPEÑO HAVARTI OR GOUDA CHEESE	4

PREHEAT BROILER. IN A BOWL, WHISK TOGETHER CILANTRO, MAYONNAISE AND SRIRACHA. STIR IN CHICKEN UNTIL COATED. SPREAD CHICKEN MIXTURE OVER BREAD SLICES AND TOP WITH CHEESE. PLACE ON A BAKING SHEET AND BROIL FOR ABOUT 1 MINUTE OR UNTIL CHEESE IS MELTED AND GOLDEN. SERVES 4.

TIP: FOR AN ADDED KICK OF HEAT, TRY USING A JALAPEÑO CHEESE BREAD.

TIP: BAKERY-STYLE BREAD LOAVES ARE GREAT FOR THIS TYPE OF SANDWICH BECAUSE YOU CAN SLICE THE BREAD AS YOU LIKE, THICK OR THIN!

SMOKY CHICKEN, ARUGULA AND AVOCADO BUNWICHES

ENJOY THE CONVENIENCE OF USING A BARBECUED DELI CHICKEN TO GET THIS SANDWICH READY IN NO TIME. SYLVIA'S FAMILY ENJOYS IT AS PART OF A PICNIC MEAL.

1/2 CUP	MAYONNAISE	125 ML
1 1/2 TSP	SMOKED PAPRIKA	7 ML
1/2 TSP	SALT	2 ML
1/2 TSP	BLACK PEPPER	2 ML
1/2 TSP	GARLIC POWDER	2 ML
1/2 TSP	SRIRACHA OR OTHER HOT PEPPER SAUCE	2 ML
4 CUPS	SHREDDED COOKED CHICKEN	1 L
2 CUPS	ARUGULA	500 ML
1	RIPE AVOCADO, SLICED	1
4	SANDWICH BUNS, SPLIT	4

IN A MEDIUM BOWL, COMBINE MAYONNAISE, PAPRIKA, SALT, PEPPER, GARLIC POWDER AND SRIRACHA. STIR IN CHICKEN UNTIL COATED. LAYER CHICKEN MIXTURE, ARUGULA AND AVOCADO IN BUNS. SERVES 4.

TIP: TO TELL IF AN AVOCADO IS RIPE, CHECK UNDER THE STEM AT THE TOP. IF IT COMES OFF EASILY AND IS GREEN UNDERNEATH, THE AVOCADO IS READY TO EAT.

VIETNAMESE-STYLE SUBS

*THERE'S NO NEED TO STAND IN LINE FOR TAKEOUT:
YOU CAN MAKE THESE POPULAR SANDWICHES
AT HOME ANYTIME.*

QUICK VEGGIE PICKLE

2	GARLIC CLOVES, MINCED	2
1	ENGLISH CUCUMBER, THINLY SLICED	1
1	LARGE CARROT, JULIENNED (CUT INTO MATCHSTICKS)	1
1	JALAPEÑO PEPPER, SEEDED AND THINLY SLICED	1
1/2 CUP	THINLY SLICED ONION	1/2
2 TBSP	SUGAR	30 ML
1/4 TSP	SALT	1 ML
3 TBSP	UNSEASONED RICE VINEGAR	45 ML

SANDWICHES

1	GARLIC CLOVE, MINCED	1
1/4 CUP	MAYONNAISE	60 ML
2 TSP	SRIRACHA	10 ML
1 TSP	FISH SAUCE	5 ML
6	CRUSTY FRENCH-STYLE ROLLS, SPLIT	6
3 CUPS	SHREDDED COOKED CHICKEN	750 ML
	FRESH CILANTRO SPRIGS	

PICKLE: IN A MEDIUM BOWL, COMBINE ALL INGREDIENTS, TOSSING TO COAT. LET STAND FOR 30 MINUTES.

SANDWICHES: IN A SMALL BOWL, COMBINE GARLIC, MAYONNAISE, SRIRACHA AND FISH SAUCE; SPREAD ON CUT SIDES OF EACH ROLL. LAYER CHICKEN AND CILANTRO

ON BOTTOM HALVES OF ROLLS. USING TONGS TO DRAIN OFF LIQUID, TOP WITH VEGGIE PICKLE. COVER WITH TOP HALVES OF ROLLS. SERVES 6.

TIP: IN PLACE OF THE ROLLS, YOU CAN USE 1 LARGE BAGUETTE, SLICED IN HALF HORIZONTALLY, THEN CUT INTO 6 PIECES.

TIP: THESE SUBS ARE ALSO DELICIOUS WARM. PREHEAT OVEN TO 400°F (200°C). TOAST SUBS IN OVEN FOR A FEW MINUTES BEFORE ADDING THE CILANTRO AND DRAINED VEGGIE PICKLE.

VARIATION: IF YOU LIKE YOUR SUBMARINE SANDWICHES EXTRA-SPICY, ADD SLICED JALAPEÑOS FOR AN EXTRA KICK OF HEAT.

HOW DO I FEEL WHEN THERE IS NO COFFEE? DEPRESSO.

GRILLED FISH SANDWICHES WITH BROCCOLI SLAW

HERE'S AN EASY RECIPE YOU'RE SURE TO ENJOY.

BROCCOLI SLAW

1/4 CUP	MAYONNAISE	60 ML
3 TBSP	APPLE CIDER VINEGAR	45 ML
1/2 TSP	CELERY SEEDS	2 ML
1/2 TSP	SALT	2 ML
1/2 TSP	BLACK PEPPER	2 ML
1	BAG (12 OZ/340 G) BROCCOLI SLAW	1

SANDWICHES

3	GARLIC CLOVES, MINCED	3
1/2 TSP	EACH SALT AND BLACK PEPPER	2 ML
2 TBSP	CANOLA OIL	30 ML
2 TBSP	PREPARED RELISH	30 ML
4	SKINLESS SALMON OR TROUT FILLETS (EACH ABOUT 4 OZ/125 G)	4
4	LETTUCE LEAVES	4
4	SOFT BUNS, SPLIT	4

SLAW: IN A BOWL, WHISK TOGETHER MAYONNAISE, VINEGAR, CELERY SEEDS, SALT AND PEPPER. ADD BROCCOLI SLAW AND TOSS TO COAT.

SANDWICHES: PREHEAT BARBECUE GRILL TO MEDIUM. IN A BOWL, COMBINE GARLIC, SALT, PEPPER, OIL AND RELISH. COAT SALMON FILLETS WELL ON BOTH SIDES. GRILL SALMON FOR ABOUT 10 MINUTES OR UNTIL FISH FLAKES EASILY WHEN TESTED WITH A FORK. ARRANGE LETTUCE AND FISH ON BOTTOM HALVES OF BUNS AND TOP WITH SLAW. COVER WITH TOP HALVES OF BUNS. SERVES 4.

HOT TUNA MELTS
WITH CHICKPEAS

A TASTY TWIST ON A CLASSIC OPEN-FACE SANDWICH.

1	CAN (6 OZ/170 G) SOLID TUNA, DRAINED	1
1 CUP	COOKED OR DRAINED RINSED CANNED CHICKPEAS	250 ML
1/2 CUP	FINELY DICED CELERY	125 ML
1/2 CUP	CHOPPED GREEN ONIONS	125 ML
1 TBSP	CHOPPED FRESH PARSLEY	15 ML
1/4 TSP	GARLIC POWDER	1 ML
1/4 CUP	MAYONNAISE	60 ML
1 TBSP	LEMON JUICE	15 ML
1 TSP	GRAINY MUSTARD	5 ML
	SALT AND BLACK PEPPER TO TASTE	
8	SLICES MOZZARELLA, SWISS OR PROVOLONE CHEESE	8
1	TOMATO, SLICED	1
4	SLICES CRUSTY BREAD	4

PREHEAT BROILER. IN A MEDIUM BOWL, USING A FORK, LIGHTLY MASH TUNA AND CHICKPEAS UNTIL TUNA IS COARSELY FLAKED. STIR IN CELERY, GREEN ONIONS, PARSLEY, GARLIC POWDER, MAYONNAISE, LEMON JUICE AND MUSTARD. SEASON TO TASTE WITH SALT AND PEPPER. PLACE BREAD SLICES ON A BAKING SHEET AND BROIL FOR 1 MINUTE OR UNTIL LIGHTLY TOASTED. SPREAD TUNA MIXTURE OVER BREAD. TOP EACH WITH 1 CHEESE SLICE, THEN TOMATO SLICES, THEN ANOTHER CHEESE SLICE. BROIL FOR 3 MINUTES OR UNTIL CHEESE IS MELTED AND GOLDEN BROWN. SERVES 4.

FRESH LOBSTER ROLLS

THIS CLASSIC FEATURES TENDER, SWEET LOBSTER
COMBINED WITH CRUNCHY CELERY AND CUCUMBER.
OUR QUICK VERSION HAS A FUN TWIST, USING
TZATZIKI FOR A LIGHT, REFRESHING FLAVOR.

1	LARGE COOKED LOBSTER (ABOUT 2 LBS/1 KG)	1
1/4 CUP	FINELY DICED ENGLISH CUCUMBER	60 ML
1/4 CUP	FINELY DICED CELERY	60 ML
2 TSP	CHOPPED FRESH DILL	10 ML
PINCH	SALT	PINCH
1/4 CUP	TZATZIKI	60 ML
2	SOFT BAKERY HOT DOG BUNS OR SMALL SUBMARINE BUNS, SPLIT	2
2	LEAF LETTUCE LEAVES	2

TWIST OFF LOBSTER TAIL AND, USING SCISSORS, CUT
ALONG UNDERSIDE TO EXPOSE MEAT. REMOVE MEAT
FROM SHELL AND PLACE IN A BOWL. PULL OFF CLAWS
AND LEGS. USING A MEAT MALLET OR SEAFOOD CRACKER,
CRACK CLAWS AND LEGS AND REMOVE MEAT FROM
SHELL. ADD TO BOWL. YOU SHOULD HAVE ABOUT 8 OZ
(250 G) MEAT. CHOP MEAT INTO BITE-SIZE PIECES AND
RETURN TO BOWL. ADD CUCUMBER, CELERY, DILL, SALT
AND TZATZIKI, TOSSING TO COMBINE. LINE BUNS WITH
LETTUCE AND FILL WITH LOBSTER MIXTURE. SERVES 2.

TIP: MAKE THE LOBSTER MIXTURE AHEAD AND STORE IT
IN THE FRIDGE FOR UP TO 6 HOURS.

TIP: IF LARGE LOBSTERS ARE NOT AVAILABLE, PICK UP
2 SMALLER ONES, EACH ABOUT 1 1/4 LBS (625 G).

HAVARTI AND EGG SANDWICHES WITH AVOCADO AND TOMATO

SOMETIMES YOU JUST WANT A SIMPLE DINNER, AND SANDWICHES ARE JUST RIGHT. EGGS ARE OFTEN CALLED THE PERFECT FOOD. WITH PROTEIN TO HELP FILL YOU UP, THESE EGG SANDWICHES WILL NOT DISAPPOINT.

2 TBSP	BUTTER	30 ML
4	LARGE EGGS	4
1/4 TSP	SALT	1 ML
1/4 TSP	BLACK PEPPER	1 ML
4	SOFT KAISER BUNS, SPLIT	4
2 TBSP	CHOPPED FRESH CHIVES OR GREEN ONIONS	30 ML
4	SLICES JALAPEÑO HAVARTI CHEESE	4
1	LARGE AVOCADO, SLICED	1
1	LARGE TOMATO, SLICED	1

IN A LARGE NONSTICK SKILLET, MELT BUTTER OVER MEDIUM HEAT. CRACK EGGS INTO SKILLET, SPACING THEM APART, AND SPRINKLE WITH SALT AND PEPPER; FRY FOR 2 MINUTES OR UNTIL WHITES ARE SET. TURN EGGS OVER AND COOK FOR 1 MINUTE OR UNTIL DESIRED DONENESS. PLACE AN EGG ON BOTTOM HALF OF EACH BUN. SPRINKLE WITH CHIVES AND TOP WITH CHEESE, AVOCADO AND TOMATO. COVER WITH TOP HALVES OF BUNS. SERVES 4.

TIP: THESE EGGS ARE GOOEY; IF YOU DON'T WANT TO LICK YOUR FINGERS, COOK THE EGGS LONGER SO THE YOLKS ARE FIRMER.

BACON VARIATION: SUBSTITUTE 8 SLICES OF COOKED BACON FOR THE CHEESE, OR USE BOTH!

DELUXE FRIED EGG SANDWICHES

EGG SANDWICHES ARE A FAVORITE DINNER ITEM FOR MANY PEOPLE. THIS DELUXE VERSION IS TOPPED OFF WITH A SPICED-UP MAYO AND HAS LOTS OF COLOR THANKS TO HERBS, CHEESE AND TOMATO.

1	LARGE AVOCADO, CHOPPED	1
1	GARLIC CLOVE, MINCED	1
1 TBSP	CHOPPED FRESH CILANTRO	15 ML
1 TBSP	LIME JUICE	15 ML
1/4 TSP	SALT, DIVIDED	1 ML
1/4 TSP	BLACK PEPPER, DIVIDED	1 ML
2 TBSP	BUTTER	30 ML
4	LARGE EGGS	4
2 TBSP	MAYONNAISE	30 ML
1 TBSP	BUFFALO HOT SAUCE	15 ML
8	SLICES BREAD, TOASTED	8
4	SLICES CHEDDAR CHEESE	4
1	TOMATO, SLICED	1

IN A BOWL, MASH AVOCADO WITH GARLIC, CILANTRO, LIME JUICE AND HALF EACH OF THE SALT AND PEPPER; SET ASIDE. IN A LARGE NONSTICK SKILLET, MELT BUTTER OVER MEDIUM HEAT. CRACK EGGS INTO SKILLET, SPACING THEM APART, AND SPRINKLE WITH REMAINING SALT AND PEPPER; FRY FOR 2 MINUTES OR UNTIL WHITES ARE SET. TURN EGGS OVER AND COOK FOR 1 MINUTE OR UNTIL DESIRED DONENESS. IN A SMALL BOWL, WHISK TOGETHER MAYONNAISE AND HOT SAUCE. SPREAD AVOCADO MIXTURE OVER 4 SLICES OF TOASTED BREAD. TOP WITH EGG,

CHEESE AND TOMATO. DRIZZLE WITH MAYONNAISE MIXTURE AND TOP WITH REMAINING BREAD. SERVES 4.

TIP: TRY TO GET AHEAD A BIT AND HAVE THINGS ON HAND IN YOUR FRIDGE TO HELP OUT WITH DINNER. HAVE THE MAYONNAISE MIXTURE MADE AHEAD, AS IT'S A GREAT SPREAD ON OTHER SANDWICHES. PEEL A HEAD OF GARLIC AND KEEP THE CLOVES IN AN AIRTIGHT CONTAINER IN THE FRIDGE SO ALL YOU HAVE TO DO IS GRAB ONE AND QUICKLY MINCE IT. HERE'S THE ONE THAT HELPS THE MOST: FRY UP YOUR EGGS (OVER-HARD IS BEST FOR THIS), LET COOL AND REFRIGERATE. THE NEXT DAY, ALL YOU HAVE TO DO IS WARM THEM UP IN THE MICROWAVE OR OVEN FOR YOUR SANDWICH — A SUPER SUPPERTIME SAVER!

SCRAMBLED EGG VARIATION: IN A BOWL, USING A FORK, WHISK EGGS WITH SALT AND PEPPER. MELT BUTTER IN PAN AND COOK EGGS, SCRAMBLING UNTIL SET AND FIRM.

I THOUGHT GROWING OLD WOULD TAKE LONGER.

EASY SAMOSA WRAPS

THESE TASTY STUFFED SANDWICHES ARE CRISPY WITHOUT DEEP-FRYING.

6 CUPS	CUBED WAXY POTATOES (ABOUT 4 MEDIUM)	1.5 L
2 TSP	CUMIN SEEDS	10 ML
	CANOLA OIL	
2	GARLIC CLOVES, MINCED	2
1	SMALL ONION, FINELY DICED	1
1 TSP	GRATED FRESH GINGER	5 ML
2 TSP	GARAM MASALA	10 ML
1 TSP	SALT	5 ML
1/2 TSP	HOT PEPPER FLAKES	2 ML
1/2 TSP	GROUND TURMERIC	2 ML
1 1/2 CUPS	GREEN PEAS	375 ML
1/4 CUP	CHOPPED FRESH CILANTRO	60 ML
4	10-INCH (25 CM) FLOUR TORTILLAS	4
	MANGO CHUTNEY	

PLACE POTATOES IN A POT, COVER WITH COLD SALTED WATER AND BRING TO A BOIL. BOIL FOR 15 MINUTES OR UNTIL TENDER. DRAIN WELL. (OR MICROWAVE POTATOES IN A COVERED MICROWAVE-SAFE CONTAINER FOR 8 TO 10 MINUTES OR UNTIL TENDER.)

MEANWHILE, IN A LARGE SKILLET OVER MEDIUM-HIGH HEAT, TOAST CUMIN SEEDS FOR 30 SECONDS. ADD 1 TBSP (15 ML) OIL, GARLIC, ONION, GINGER, GARAM MASALA, SALT, HOT PEPPER FLAKES AND TURMERIC; SAUTÉ FOR 5 MINUTES. ADD POTATOES AND GREEN PEAS; SAUTÉ

UNTIL JUST HEATED THROUGH. REMOVE FROM HEAT AND STIR IN CILANTRO.

SPOON POTATO FILLING ONTO TORTILLAS. FOLD TORTILLAS LIKE A BURRITO, ENCLOSING FILLING. IN THE SAME SKILLET, HEAT $\frac{1}{2}$ TSP (2 ML) OIL OVER MEDIUM HEAT. COOK 2 WRAPS UNTIL GOLDEN AND CRISP ON THE BOTTOM, THEN FLIP OVER AND COOK THE OTHER SIDE. REPEAT WITH REMAINING WRAPS. SERVE WITH MANGO CHUTNEY. SERVES 4.

TIP: WAXY POTATO VARIETIES INCLUDE YUKON GOLD, RED-SKINNED AND PURPLE.

TIP: GARAM MASALA IS A BLEND OF SPICES USED IN INDIAN CUISINE. IT IS COMMONLY MADE UP OF CUMIN, CORIANDER, CARDAMOM, PEPPER, CINNAMON, CLOVES AND NUTMEG.

IF I AGREE WITH YOU, WE'LL BOTH BE WRONG.

GRILLED PORTOBELLO AND ROASTED RED PEPPER SANDWICHES

EMILY ENJOYS GRILLING UP PORTOBELLOS OUTSIDE IN THE SUMMER, BUT THEY ARE JUST AS EASY TO COOK ON A GRILL PAN AT OTHER TIMES OF THE YEAR.

I	GARLIC CLOVE, MINCED	I
I TSP	CHOPPED FRESH THYME (OR 1/2 TSP/2 ML DRIED)	5 ML
1/2 TSP	SALT	2 ML
1/2 TSP	BLACK PEPPER	2 ML
2 TBSP	EXTRA VIRGIN OLIVE OIL	30 ML
4	PORTOBELLO MUSHROOMS, STEMS AND GILLS REMOVED	4
1/2 CUP	HUMMUS	125 ML
4	SOFT KAISER BUNS, SPLIT AND LIGHTLY TOASTED	4
	BALSAMIC GLAZE (OPTIONAL)	
1/2 CUP	THINLY SLICED ROASTED RED BELL PEPPERS	125 ML
8	LARGE FRESH BASIL LEAVES	8

PREHEAT BARBECUE GRILL TO MEDIUM-HIGH. IN A SMALL BOWL, STIR TOGETHER GARLIC, THYME, SALT, PEPPER AND OIL. RUB MIXTURE ALL OVER MUSHROOMS. GRILL MUSHROOMS, TURNING OCCASIONALLY, FOR ABOUT 10 MINUTES OR UNTIL TENDER AND GOLDEN. SPREAD HUMMUS OVER BOTTOM HALVES OF BUNS. TOP EACH WITH A MUSHROOM AND DRIZZLE WITH BALSAMIC GLAZE, IF USING. TOP WITH ROASTED RED PEPPERS AND BASIL LEAVES. COVER WITH TOP HALVES OF BUNS. SERVES 4.

TIP: USE YOUR FAVORITE HUMMUS FLAVOR IF PLAIN IS TOO BORING FOR YOU.

PIZZA AND PASTA

EMILY'S BASIC PIZZA DOUGH

THIS IS EMILY'S TRIED-AND-TRUE THIN-CRUST RECIPE FROM HER COOKBOOK PER LA FAMIGLIA.

1/8 TSP	SUGAR	0.5 ML
2/3 CUP	WARM WATER	150 ML
2 1/4 TSP	ACTIVE DRY YEAST (ONE 1/4-OZ/8 G ENVELOPE)	11 ML
2 TBSP	EXTRA VIRGIN OLIVE OIL	30 ML
1/4 TSP	SALT	1 ML
1 1/2 CUPS	ALL-PURPOSE FLOUR (APPROX.)	375 ML

IN A LARGE BOWL, DISSOLVE SUGAR IN WARM WATER. SPRINKLE WITH YEAST AND LET STAND FOR 5 TO 10 MINUTES OR UNTIL FROTHY (IF IT DOESN'T FOAM, TOSS IT OUT AND BUY SOME FRESH YEAST). WHISK IN OLIVE OIL AND SALT. ADD FLOUR AND STIR UNTIL DOUGH COMES TOGETHER. SCRAPE OUT ONTO A FLOURED SURFACE AND KNEAD GENTLY, ADDING A BIT MORE FLOUR IF NEEDED, JUST UNTIL A SMOOTH DOUGH FORMS, ABOUT 8 MINUTES. PLACE IN A GREASED BOWL AND COVER WITH PLASTIC WRAP; LET STAND IN A WARM PLACE FOR ABOUT 1 HOUR OR UNTIL DOUBLED IN BULK. PRESS INTO A 14-INCH (35 CM) CIRCLE. MAKES ABOUT 1 LB (500 G) DOUGH.

TIP: AFTER KNEADING THE DOUGH, PLACE IT IN A GREASED SEALABLE PLASTIC BAG AND REFRIGERATE FOR UP TO 1 DAY OR FREEZE FOR UP TO 2 WEEKS. FROM REFRIGERATOR, LET COME TO ROOM TEMPERATURE BEFORE USING. IF FROZEN, THAW IN REFRIGERATOR OVERNIGHT, THEN BRING TO ROOM TEMPERATURE BEFORE USING.

MIGHTY MEAT SAUCE

THIS HEARTY MEAT SAUCE IS PERFECT TO TOSS WITH YOUR FAVORITE PASTA OR TO MAKE LASAGNA OR PIZZA.

1/4 CUP	EXTRA VIRGIN OLIVE OIL, DIVIDED	60 ML
8 OZ	GROUND PORK	250 G
8 OZ	GROUND VEAL	250 G
8 OZ	LEAN GROUND BEEF	250 G
3	LARGE GARLIC CLOVES, MINCED	3
1	ONION, CHOPPED	1
1 TBSP	DRIED OREGANO	15 ML
1 TSP	SALT	5 ML
1/2 TSP	HOT PEPPER FLAKES	2 ML
1/3 CUP	DRY WHITE WINE	75 ML
2	JARS (EACH 24 OZ/700 ML) STRAINED TOMATOES (PASSATA DI POMODORO)	2
1/2 CUP	WATER	125 ML
6	FLAT-LEAF (ITALIAN) PARSLEY SPRIGS	6
2	BASIL SPRIGS	2

IN A LARGE POT, HEAT 2 TBSP (30 ML) OIL OVER MEDIUM-HIGH HEAT. COOK PORK, VEAL, BEEF, GARLIC, ONION, OREGANO, SALT AND HOT PEPPER FLAKES, STIRRING AND BREAKING MEATS UP WITH A SPOON, FOR ABOUT 8 MINUTES OR UNTIL MEATS ARE NO LONGER PINK. STIR IN WINE AND COOK, STIRRING, FOR 1 MINUTE. ADD TOMATOES. POUR WATER INTO 1 STRAINED TOMATO JAR, SEAL AND SHAKE; POUR INTO OTHER TOMATO JAR, SEAL AND SHAKE. ADD LIQUID TO POT. STIR IN PARSLEY, BASIL AND REMAINING OIL; BRING TO A BOIL. REDUCE HEAT, PARTIALLY COVER AND SIMMER, STIRRING OCCASIONALLY, FOR 45 MINUTES. SERVES 4 TO 6.

DEEP-DISH PEPPERONI AND SAUSAGE PIZZA

THIS CHICAGO-STYLE PIZZA IS DELICIOUSLY DIFFERENT. THE THICK CRUST IS LAYERED "UPSIDE DOWN" — THE CHEESE IS TOPPED BY THE TOMATO SAUCE.

CRUST

2 CUPS	ALL-PURPOSE FLOUR	500 ML
1/4 CUP	CORNMEAL	60 ML
2 1/4 TSP	QUICK-RISING (INSTANT) YEAST	11 ML
1 TSP	SALT	5 ML
1 TSP	SUGAR	5 ML
3/4 CUP	WARM WATER	175 ML
3 TBSP	OLIVE OIL	45 ML

SAUCE

1 TBSP	CANOLA OIL	15 ML
1	SMALL ONION, FINELY CHOPPED	1
1	GREEN BELL PEPPER, FINELY CHOPPED	1
1 CUP	SLICED MUSHROOMS	250 ML
2	GARLIC CLOVES, MINCED	2
1 TSP	DRIED ITALIAN SEASONING	5 ML
1/2 TSP	HOT PEPPER FLAKES	2 ML
1/2 TSP	SUGAR	2 ML
1 1/2 CUPS	TOMATO BASIL PASTA SAUCE	375 ML

TOPPING

2 CUPS	SHREDDED MOZZARELLA CHEESE	500 ML
2 CUPS	SLICED PEPPERONI	500 ML
2 CUPS	CRUMBLED COOKED SAUSAGE	500 ML
1 CUP	SLICED PITTED BLACK OLIVES	250 ML
1/4 CUP	GRATED PARMESAN CHEESE	60 ML

CRUST: GENEROUSLY GREASE THE BOTTOM AND SIDES OF A 13- BY 9-INCH (33 BY 23 CM) METAL BAKING PAN. IN THE BOWL OF A STAND MIXER, COMBINE ALL INGREDIENTS. BEAT ON HIGH FOR 1 MINUTE, THEN SCOOP DOUGH INTO PREPARED PAN. COVER WITH PLASTIC WRAP AND LET STAND IN A WARM PLACE FOR 30 TO 45 MINUTES OR UNTIL DOUBLED IN SIZE.

SAUCE: IN A SKILLET, HEAT OIL OVER MEDIUM-HIGH HEAT. SAUTÉ ONION, GREEN PEPPER AND MUSHROOMS FOR 10 MINUTES. REDUCE HEAT TO MEDIUM AND STIR IN GARLIC, ITALIAN SEASONING, HOT PEPPER FLAKES, SUGAR AND PASTA SAUCE; COOK FOR 10 MINUTES, UNTIL SAUCE IS THICK.

MEANWHILE, PREHEAT OVEN TO 400°F (200°C). WHEN DOUGH IS READY, USE YOUR FINGERTIPS TO GENTLY PRESS DOUGH INTO THE BOTTOM, CORNERS AND 1½ INCHES (4 CM) UP THE SIDES OF THE PAN (ADD A DRIZZLE OF OIL IF DOUGH IS TOO STICKY).

TOPPING: SPRINKLE MOZZARELLA OVER DOUGH, THEN ARRANGE PEPPERONI, SAUSAGE AND OLIVES ON TOP. SPREAD TOMATO SAUCE OVER TOP, THEN SPRINKLE WITH PARMESAN. BAKE FOR 40 TO 45 MINUTES OR UNTIL CRUST IS GOLDEN BROWN. LET COOL FOR 10 MINUTES BEFORE SERVING. SERVES 8.

TIP: A DEEP 12-INCH (30 CM) CAST-IRON SKILLET IS A GREAT ALTERNATIVE TO THE BAKING PAN.

BUTTERNUT SQUASH, BACON AND VEGETABLE PIZZA

THIS SAVORY PIZZA HAS A DELICIOUS ADDITION: IT IS FINISHED WITH A DRIZZLE OF HONEY. YOU CAN PURCHASE PREMADE PIZZA DOUGH OR USE EMILY'S TRIED-AND-TRUE PIZZA DOUGH RECIPE (PAGE 84).

4 CUPS	CUBED BUTTERNUT SQUASH	1 L
1/2	ONION, THINLY SLICED	1/2
1 TBSP	CANOLA OIL	15 ML
6	SLICES BACON, CHOPPED	6
3	GARLIC CLOVES, THINLY SLICED	3
2 CUPS	CHOPPED BROCCOLI	500 ML
1/2 TSP	SALT	2 ML
1/2 TSP	BLACK PEPPER	2 ML
1 LB	PIZZA DOUGH	500 G
1 1/2 CUPS	SHREDDED MOZZARELLA CHEESE	375 ML
1 TSP	DRIED THYME	5 ML
1/2 TSP	HOT PEPPER FLAKES	2 ML
1/4 CUP	GRATED PARMESAN CHEESE	60 ML
1 TBSP	LIQUID HONEY	15 ML

PREHEAT OVEN TO 425°F (220°C), WITH RACK IN CENTER. PLACE SQUASH AND ONION ON A FOIL- OR PARCHMENT-LINED RIMMED BAKING SHEET, DRIZZLE WITH OIL AND TOSS TO COAT. SPREAD OUT IN A SINGLE LAYER. BAKE FOR 10 MINUTES, THEN STIR IN BACON, GARLIC, BROCCOLI, SALT AND BLACK PEPPER. BAKE FOR 15 MINUTES, STIRRING OCCASIONALLY, UNTIL MOISTURE FROM VEGETABLES HAS EVAPORATED AND BACON IS CRISP.

INCREASE OVEN TEMPERATURE TO 475°F (240°C) AND MOVE RACK TO LOWEST POSITION. PRESS DOUGH INTO A 14-INCH (35 CM) CIRCLE ON A LIGHTLY OILED FOIL-LINED RIMMED BAKING SHEET. SPRINKLE MOZZARELLA OVER DOUGH, THEN SPRINKLE WITH VEGETABLE MIXTURE, THYME AND HOT PEPPER FLAKES. BAKE FOR 20 MINUTES, THEN SPRINKLE PARMESAN OVER TOP. BAKE FOR 5 MINUTES OR UNTIL CHEESE IS GOLDEN BROWN. DRIZZLE WITH HONEY BEFORE SERVING. SERVES 5 TO 6.

TIP: TO SPEED THINGS UP, BUY PRECHOPPED SQUASH.

VARIATION: AS AN ALTERNATIVE TO THE HONEY DRIZZLE, YOU CAN USE PURE MAPLE SYRUP.

TEACH A CHILD TO BE POLITE AND COURTEOUS
AT HOME AND, WHEN HE GROWS UP,
HE'LL NEVER BE ABLE TO MERGE ONTO THE FREEWAY.

PUTTANESCA PITA PIZZA

PUTTANESCA SAUCE IS TYPICALLY SERVED ON PASTA,
BUT YOU'VE GOT TO TRY IT ON PIZZA — IT'S DELICIOUS!

4	6- TO 7-INCH (15 TO 18 CM) PITAS	4
2 TBSP	EXTRA VIRGIN OLIVE OIL	30 ML
1	RED OR YELLOW BELL PEPPER, CUT INTO $1/2$-INCH (1 CM) PIECES	1
3	GARLIC CLOVES, MINCED	3
1 TSP	DRIED ITALIAN SEASONING	5 ML
$1/2$ TSP	HOT PEPPER FLAKES	2 ML
1 CUP	TOMATO PASTA SAUCE	250 ML
$1/2$ CUP	SLICED PITTED DRAINED OLIVES	125 ML
1 TBSP	CAPERS, DRAINED AND CHOPPED	15 ML
2 TSP	ANCHOVY PASTE	10 ML
2 CUPS	SHREDDED MOZZARELLA CHEESE	500 ML

PREHEAT OVEN TO 425°F (220°C). SET PITAS OUT ON A
LIGHTLY GREASED FOIL-LINED BAKING SHEET; SET ASIDE.
IN A SKILLET, HEAT OIL OVER MEDIUM-HIGH HEAT. SAUTÉ
RED PEPPER FOR 3 MINUTES. STIR IN GARLIC, ITALIAN
SEASONING, HOT PEPPER FLAKES, PASTA SAUCE, OLIVES,
CAPERS AND ANCHOVY PASTE; REDUCE HEAT TO MEDIUM
AND COOK, STIRRING OCCASIONALLY, FOR 7 TO 10 MINUTES
OR UNTIL THICKENED. SPREAD TOMATO SAUCE OVER PITAS
TO WITHIN $1/2$ INCH (1 CM) OF EDGE. SPRINKLE CHEESE ON
TOP. BAKE FOR 10 TO 12 MINUTES OR UNTIL PITAS ARE
CRISP AND CHEESE IS GOLDEN. SERVES 4.

TIP: ANCHOVY PASTE BOOSTS THE FLAVOR OF ANY
DISH YOU ADD IT TO. IT CAN USUALLY BE FOUND IN THE
CONDIMENT SECTION OF THE GROCERY STORE.

Grilled Portobello and Roasted Red Pepper Sandwiches (page 82)

Four-Cheese Cannelloni (page 108)

Roasted Cauliflower Pasta with Parmesan Hazelnut Crunch (page 110)

SAUSAGE AND RAPINI PASTA

RAPINI OFFERS UP A BITE TO THIS HEARTY PASTA DISH.

I CUP	WATER	250 ML
I	BUNCH RAPINI, TRIMMED AND COARSELY CHOPPED	I
1/4 CUP	EXTRA VIRGIN OLIVE OIL, DIVIDED	60 ML
2	ITALIAN SAUSAGES (BULK OR CASINGS REMOVED)	2
4	GARLIC CLOVES, MINCED	4
1/4 TSP	HOT PEPPER FLAKES	I ML
1/4 TSP	SALT	I ML
I LB	DRIED RIGATONI PASTA	500 G
1/3 CUP	GRATED PARMESAN CHEESE	75 ML

IN A LARGE NONSTICK SKILLET, BRING WATER TO A BOIL OVER MEDIUM-HIGH HEAT. ADD RAPINI, REDUCE HEAT TO MEDIUM, COVER AND STEAM, STIRRING OCCASIONALLY, FOR ABOUT 7 MINUTES OR UNTIL TENDER. DRAIN WELL AND SET ASIDE. RETURN SKILLET TO MEDIUM HEAT AND ADD 2 TBSP (30 ML) OIL. COOK SAUSAGE, BREAKING IT UP WITH A SPOON, FOR ABOUT 6 MINUTES OR UNTIL NO LONGER PINK. ADD RAPINI, GARLIC, HOT PEPPER FLAKES AND SALT; COOK, STIRRING, FOR 5 MINUTES OR UNTIL RAPINI IS STARTING TO BECOME GOLDEN.

MEANWHILE, IN A LARGE POT OF BOILING SALTED WATER, COOK PASTA FOR ABOUT 10 MINUTES OR UNTIL AL DENTE. DRAIN WELL AND RETURN TO POT. ADD SAUSAGE MIXTURE AND TOSS TO COAT. DRIZZLE WITH REMAINING OIL AND SPRINKLE WITH CHEESE. SERVES 4.

STUFFED PIZZA BRAID

BY COMBINING TRADITIONAL PIZZA TOPPINGS A
LITTLE DIFFERENTLY, YOU MAKE A SPLENDID FILLING,
PACKED WITH MEAT AND VEGETABLES, FOR
THIS UNIQUE STUFFED BREAD.

2 TBSP	OLIVE OIL	30 ML
12 OZ	LEAN GROUND VEAL OR PORK	375 G
1	ONION, CHOPPED	1
1 TBSP	DRIED OREGANO	15 ML
PINCH	HOT PEPPER FLAKES	PINCH
2 CUPS	CHOPPED BROCCOLI	500 ML
4 CUPS	LIGHTLY PACKED BABY SPINACH	1 L
PINCH	SALT	PINCH
PINCH	BLACK PEPPER	PINCH
1	JAR (12 OZ/340 ML) ROASTED RED BELL PEPPERS, DRAINED AND CHOPPED	1
1/3 CUP	CHOPPED PITTED DRAINED BLACK OIL-CURED OR KALAMATA OLIVES	75 ML
2 CUPS	DICED PROVOLONE OR MOZZARELLA CHEESE	500 ML
1 1/2 LBS	HOMEMADE OR STORE-BOUGHT PIZZA OR BREAD DOUGH	750 G

IN A LARGE, DEEP SKILLET, HEAT OIL OVER MEDIUM-HIGH
HEAT. COOK VEAL, ONION, OREGANO AND HOT PEPPER
FLAKES, STIRRING AND BREAKING MEAT UP WITH A SPOON,
FOR 5 MINUTES OR UNTIL ONION IS SOFTENED AND VEAL
IS NO LONGER PINK. ADD BROCCOLI, COVER AND COOK FOR
3 MINUTES OR UNTIL BRIGHT GREEN AND TENDER-CRISP.
ADD SPINACH, SALT AND PEPPER; COOK, STIRRING, FOR
ABOUT 2 MINUTES OR UNTIL SPINACH IS WILTED. REMOVE

FROM HEAT AND STIR IN ROASTED PEPPERS AND OLIVES. LET COOL SLIGHTLY, THEN STIR IN CHEESE.

PREHEAT OVEN TO 400°F (200°C). ON A LIGHTLY FLOURED SURFACE, ROLL OUT DOUGH INTO A 16- BY 12-INCH (40 BY 30 CM) RECTANGLE. PLACE ON A GREASED OR PARCHMENT-LINED LARGE BAKING SHEET AND RESHAPE. MOUND MEAT MIXTURE IN CENTER OF DOUGH, LEAVING A 2-INCH (5 CM) BORDER AT THE SHORT ENDS AND A 3-INCH (7.5 CM) BORDER ON THE LONG SIDES. CUT DIAGONAL SLASHES, ABOUT 1 INCH (2.5 CM) APART, ALONG BOTH LONG SIDES OF DOUGH. CRISSCROSS STRIPS OVER FILLING TO COVER, CREATING A BRAIDED LOOK. BAKE FOR ABOUT 20 MINUTES OR UNTIL GOLDEN BROWN. LET COOL SLIGHTLY BEFORE SERVING. SERVES 6.

TIP: YOU CAN SERVE THIS WITH SOME PASTA SAUCE ALONGSIDE. IT IS PERFECT WITH JUST A SALAD FOR DINNER.

SPAGHETTI PIE

COMFORT FOOD AT ITS BEST! THIS TWIST ON SPAGHETTI AND MEATBALLS IS BOUND TO BECOME A FAMILY FAVORITE. YOU CAN PREPARE THE PIE THE NIGHT BEFORE AND POP IT IN THE OVEN WHEN YOU'RE READY TO BAKE. ADD A FEW EXTRA MINUTES OF BAKING TIME TO MAKE SURE THE PIE IS HEATED THROUGH.

8 OZ	DRIED SPAGHETTI	250 G
2 TSP	CANOLA OIL	10 ML
1	SMALL ONION, FINELY CHOPPED	1
1 LB	LEAN GROUND BEEF	500 G
3	GARLIC CLOVES, MINCED	3
2 CUPS	CANNED CRUSHED TOMATOES	500 ML
2 TSP	DRIED BASIL	10 ML
1 TSP	DRIED OREGANO	5 ML
1 TSP	BLACK PEPPER	5 ML
1/2 TSP	HOT PEPPER FLAKES	2 ML
2	LARGE EGGS, LIGHTLY BEATEN	2
1 CUP	SHREDDED MOZZARELLA CHEESE	250 ML
3/4 CUP	COTTAGE CHEESE	175 ML
1/2 CUP	SHREDDED CHEDDAR CHEESE	125 ML
1/2 CUP	GRATED PARMESAN CHEESE	125 ML

PREHEAT OVEN TO 400°F (200°C). LIGHTLY GREASE A 10-INCH (25 CM) DEEP-DISH PIE PLATE; SET ASIDE. IN A LARGE POT OF BOILING SALTED WATER, COOK SPAGHETTI FOR 7 MINUTES OR UNTIL ALMOST AL DENTE (DO NOT OVERCOOK, AS PASTA WILL CONTINUE TO COOK IN THE OVEN). DRAIN WELL AND SET ASIDE.

MEANWHILE, IN A LARGE SKILLET, HEAT OIL OVER MEDIUM-HIGH HEAT. SAUTÉ ONION FOR 3 MINUTES OR UNTIL SOFTENED. ADD BEEF AND GARLIC; COOK, STIRRING AND BREAKING MEAT UP WITH A SPOON, FOR ABOUT 10 MINUTES OR UNTIL MEAT IS NO LONGER PINK. STIR IN TOMATOES, BASIL, OREGANO, BLACK PEPPER AND HOT PEPPER FLAKES.

IN A LARGE BOWL, COMBINE EGGS, MOZZARELLA, COTTAGE CHEESE AND CHEDDAR. STIR IN BEEF MIXTURE AND PASTA UNTIL WELL COMBINED. SCRAPE MIXTURE INTO PREPARED PAN, SMOOTH TOP AND LOOSELY COVER WITH FOIL. PLACE PIE ON A RIMMED BAKING SHEET. BAKE FOR 25 MINUTES, THEN UNCOVER AND SPRINKLE WITH PARMESAN. BAKE FOR 15 MINUTES OR UNTIL TOP IS GOLDEN BROWN. LET COOL FOR 5 MINUTES BEFORE SERVING. SERVES 4 TO 6.

TIP: FOR THIS RECIPE, DO NOT SUBSTITUTE TOMATO SAUCE, AS THE FLAVOR IS LESS CONCENTRATED THAN CANNED CRUSHED TOMATOES.

TIP: FOR A TALLER PIE, BAKE IT IN A GREASED 9-INCH (23 CM) SPRINGFORM PAN.

PRESSURE COOKER SAUSAGE LASAGNA

USING A PRESSURE COOKER AND NO-BOIL LASAGNA NOODLES MEANS GETTING THIS LAYERED PASTA ON THE TABLE FAST! YOUR PRESSURE COOKER NEEDS TO BE AT LEAST 9 INCHES (23 CM) ACROSS TO FIT THE PAN.

2 TBSP	CANOLA OIL	30 ML
1/2	ONION, FINELY CHOPPED	1/2
I LB	SWEET ITALIAN SAUSAGE (BULK OR CASINGS REMOVED)	500 G
3	GARLIC CLOVES, MINCED	3
I TSP	DRIED OREGANO	5 ML
I TSP	DRIED BASIL	5 ML
1/4 TSP	HOT PEPPER FLAKES	I ML
2 CUPS	TOMATO PASTA SAUCE	500 ML
I	LARGE EGG, LIGHTLY BEATEN	I
2 CUPS	SHREDDED MOZZARELLA CHEESE, DIVIDED	500 ML
I CUP	RICOTTA CHEESE	250 ML
6	NO-BOIL DRIED LASAGNA NOODLES	6
1/4 CUP	GRATED PARMESAN CHEESE	60 ML

POUR I CUP (250 ML) WATER INTO A PRESSURE COOKER AND PLACE A TRIVET IN THE BOTTOM; SET ASIDE. TO MAKE A FOIL SLING FOR EASY REMOVAL OF THE LASAGNA WHEN IT IS FINISHED COOKING, TEAR A 24-INCH (60 CM) LENGTH OF FOIL. FOLD FOIL LENGTHWISE INTO THIRDS AND PRESS FLAT; SET ASIDE.

IN A LARGE SKILLET, HEAT OIL OVER MEDIUM-HIGH HEAT. SAUTÉ ONION FOR 3 MINUTES. ADD SAUSAGE, GARLIC, OREGANO, BASIL AND HOT PEPPER FLAKES; COOK

FOR 5 MINUTES, STIRRING AND BREAKING MEAT UP WITH A SPOON, UNTIL MEAT IS NO LONGER PINK. REDUCE HEAT TO MEDIUM, STIR IN PASTA SAUCE AND COOK FOR 7 MINUTES.

MEANWHILE, IN A MEDIUM BOWL, STIR TOGETHER EGG, $1\frac{1}{2}$ CUPS (375 ML) MOZZARELLA AND RICOTTA. LINE THE BOTTOM OF AN 8-INCH (20 CM) SPRINGFORM PAN WITH 2 LASAGNA NOODLES, BREAKING THEM INTO PIECES TO FIT PAN. SPREAD ONE-THIRD OF THE MEAT MIXTURE ON TOP, FOLLOWED BY HALF THE RICOTTA MIXTURE. REPEAT LAYERS, ENDING WITH MEAT SAUCE (PAN WILL BE QUITE FULL). COVER WITH FOIL. PLACE PAN ON TOP OF SLING, THEN LOWER ON TOP OF TRIVET IN COOKER. FOLD DOWN ENDS OF SLING, TUCKING INSIDE COOKER. LOCK LID AND BRING COOKER UP TO FULL PRESSURE OVER HIGH HEAT. REDUCE HEAT TO MEDIUM-LOW, JUST TO MAINTAIN EVEN PRESSURE, AND COOK FOR 20 MINUTES. REMOVE FROM HEAT AND LET PRESSURE DROP NATURALLY.

PREHEAT BROILER. USING SLING, CAREFULLY LIFT PAN FROM COOKER. REMOVE FOIL AND PLACE PAN ON A BAKING SHEET. IN A BOWL, COMBINE REMAINING MOZZARELLA AND PARMESAN. SPRINKLE CHEESE MIXTURE OVER LASAGNA. BROIL UNTIL CHEESE IS BROWNED. LET COOL FOR 10 MINUTES BEFORE SERVING. SERVES 6 TO 8.

TIP: NO-BOIL LASAGNA NOODLES ARE ALSO LABELLED "EXPRESS" OR "OVEN-READY."

TIP: LASAGNA FREEZES WELL. CUT COOLED LASAGNA INTO SINGLE PORTIONS, WRAP IN PLASTIC WRAP AND STORE IN FREEZER-SAFE CONTAINERS.

PASTA WITH TOMATOES AND PANCETTA

THE COMBINATION OF PANCETTA AND CHEESE BRINGS YOU DOWN-HOME TO REAL, RUSTIC CUISINE.

1 TBSP	EXTRA VIRGIN OLIVE OIL	15 ML
4 OZ	PANCETTA OR BACON (SEE TIP), DICED	125 G
4	GARLIC CLOVES, MINCED	4
1	ONION, FINELY CHOPPED	1
1/4 TSP	HOT PEPPER FLAKES	1 ML
1	CAN (28 OZ/796 ML) PLUM (ROMA) TOMATOES, WITH JUICE	1
12 OZ	DRIED SPAGHETTI	375 G
1/3 CUP	GRATED PARMESAN OR ROMANO CHEESE	75 ML
1/4 CUP	CHOPPED FRESH PARSLEY	60 ML

IN A LARGE SKILLET OR SAUCEPAN, HEAT OIL OVER MEDIUM HEAT. COOK PANCETTA, STIRRING, FOR 5 MINUTES OR UNTIL CRISP. ADD GARLIC AND ONION; SAUTÉ FOR 5 MINUTES OR UNTIL ONION IS SOFTENED. ADD HOT PEPPER FLAKES AND STIR TO COAT. STIR IN TOMATOES WITH JUICE, BREAKING THEM UP WITH A SPOON; BOIL GENTLY FOR ABOUT 15 MINUTES OR UNTIL THICKENED.

MEANWHILE, IN A LARGE POT OF BOILING SALTED WATER, COOK SPAGHETTI FOR ABOUT 10 MINUTES OR UNTIL AL DENTE. DRAIN WELL AND RETURN TO POT. ADD SAUCE AND STIR TO COAT WELL. STIR IN HALF EACH OF THE CHEESE AND PARSLEY. SERVE SPRINKLED WITH REMAINING CHEESE AND PARSLEY. SERVES 4.

TIP: IF USING BACON, OMIT THE OIL.

STOVETOP MAC AND CHEESE WITH BACON

YOU CAN SKIP THE STEP OF BOILING A POT OF WATER TO COOK THE PASTA FOR THIS RECIPE — THAT MEANS ONE LESS POT TO WASH.

6	SLICES BACON, CHOPPED	6
1/2	SMALL ONION, FINELY CHOPPED	1/2
3 CUPS	MILK	750 ML
I CUP	WATER	250 ML
2	GARLIC CLOVES, MINCED	2
2 1/2 CUPS	DRIED MACARONI PASTA	625 ML
I TSP	DRY MUSTARD	5 ML
3 CUPS	SHREDDED SHARP (OLD) CHEDDAR CHEESE	750 ML
	SALT AND BLACK PEPPER TO TASTE	

IN A 10-INCH (25 CM) SKILLET OVER MEDIUM-HIGH HEAT, COOK BACON AND ONION, STIRRING OFTEN, FOR ABOUT 5 MINUTES OR UNTIL BACON IS CRISP AND ONION IS TENDER. TRANSFER TO A PLATE. IN THE SAME SKILLET, OVER MEDIUM HEAT, COMBINE MILK AND WATER, THEN STIR IN GARLIC, MACARONI AND MUSTARD; BOIL GENTLY, STIRRING OFTEN, FOR 10 TO 12 MINUTES OR UNTIL PASTA IS ALMOST TENDER. ADD CHEESE, I CUP (250 ML) AT A TIME, STIRRING UNTIL MELTED. REMOVE FROM HEAT AND STIR IN BACON MIXTURE. SEASON WITH SALT AND PEPPER. SERVES 5 TO 6.

TIP: IF YOU HAVE EXTRA TIME, USE AN OVENPROOF SKILLET AND BROIL THE MACARONI FOR A FEW MINUTES, UNTIL THE TOP IS GOLDEN BROWN.

BACON AND SPINACH SPAGHETTI FRITTATA

*THIS FRITTATA IS HEARTY ENOUGH FOR DINNER
AND MAKES FABULOUS LEFTOVERS, SO YOU CAN
ALSO HAVE A GREAT BREAKFAST!*

8 OZ	DRIED SPAGHETTI	250 G
8	LARGE EGGS	8
1/2 TSP	SALT	2 ML
1/4 TSP	BLACK PEPPER	1 ML
2 CUPS	CHOPPED BABY SPINACH	500 ML
1/2 CUP	CHOPPED CRISPLY COOKED BACON	125 ML
1/2 CUP	RICOTTA CHEESE	125 ML
1/4 CUP	GRATED PARMESAN CHEESE	60 ML
2 TBSP	CHOPPED FRESH BASIL	30 ML
3 TBSP	CANOLA OIL	45 ML

IN A LARGE POT OF BOILING SALTED WATER, COOK
SPAGHETTI FOR ABOUT 10 MINUTES OR UNTIL AL DENTE.
DRAIN WELL AND SET ASIDE. IN A LARGE BOWL, USING A
FORK, BEAT EGGS, SALT AND PEPPER. ADD SPAGHETTI,
SPINACH AND BACON, TOSSING TO COAT. SPOON LARGE
DOLLOPS OF RICOTTA INTO SPAGHETTI MIXTURE. ADD
PARMESAN AND BASIL, STIRRING GENTLY TO COMBINE.
IN A LARGE NONSTICK SKILLET, HEAT OIL OVER MEDIUM
HEAT. POUR IN SPAGHETTI MIXTURE AND, USING A FORK,
STIR SPAGHETTI TO DISTRIBUTE IT EVENLY. COOK FOR
ABOUT 10 MINUTES, JIGGLING THE PAN TO MAKE SURE
IT DOESN'T STICK, UNTIL ALMOST SET. PLACE A LARGE
PLATE OVER THE PAN AND INVERT FRITTATA ONTO PLATE.
SLIDE FRITTATA BACK INTO PAN AND COOK FOR ABOUT

10 MINUTES OR UNTIL NO LIQUID APPEARS WHEN FRITTATA IS PIERCED WITH A FORK. SERVES 6.

TIP: IF YOU HAVE ABOUT 3 CUPS (750 ML) OF LEFTOVER PASTA THAT WAS TOSSED WITH SAUCE, YOU CAN USE IT IN THIS RECIPE IN PLACE OF THE COOKED SPAGHETTI. HEAT UP SOME EXTRA SAUCE TO SERVE ALONGSIDE.

VARIATION: SUBSTITUTE 1 CUP (250 ML) CHOPPED COOKED SAUSAGE FOR THE BACON.

EATING IN IS THE NEW GOING OUT.

CREAMY SMOKED SALMON ON FETTUCCINI

THIS PASTA DISH IS A FAVORITE IN SYLVIA'S FAMILY. THE LEMON ZEST AND CAPERS LIVEN UP THE FLAVOR.

I LB	DRIED FETTUCCINI PASTA	500 G
8 OZ	BRICK-STYLE CREAM CHEESE, SOFTENED AND CUT INTO CUBES	250 G
1/2 CUP	MILK	125 ML
1/4 CUP	CHOPPED FRESH DILL (OR 2 TSP/10 ML DRIED)	60 ML
I TBSP	FINELY CHOPPED DRAINED CAPERS	15 ML
2 TSP	GRATED LEMON ZEST	10 ML
I TSP	BLACK PEPPER	5 ML
1/2 TSP	GARLIC POWDER	2 ML
4 CUPS	LIGHTLY PACKED BABY SPINACH, COARSELY CHOPPED	I L
8 OZ	SMOKED SALMON, CHOPPED	250 G

IN A LARGE POT OF BOILING SALTED WATER, COOK PASTA FOR 7 MINUTES OR UNTIL AL DENTE. DRAIN WELL, RESERVING 1/2 CUP (125 ML) PASTA WATER, AND SET ASIDE. IN THE SAME POT, OVER MEDIUM HEAT, COMBINE CREAM CHEESE, MILK, DILL, CAPERS, LEMON ZEST, PEPPER AND GARLIC POWDER, STIRRING UNTIL SMOOTH. ADD SPINACH AND COOK FOR I MINUTE. REMOVE FROM HEAT AND GENTLY STIR IN SALMON. ADD SOME RESERVED PASTA WATER IF SAUCE IS TOO THICK. ADD PASTA AND TOSS TO COAT. SERVES 4.

SPAGHETTI WITH CLAM SAUCE

THE CONVENIENCE OF CANNED CLAMS MAKES THIS PASTA SUPER-EASY. THE FLAVOR OF FRESH TOMATOES ADDS A COLORFUL SUMMERY BITE.

2 TBSP	CANOLA OIL	30 ML
3	GARLIC CLOVES, MINCED	3
1/4 TSP	HOT PEPPER FLAKES	1 ML
4	SMALL PLUM (ROMA) TOMATOES, CHOPPED	4
2 TBSP	CHOPPED FRESH BASIL	30 ML
1/4 TSP	SALT	1 ML
1	CAN (5 OZ/142 G) BABY CLAMS, RINSED AND DRAINED	1
1/3 CUP	DRY WHITE WINE	75 ML
8 OZ	DRIED SPAGHETTI	250 G

IN A LARGE SKILLET, HEAT OIL OVER MEDIUM HEAT. SAUTÉ GARLIC AND HOT PEPPER FLAKES FOR 1 MINUTE. ADD TOMATOES, BASIL AND SALT; SIMMER, STIRRING OCCASIONALLY, FOR 8 MINUTES. ADD CLAMS AND WINE; SIMMER FOR 5 MINUTES OR UNTIL HEATED THROUGH.

MEANWHILE, IN A LARGE POT OF BOILING SALTED WATER, COOK SPAGHETTI FOR ABOUT 10 MINUTES OR UNTIL AL DENTE. DRAIN WELL AND ADD TO SAUCE, TOSSING TO COMBINE. SERVES 2.

CHORIZO AND SHRIMP ORZO PAELLA

EMILY'S FRIEND AMY LOVES ONE-SKILLET MEALS THAT WILL FEED HER YOUNG FAMILY, AND THIS ONE IS A WINNER. ORZO COOKS IN MUCH LESS TIME THAN TRADITIONAL PAELLA RICE, FOR A SPEEDY DINNER.

1 TBSP	OLIVE OIL	15 ML
3	GARLIC CLOVES, CHOPPED	3
1	ONION, CHOPPED	1
1/2 CUP	CHOPPED DRIED SPANISH CHORIZO (ABOUT 1 1/2 OZ/45 G)	125 ML
1 TSP	SPANISH SWEET OR SMOKED PAPRIKA	5 ML
2 3/4 CUPS	READY-TO-USE CHICKEN BROTH	675 ML
PINCH	SAFFRON THREADS (OPTIONAL)	PINCH
2	PLUM (ROMA) TOMATOES, SEEDED AND DICED	2
1 1/2 CUPS	DRIED ORZO PASTA	375 ML
1/2 CUP	DRY WHITE WINE	125 ML
20	LARGE SHRIMP (THAWED IF FROZEN), PEELED AND DEVEINED	20
1	ROASTED RED BELL PEPPER, BLOTTED DRY AND CUT INTO STRIPS	1
	CHOPPED FRESH PARSLEY	
	LEMON WEDGES	

IN A LARGE SKILLET, HEAT OIL OVER MEDIUM HEAT. SAUTÉ GARLIC, ONION, CHORIZO AND PAPRIKA FOR ABOUT 4 MINUTES OR UNTIL GOLDEN. MEANWHILE, HEAT BROTH WITH SAFFRON (IF USING) IN THE MICROWAVE ON HIGH FOR 90 SECONDS. STIR TOMATOES AND ORZO INTO SKILLET, COATING IN PAN OILS. STIR IN WARM BROTH AND WINE; BRING TO A BOIL. REDUCE HEAT, COVER AND

SIMMER FOR 6 MINUTES. ARRANGE SHRIMP AND ROASTED PEPPER OVER ORZO, COVER AND COOK FOR 3 MINUTES OR UNTIL SHRIMP ARE PINK, FIRM AND OPAQUE AND ORZO IS TENDER. SPRINKLE WITH PARSLEY AND SERVE WITH LEMON WEDGES. SERVES 4.

TIP: TO OMIT WINE, INCREASE THE AMOUNT OF CHICKEN BROTH TO 3¼ CUPS (800 ML).

TIP: CHORIZO SAUSAGE IS AVAILABLE EITHER FRESH OR DRIED. FOR THIS RECIPE, BE SURE TO USE AN AIR-DRIED, SEMI-DRY OR DRY-CURED CHORIZO VARIETY.

ALL I ASK IS A CHANCE TO PROVE THAT MONEY CAN'T MAKE ME HAPPY.

CRAB LINGUINE ALFREDO

THIS RICH PASTA DISH IS BEST SERVED RIGHT AWAY. ADDING A TOUCH OF TOMATO PASTE CREATES A LIGHT ROSE SAUCE THAT COATS THE PASTA BEAUTIFULLY.

I TBSP	BUTTER	15 ML
2	GARLIC CLOVES, MINCED	2
I	SHALLOT, MINCED	I
I TSP	CHOPPED FRESH TARRAGON	5 ML
2	CANS (EACH 4 OZ/120 G) CRABMEAT, DRAINED WELL	2
2 CUPS	HEAVY OR WHIPPING (35%) CREAM	500 ML
2 TBSP	TOMATO PASTE	30 ML
10 OZ	FRESH LINGUINE PASTA	300 G
2 TBSP	CHOPPED FRESH PARSLEY	30 ML

IN A LARGE SKILLET, MELT BUTTER OVER MEDIUM HEAT. SAUTÉ GARLIC, SHALLOT AND TARRAGON FOR ABOUT 2 MINUTES OR UNTIL SOFTENED. ADD CRAB AND BREAK UP WITH A SPOON. STIR IN CREAM AND TOMATO PASTE; BRING TO A BOIL. REDUCE HEAT AND SIMMER, STIRRING OFTEN, FOR ABOUT 5 MINUTES OR UNTIL SAUCE IS THICK ENOUGH TO COAT BACK OF SPOON.

MEANWHILE, IN A LARGE POT OF BOILING SALTED WATER, COOK PASTA FOR ABOUT 5 MINUTES OR UNTIL AL DENTE. DRAIN WELL AND STIR INTO SAUCE, COATING WELL. SPRINKLE WITH PARSLEY. SERVES 4.

TIP: FRESH PASTA PACKAGE SIZES VARY, AND THERE IS ENOUGH SAUCE HERE TO COAT UP TO 12 OZ (375 G) OF FRESH PASTA. IF USING LESS THAN 8 OZ (250 G), SIMPLY CUT THE SAUCE INGREDIENTS IN HALF.

FRIED EGG FETTUCCINI AND GREENS

THIS VEGETARIAN PASTA IS A SUPER WAY TO ENJOY SOME GREENS. TOPPED OFF WITH EGGS, IT IS FILLING TOO.

1/4 CUP	EXTRA VIRGIN OLIVE OIL	60 ML
4 CUPS	SHREDDED KALE	1 L
3	GARLIC CLOVES, MINCED	3
1/4 TSP	HOT PEPPER FLAKES	1 ML
1/4 CUP	GRATED PARMESAN CHEESE	60 ML
1	CAN (19 OZ/540 ML) PETITE-CUT GARLIC AND OLIVE OIL DICED TOMATOES, WITH JUICE	1
8 OZ	DRIED FETTUCCINI PASTA	250 G
2 TBSP	BUTTER	30 ML
4	LARGE EGGS	4

IN A LARGE, DEEP NONSTICK SKILLET, HEAT OIL OVER MEDIUM HEAT. SAUTÉ KALE UNTIL WILTED. ADD GARLIC AND HOT PEPPER FLAKES; SAUTÉ FOR 2 MINUTES. STIR IN CHEESE AND TOMATOES WITH JUICE; SIMMER, STIRRING OCCASIONALLY, FOR 10 MINUTES.

MEANWHILE, IN A LARGE POT OF BOILING SALTED WATER, COOK PASTA FOR ABOUT 10 MINUTES OR UNTIL AL DENTE. DRAIN WELL AND RETURN TO POT. ADD KALE MIXTURE AND TOSS WITH PASTA; KEEP WARM. IN A NONSTICK SKILLET, HEAT BUTTER OVER MEDIUM-HIGH HEAT. FRY EGGS, SPACING THEM APART, UNTIL YOLKS ARE SET. DIVIDE PASTA ONTO SERVING PLATES AND TOP EACH WITH AN EGG. SERVES 4.

FOUR-CHEESE CANNELLONI

FRESH PASTA MAKES IT SUPER-EASY TO FILL AND ROLL CANNELLONI, SO YOU CAN ENJOY THIS WEEKEND FAVORITE DURING THE WEEK.

1 CUP	RICOTTA CHEESE	250 ML
1/2 CUP	SHREDDED PROVOLONE OR MOZZARELLA CHEESE	125 ML
1/2 CUP	SHREDDED ASIAGO CHEESE	125 ML
1/3 CUP	GRATED PARMESAN CHEESE	75 ML
1	SMALL GARLIC CLOVE, MINCED	1
2 TBSP	CHOPPED FRESH PARSLEY	30 ML
1/4 TSP	SALT	1 ML
1/4 TSP	BLACK PEPPER	1 ML
1	LARGE EGG, LIGHTLY BEATEN	1
8	SHEETS (EACH ABOUT 8 BY 5 INCHES/ 20 BY 12.5 CM) FRESH PASTA	8
4 CUPS	TOMATO PASTA SAUCE	1 L

PREHEAT OVEN TO 375°F (190°C). IN A BOWL, STIR TOGETHER RICOTTA, PROVOLONE, ASIAGO AND PARMESAN. STIR IN GARLIC, PARSLEY, SALT, PEPPER AND EGG UNTIL WELL COMBINED. SPOON ONE-EIGHTH OF THE CHEESE MIXTURE ONTO A SHORT EDGE OF A PASTA SHEET. ROLL UP. REPEAT WITH REMAINING CHEESE MIXTURE AND PASTA SHEETS. SPREAD HALF THE TOMATO SAUCE IN AN 11- BY 7-INCH (28 BY 18 CM) BAKING DISH. NESTLE CANNELLONI INTO SAUCE. SPREAD REMAINING SAUCE OVER TOP. COVER WITH FOIL AND BAKE FOR ABOUT 45 MINUTES OR UNTIL PASTA IS TENDER AND PUFFED. SERVES 4.

TIP: PASTA SHEETS THAT ARE A BIT LONGER OR WIDER WILL WORK FINE TOO.

Gnocchi and Beef Stew (page 126)

Asian-Style Beef Tacos with Spicy Coleslaw (page 128)

Steak Nachos (page 130)

Lamb Meatballs with Lemony Garlic Potatoes (page 150)

TORTELLINI CASSEROLE

*COMFORTING CASSEROLES MAKE DINNER
WITH YOUR FAMILY MEMORABLE AND DELICIOUS.*

1 TBSP	CANOLA OIL	15 ML
2	GARLIC CLOVES, MINCED	2
1	SMALL ONION, FINELY CHOPPED	1
2 TSP	DRIED OREGANO	10 ML
2 CUPS	TOMATO BASIL PASTA SAUCE	500 ML
1/2 CUP	RICOTTA CHEESE	125 ML
3 TBSP	CHOPPED FRESH PARSLEY, DIVIDED	45 ML
1 LB	FRESH CHEESE OR MEAT TORTELLINI PASTA	500 G
1/2 CUP	SHREDDED MOZZARELLA CHEESE	125 ML

PREHEAT BROILER. IN A SKILLET, HEAT OIL OVER MEDIUM HEAT. SAUTÉ GARLIC, ONION AND OREGANO FOR 3 MINUTES OR UNTIL ONION IS SOFTENED. ADD PASTA SAUCE AND BRING TO A BOIL. REDUCE HEAT AND SIMMER, STIRRING OCCASIONALLY, FOR 5 MINUTES. REMOVE FROM HEAT AND STIR IN RICOTTA AND 2 TBSP (30 ML) PARSLEY.

MEANWHILE, IN A LARGE POT OF BOILING SALTED WATER, COOK PASTA FOR ABOUT 8 MINUTES OR UNTIL AL DENTE. DRAIN WELL AND RETURN TO POT. ADD SAUCE AND TOSS TO COAT. SCRAPE INTO A SHALLOW CASSEROLE DISH AND SPRINKLE WITH MOZZARELLA. BROIL FOR 2 MINUTES OR UNTIL CHEESE IS MELTED AND GOLDEN. SPRINKLE WITH REMAINING PARSLEY. SERVES 4 TO 6.

ROASTED CAULIFLOWER PASTA WITH PARMESAN HAZELNUT CRUNCH

CAULIFLOWER IS INCREDIBLY FLAVORFUL WHEN ROASTED. WHEN COMBINED, THESE SIMPLE INGREDIENTS RESULT IN A DELICIOUS MEAL WITH A CRISP TOPPING.

5	GARLIC CLOVES, SLICED	5
8 CUPS	CHOPPED CAULIFLOWER (ABOUT 1 LARGE HEAD)	2 L
3 TBSP	CANOLA OIL	45 ML
1 TSP	DRIED ROSEMARY, CRUSHED	5 ML
1/2 TSP	SALT	2 ML
1/2 TSP	BLACK PEPPER	2 ML
1/2 TSP	HOT PEPPER FLAKES	2 ML
3 TBSP	BUTTER, DIVIDED	45 ML
1/2 CUP	PANKO	125 ML
1/2 CUP	FINELY CHOPPED HAZELNUTS	125 ML
1/4 CUP	GRATED PARMESAN CHEESE	60 ML
1 TSP	DRIED THYME	5 ML
1 LB	DRIED SHORT PASTA (SUCH AS PENNE, FARFALLE OR GEMELLI)	500 G

PREHEAT OVEN TO 425°F (220°C). PLACE GARLIC AND CAULIFLOWER ON A FOIL-LINED BAKING SHEET, DRIZZLE WITH OIL AND TOSS TO COAT. SPREAD IN A SINGLE LAYER AND SPRINKLE WITH ROSEMARY, SALT, BLACK PEPPER AND HOT PEPPER FLAKES. BAKE FOR 25 MINUTES OR UNTIL CAULIFLOWER IS GOLDEN BROWN AND CRISP.

MEANWHILE, IN A SMALL SKILLET, MELT 2 TBSP (30 ML) BUTTER OVER MEDIUM HEAT. ADD PANKO AND HAZELNUTS; COOK, STIRRING OCCASIONALLY, FOR 3 TO 5 MINUTES OR UNTIL GOLDEN AND TOASTED. IMMEDIATELY TRANSFER

TO A BOWL AND LET COOL FOR 10 MINUTES, THEN STIR IN PARMESAN AND THYME; SET ASIDE.

START COOKING PASTA ABOUT 10 TO 15 MINUTES BEFORE CAULIFLOWER IS DONE. IN A LARGE POT OF BOILING SALTED WATER, COOK PASTA ACCORDING TO PACKAGE DIRECTIONS UNTIL AL DENTE. DRAIN WELL AND RETURN TO POT. ADD REMAINING BUTTER AND ROASTED CAULIFLOWER, INCLUDING ANY OIL AND CRISPY BITS FROM THE BAKING SHEET. TOSS TO COMBINE. TRANSFER TO A SERVING DISH AND SPRINKLE WITH CRUMB TOPPING. SERVES 6.

TIP: THE CRUMB TOPPING CAN BE MADE IN ADVANCE. STORE IN AN AIRTIGHT CONTAINER IN THE REFRIGERATOR FOR UP TO 3 DAYS.

IF THE WORLD WERE A LOGICAL PLACE, MEN WOULD BE THE ONES WHO RIDE HORSES SIDESADDLE.

CAPRESE PASTA WITH HALLOUMI

THE COLORS OF ITALY'S FLAG — RED, WHITE AND GREEN — PLAY A BIG PART IN THIS TWIST ON THE CLASSIC SALAD, WHICH TASTES JUST AS DELICIOUS AS A PASTA!

12 OZ	DRIED PENNE OR FUSILLI PASTA	375 G
3 TBSP	EXTRA VIRGIN OLIVE OIL, DIVIDED	45 ML
8 OZ	HALLOUMI, CUT INTO BITE-SIZE PIECES	250 G
4	GARLIC CLOVES, SLIVERED	4
2	VINE-RIPENED TOMATOES, CHOPPED	2
2 TBSP	CHOPPED FRESH BASIL	30 ML
	BALSAMIC GLAZE	

IN A LARGE POT OF BOILING SALTED WATER, COOK PASTA FOR ABOUT 8 MINUTES OR UNTIL AL DENTE. DRAIN WELL AND RETURN TO POT; KEEP WARM. IN A NONSTICK SKILLET, HEAT 1 TBSP (15 ML) OIL OVER MEDIUM-HIGH HEAT. FRY HALLOUMI FOR ABOUT 5 MINUTES OR UNTIL STARTING TO BROWN. TRANSFER TO A PLATE. ADD REMAINING OIL TO SKILLET AND SAUTÉ GARLIC AND TOMATOES FOR 3 MINUTES OR UNTIL TOMATOES START TO BREAK DOWN. RETURN HALLOUMI TO SKILLET, ALONG WITH BASIL, AND COOK UNTIL HEATED THROUGH. TOSS SAUCE WITH PASTA, COATING WELL. SERVE DRIZZLED WITH BALSAMIC GLAZE. SERVES 4.

BEEF AND VEAL

GRILLED STEAK WITH HERB BUTTER MUSHROOMS

BIG STEAKS ARE JUST AS EASY TO COOK AND SHARE.

2 TBSP	CHOPPED FRESH PARSLEY, DIVIDED	30 ML
I TBSP	CHOPPED FRESH CHIVES	15 ML
2 TBSP	BUTTER, SOFTENED	30 ML
I LB	MIXED SHIITAKE AND OYSTER MUSHROOMS, TRIMMED AND SLICED	500 G
2	GARLIC CLOVES, MINCED	2
I	SHALLOT, FINELY CHOPPED	I
I TBSP	CHOPPED FRESH THYME	15 ML
$3/4$ TSP	SALT, DIVIDED	3 ML
I CUP	READY-TO-USE BEEF BROTH	250 ML
2 LB	BEEF TOP SIRLOIN GRILLING STEAK, ABOUT I INCH (2.5 CM) THICK	I KG
2 TBSP	CANOLA OIL	30 ML
$1/2$ TSP	HOT PEPPER FLAKES	2 ML

IN A BOWL, STIR TOGETHER I TBSP (15 ML) PARSLEY, CHIVES AND BUTTER. SPOON 2 TBSP (30 ML) OF THE BUTTER MIXTURE INTO A LARGE NONSTICK SKILLET OVER MEDIUM-HIGH HEAT. SAUTÉ MUSHROOMS, GARLIC, SHALLOT, THYME AND $1/4$ TSP (I ML) SALT FOR 10 MINUTES OR UNTIL MUSHROOMS ARE GOLDEN. STIR IN BROTH AND BRING TO A BOIL; BOIL FOR 2 MINUTES. STIR IN REMAINING PARSLEY; KEEP WARM.

PREHEAT BARBECUE GRILL TO MEDIUM-HIGH. TRIM ANY VISIBLE FAT FROM STEAK. BRUSH STEAK WITH OIL AND SPRINKLE WITH HOT PEPPER FLAKES AND REMAINING SALT. PLACE STEAK ON GREASED GRILL AND GRILL, TURNING

ONCE, FOR ABOUT 8 MINUTES FOR MEDIUM-RARE OR TO DESIRED DONENESS. TRANSFER STEAK TO A CUTTING BOARD AND SPREAD REMAINING BUTTER MIXTURE OVER STEAK. LET STAND FOR 5 MINUTES, THEN THINLY SLICE STEAK AGAINST THE GRAIN AND PLACE ON A SERVING PLATTER WITH MUSHROOMS. SERVES 6 TO 8.

TIP: DOUBLE UP ON THE BUTTER AND HERB MIXTURE AND ROLL HALF OF IT UP IN PLASTIC WRAP TO SAVE FOR ANOTHER STEAK DINNER NEXT WEEK! IF YOU ARE KEEPING IT LONGER, SIMPLY POP IT IN THE FREEZER.

TIP: IF YOU CAN'T FIND ONE BIG TOP SIRLOIN GRILLING STEAK, ASK YOUR BUTCHER IF THERE'S ONE BEHIND THE COUNTER. IN A PINCH, YOU CAN USE 4 TO 6 SMALLER BEEF STRIP LOIN STEAKS TO GET DINNER HAPPENING WITH THOSE TASTY MUSHROOMS.

ALL I KNOW IS, ONE OF US IS RIGHT AND THE OTHER IS YOU.

SPICY BEEF KEBABS WITH PINEAPPLE SLAW

CONVENIENT BOTTLED JERK SEASONING PASTE ADDS A LOAD OF FLAVOR TO THESE JAMAICAN-STYLE KEBABS. SERVE BUNS ON THE SIDE TO ROUND OUT THE MEAL.

PINEAPPLE SLAW

1	GREEN ONION, SLICED	1
5 CUPS	CABBAGE COLESLAW MIX (ABOUT 1 LB/500 G)	1.25 L
1 CUP	DRAINED CANNED PINEAPPLE TIDBITS, JUICE RESERVED FOR KEBABS	250 ML
1/4 CUP	CHOPPED FRESH CILANTRO	60 ML
1/2 TSP	SALT	2 ML
1/2 TSP	BLACK PEPPER	2 ML
1/2 TSP	SUGAR	2 ML
2 TBSP	LIME JUICE	30 ML
1 TBSP	CANOLA OIL	15 ML
1 TBSP	MAYONNAISE	15 ML

KEBABS

2	GARLIC CLOVES, MINCED	2
3 TBSP	CANOLA OIL	45 ML
3 TBSP	RESERVED PINEAPPLE JUICE	45 ML
1 1/2 TBSP	JERK SEASONING PASTE	22 ML
1 1/2 LBS	BEEF TOP SIRLOIN STEAK, CUT INTO 1 1/2-INCH (4 CM) CUBES	750 G
1	RED BELL PEPPER, CUT INTO 1 1/2-INCH (4 CM) PIECES	1
1	ONION, CUT INTO 1 1/2-INCH (4 CM) PIECES	1
	FLAT METAL SKEWERS OR BAMBOO SKEWERS	

SLAW: IN A MEDIUM BOWL, COMBINE ALL INGREDIENTS. COVER AND REFRIGERATE UNTIL READY TO SERVE.

KABOBS: IN A LARGE BOWL, COMBINE GARLIC, OIL, PINEAPPLE JUICE AND JERK SEASONING. STIR IN BEEF, RED PEPPER AND ONION, TOSSING UNTIL WELL COMBINED. COVER AND REFRIGERATE FOR AT LEAST 30 MINUTES OR OVERNIGHT.

MEANWHILE, IF USING BAMBOO SKEWERS, SOAK IN WATER FOR 30 MINUTES. PREHEAT BARBECUE GRILL TO MEDIUM-HIGH. THREAD ALTERNATING PIECES OF BEEF AND VEGETABLES ONTO SKEWERS; DISCARD MARINADE. GRILL SKEWERS, TURNING ONCE, FOR 4 MINUTES FOR MEDIUM-RARE OR TO DESIRED DONENESS. SERVE WITH SLAW. SERVES 6 TO 8.

TIP: KEBABS CAN ALSO BE BROILED. PREHEAT BROILER WITH RACK SET IN TOP THIRD OF OVEN. LAY SKEWERS ON A FOIL-LINED RIMMED BAKING SHEET. BROIL, TURNING ONCE, FOR 8 MINUTES OR UNTIL BEEF IS COOKED TO DESIRED DONENESS.

LEMONGRASS BEEF SKEWERS WITH DIPPING SAUCE

IF YOU'RE LOOKING FOR A FLAVOR-PACKED MEAL, HERE'S ONE YOUR FAMILY WILL LOVE. SERVE THESE SUCCULENT BEEF SKEWERS WITH RICE AND A SIDE SALAD.

3	GREEN ONIONS, FINELY CHOPPED	3
3	GARLIC CLOVES, MINCED	3
3 TBSP	MINCED LEMONGRASS, WHITE BULB PART ONLY (1 STALK)	45 ML
1 TBSP	PACKED BROWN SUGAR	15 ML
1/4 TSP	BLACK PEPPER	1 ML
3 TBSP	CANOLA OIL	45 ML
1 TBSP	FISH SAUCE	15 ML
1 TBSP	SOY SAUCE	15 ML
1 LB	BEEF FLANK STEAK, SLICED AGAINST THE GRAIN INTO 1/4-INCH (0.5 CM) PIECES	500 G
	METAL OR BAMBOO SKEWERS	
3 TBSP	PLUM SAUCE	45 ML
2 TBSP	HOISIN SAUCE	30 ML
1 TBSP	WATER	15 ML
2 TBSP	FINELY CHOPPED SALTED PEANUTS	30 ML

IN A MEDIUM BOWL, COMBINE GREEN ONIONS, GARLIC, LEMONGRASS, BROWN SUGAR, PEPPER, OIL, FISH SAUCE AND SOY SAUCE. ADD BEEF AND STIR UNTIL WELL COATED. COVER AND REFRIGERATE FOR AT LEAST 1 HOUR OR OVERNIGHT.

MEANWHILE, IF USING BAMBOO SKEWERS, SOAK IN WATER FOR 30 MINUTES. PREHEAT BARBECUE GRILL TO HIGH. IN A SMALL BOWL, COMBINE PLUM SAUCE, HOISIN AND WATER; SET ASIDE. THREAD BEEF ONTO SKEWERS; DISCARD MARINADE. GRILL SKEWERS FOR 3 TO 4 MINUTES PER SIDE OR UNTIL BEEF IS BROWNED AND SLIGHTLY CHARRED. SERVE BEEF SKEWERS SPRINKLED WITH PEANUTS, WITH DIPPING SAUCE ON THE SIDE. SERVES 6 TO 8.

TIP: PRECHOPPED LEMONGRASS IS A GREAT CONVENIENCE ITEM THAT IS AVAILABLE IN FROZEN FORM OR IN TUBES OF PASTE. TO MINCE FRESH LEMONGRASS, USE THE WHITE BULB PART ONLY (ABOUT 6 INCHES/15 CM). CUT OFF THE TOUGH ROOT END AND REMOVE A FEW OF THE TOUGH OUTER LAYERS. LIGHTLY SMASH LEMONGRASS WITH THE FLAT PART OF A KNIFE OR WITH A ROLLING PIN. SLICE VERY THINLY, THEN FINELY CHOP.

TIP: THE EASIEST WAY TO THINLY SLICE BEEF IS TO FREEZE IT FIRST FOR ABOUT 30 MINUTES. THIS GIVES IT A CHANCE TO FIRM UP.

BEEF AND VEGETABLE STIR-FRY ON A CRISPY NOODLE PANCAKE

STIR-FRIES COME TOGETHER QUICKLY, SO HAVE THE INGREDIENTS PREPARED BEFORE YOU BEGIN COOKING.

1 TBSP	CORNSTARCH	15 ML
2 TSP	GRATED FRESH GINGER	10 ML
1/4 CUP	HOISIN SAUCE	60 ML
2 TBSP	SOY SAUCE	30 ML
1 TBSP	SAMBAL OELEK OR CHILI GARLIC SAUCE	15 ML
1 TSP	SESAME OIL	5 ML
1 LB	FRESH ASIAN EGG NOODLES (SEE TIP)	500 G
1/4 CUP	CANOLA OIL, DIVIDED	60 ML
1 LB	BONELESS BEEF STEAK (SUCH AS SIRLOIN TIP, FLANK OR STRIP LOIN), CUT INTO THIN STRIPS	500 G
2	RED OR YELLOW BELL PEPPERS, CUT INTO THIN STRIPS	2
1	GARLIC CLOVE, MINCED	1
2 CUPS	CHOPPED BROCCOLI	500 ML
1/4 CUP	WATER	60 ML
3	GREEN ONIONS, SLICED	3

IN A SMALL BOWL, COMBINE CORNSTARCH, GINGER, HOISIN, SOY SAUCE, SAMBAL OELEK AND SESAME OIL; SET ASIDE. IN A LARGE POT OF BOILING SALTED WATER, COOK NOODLES FOR 40 SECONDS OR UNTIL JUST TENDER; DRAIN WELL AND SET ASIDE. IN A LARGE NONSTICK SKILLET, HEAT 1 TBSP (15 ML) CANOLA OIL OVER MEDIUM-HIGH HEAT. ADD NOODLES, PRESSING GENTLY WITH THE BACK OF A SPATULA UNTIL FLAT AND COMPACT; COOK FOR ABOUT 5 MINUTES OR UNTIL LIGHTLY BROWNED

AND CRISP ON THE BOTTOM. REMOVE SKILLET FROM HEAT AND GENTLY SLIDE NOODLE PANCAKE ONTO A LARGE PLATE. ADD ANOTHER 1 TBSP (15 ML) OIL TO THE SKILLET AND CAREFULLY RETURN PANCAKE TO SKILLET, WITH THE UNCOOKED SIDE DOWN. COOK FOR 5 MINUTES OR UNTIL BROWNED ON THE BOTTOM. REDUCE HEAT TO LOW AND KEEP WARM.

MEANWHILE, IN ANOTHER LARGE NONSTICK SKILLET, HEAT 1 TBSP (15 ML) OIL OVER MEDIUM-HIGH HEAT. ADD HALF THE BEEF IN A SINGLE LAYER AND COOK FOR 2 MINUTES WITHOUT STIRRING, THEN STIR BEEF AND COOK FOR 1 MINUTE. TRANSFER BEEF TO A BOWL AND REPEAT WITH THE REMAINING BEEF. IN SAME SKILLET, WITHOUT CLEANING IT, HEAT REMAINING OIL OVER MEDIUM-HIGH HEAT. SAUTÉ RED PEPPERS, GARLIC AND BROCCOLI FOR 2 MINUTES. ADD WATER, COVER AND COOK FOR 1 MINUTE. UNCOVER AND STIR IN HOISIN MIXTURE; COOK FOR 1 MINUTE. STIR IN GREEN ONIONS AND BEEF, ALONG WITH ANY ACCUMULATED JUICES; COOK, STIRRING CONSTANTLY, FOR ABOUT 30 SECONDS OR UNTIL HEATED THROUGH. TRANSFER NOODLE PANCAKE TO A CUTTING BOARD AND CUT INTO 6 WEDGES. SERVE WITH BEEF MIXTURE LADLED OVER TOP. SERVES 6.

TIP: FRESH ASIAN EGG NOODLES ARE SOMETIMES LABELED "WONTON NOODLES." THEY CAN USUALLY BE FOUND IN THE REFRIGERATED ASIAN INGREDIENT SECTION OF GROCERY STORES OR ASIAN SPECIALTY MARKETS.

STUFFED SKILLET PEPPERS

STUFFED PEPPERS HAVE ALWAYS BEEN A FAVORITE
DINNER FOR EMILY'S FAMILY, BUT SOME (THE KIDS)
DON'T HAVE THE PATIENCE TO WAIT FOR THEM TO COOK
IN THE OVEN. THIS SKILLET VERSION IS A QUICKER WAY
TO SERVE UP SUPPER, SO EVERYONE IS HAPPY!

1 TBSP	CANOLA OIL	15 ML
4	GARLIC CLOVES, MINCED	4
1	SMALL ONION, CHOPPED	1
1	GREEN BELL PEPPER, DICED	1
12 OZ	BONELESS FAST-FRY BEEF STEAKS, DICED	375 G
1 TSP	DRIED OREGANO	5 ML
1/4 TSP	HOT PEPPER FLAKES	1 ML
1/4 TSP	SALT	1 ML
1/4 TSP	BLACK PEPPER	1 ML
2/3 CUP	SHREDDED MOZZARELLA CHEESE	150 ML
1/4 CUP	GRATED PARMESAN CHEESE	60 ML
1/4 CUP	ITALIAN-SEASONED DRY BREAD CRUMBS	60 ML
2	RED BELL PEPPERS, HALVED LENGTHWISE	2
1 CUP	TOMATO BASIL PASTA SAUCE	250 ML
1/3 CUP	WATER	75 ML

IN A LARGE NONSTICK SKILLET, HEAT OIL OVER MEDIUM
HEAT. SAUTÉ GARLIC, ONION AND GREEN PEPPER FOR
5 MINUTES OR UNTIL SOFTENED. STIR IN STEAK,
OREGANO, HOT PEPPER FLAKES, SALT AND BLACK PEPPER;
COOK, STIRRING, FOR 5 MINUTES OR UNTIL JUST A HINT
OF PINK REMAINS IN BEEF. TRANSFER TO A BOWL AND

STIR IN MOZZARELLA, PARMESAN AND BREAD CRUMBS. SPOON MIXTURE INTO RED PEPPER HALVES, DIVIDING EVENLY. PLACE STUFFED PEPPERS IN THE SKILLET AND POUR PASTA SAUCE AND WATER AROUND PEPPERS; BRING TO A SIMMER OVER MEDIUM HEAT. REDUCE HEAT, COVER AND SIMMER FOR 10 MINUTES OR UNTIL PEPPERS ARE SOFT AND CHEESE IS MELTED. SERVES 4.

TIP: USE BELL PEPPERS IN DIFFERENT COLORS, FOR A BEAUTIFUL PREPARATION.

VARIATION: WANT A SPICY MEXICAN TWIST TO THIS SKILLET SUPPER? ADD 1 TSP (5 ML) CHILI POWDER WITH THE OREGANO AND REPLACE THE MOZZARELLA AND PARMESAN CHEESES WITH 3/4 CUP (175 ML) SHREDDED JALAPEÑO HAVARTI. SWAP OUT THE PASTA SAUCE FOR SALSA, AND THERE YOU HAVE IT!

CHUNKY STEAK CHILI

INSPIRED BY CHILI COOKOFFS ACROSS NORTH AMERICA, WE CREATED THIS COMBO OF STEAK AND BAKED BEANS.

I TBSP	CANOLA OIL	15 ML
2 LBS	BEEF TOP SIRLOIN STEAK, TRIMMED AND CUT INTO I-INCH (2.5 CM) CUBES	I KG
4	GARLIC CLOVES, MINCED	4
2	CELERY STALKS, DICED	2
I	LARGE RED OR ORANGE BELL PEPPER, DICED	I
I	LARGE ONION, CHOPPED	I
I TBSP	CHILI POWDER	15 ML
2 TSP	DRIED OREGANO	10 ML
I TSP	GROUND CUMIN	5 ML
1/2 TSP	SALT	2 ML
1/4 TSP	CAYENNE PEPPER	I ML
1/4 TSP	BLACK PEPPER	I ML
I	CAN (28 OZ/796 ML) DICED TOMATOES, WITH JUICE	I
3/4 CUP	READY-TO-USE BEEF BROTH	175 ML
I	CAN (14 OZ/398 ML) BAKED BEANS IN TOMATO SAUCE	I
I	CAN (19 OZ/540 ML) RED KIDNEY OR BLACK BEANS, RINSED AND DRAINED (2 CUPS/500 ML)	I
I TBSP	WORCESTERSHIRE SAUCE	15 ML

IN A LARGE, SHALLOW SAUCEPAN, HEAT OIL OVER MEDIUM-HIGH HEAT. IN BATCHES AS NECESSARY, BROWN BEEF AND TRANSFER TO A BOWL. REDUCE HEAT TO MEDIUM AND SAUTÉ GARLIC, CELERY, RED PEPPER AND ONION

FOR 5 MINUTES. STIR IN CHILI POWDER, OREGANO, CUMIN, SALT, CAYENNE AND BLACK PEPPER; SAUTÉ FOR 2 MINUTES OR UNTIL VEGETABLES ARE SOFTENED. RETURN BEEF TO PAN, ALONG WITH ANY ACCUMULATED JUICES. STIR IN TOMATOES WITH JUICE AND BROTH; BRING TO A BOIL. STIR IN BAKED BEANS, KIDNEY BEANS AND WORCESTERSHIRE SAUCE; REDUCE HEAT AND SIMMER, STIRRING OCCASIONALLY, FOR 20 MINUTES OR UNTIL SLIGHTLY THICKENED. SERVES 6.

TIP: SERVE THIS CHILI WITH CORNBREAD OR MAKE A SIMPLE BREAD BOWL BY HOLLOWING OUT A KAISER ROLL AND SERVING THE CHILI IN IT. THIS CHUNKY CHILI IS ALSO DELICIOUS LADLED OVER YOUR FAVORITE CREAMY MASHED POTATOES.

I'M NOT ARGUING. I'M EXPLAINING WHY I'M RIGHT.

GNOCCHI AND BEEF STEW

HERE'S A THICK, COMFORTING STEW.

1¼ LBS	BEEF STRIP LOIN STEAKS, TRIMMED AND CUT INTO 1-INCH (2.5 CM) CUBES	625 G
2 TBSP	ALL-PURPOSE FLOUR	30 ML
2 TSP	DRIED ITALIAN SEASONING	10 ML
1 TSP	EACH SALT AND BLACK PEPPER, DIVIDED	5 ML
1 TBSP	CANOLA OIL	15 ML
2	CARROTS, CHOPPED	2
2	GARLIC CLOVES, MINCED	2
1	ONION, CHOPPED	1
1	CELERY STALK, CHOPPED	1
2½ CUPS	READY-TO-USE BEEF BROTH	625 ML
2 TBSP	TOMATO PASTE	30 ML
2	BAY LEAVES	2
1 LB	FRESH POTATO GNOCCHI	500 G

TOSS STEAK WITH FLOUR, ITALIAN SEASONING AND HALF EACH OF THE SALT AND PEPPER. IN A LARGE, SHALLOW SAUCEPAN, HEAT OIL OVER MEDIUM-HIGH HEAT. IN BATCHES AS NECESSARY, BROWN BEEF AND TRANSFER TO A PLATE. REDUCE HEAT TO MEDIUM AND SAUTÉ CARROTS, GARLIC, ONION AND CELERY FOR 5 MINUTES OR UNTIL SOFTENED. STIR IN BROTH, TOMATO PASTE, BAY LEAVES AND REMAINING SALT AND PEPPER; BRING TO A BOIL. RETURN STEAK TO THE PAN, ALONG WITH ANY ACCUMULATED JUICES. STIR IN GNOCCHI, REDUCE HEAT AND SIMMER GENTLY FOR ABOUT 5 MINUTES OR UNTIL SAUCE IS THICKENED AND GNOCCHI IS TENDER. DISCARD BAY LEAVES. SERVES 4 TO 6.

Apricot Cranberry Stuffed Pork Tenderloin (page 154)

Caesar Pork Burgers (page 162)

Roast Chicken, Potatoes and Chickpeas (page 172)

ONE-POT BEEF STROGANOFF

ONE POT MEANS LESS CLEANUP WITH THIS STREAMLINED REMAKE OF A FLAVORFUL CLASSIC.

1 TBSP	CANOLA OIL	15 ML
1	ONION, THINLY SLICED	1
2	GARLIC CLOVES, MINCED	2
1 LB	LEAN GROUND BEEF	500 G
2 CUPS	SLICED MUSHROOMS	500 ML
2 TSP	DRIED THYME	10 ML
1 1/2 TSP	BLACK PEPPER	7 ML
1 TSP	PAPRIKA	5 ML
1 TSP	DIJON MUSTARD	5 ML
12 OZ	DRIED BROAD EGG NOODLES	375 G
4 CUPS	READY-TO-USE BEEF BROTH	1 L
1 TSP	WORCESTERSHIRE SAUCE	5 ML
1/2 CUP	SOUR CREAM OR PLAIN YOGURT	125 ML
1/4 CUP	CHOPPED FRESH PARSLEY	60 ML

IN A LARGE POT, HEAT OIL OVER MEDIUM-HIGH HEAT. SAUTÉ ONION FOR 5 MINUTES. ADD GARLIC AND SAUTÉ FOR 30 SECONDS. ADD BEEF, MUSHROOMS, THYME, PEPPER, PAPRIKA AND MUSTARD; COOK, BREAKING BEEF UP WITH A SPOON, FOR 8 MINUTES OR UNTIL BEEF IS NO LONGER PINK. STIR IN NOODLES, BROTH AND WORCESTERSHIRE; BOIL, STIRRING OCCASIONALLY, FOR 5 MINUTES. REDUCE HEAT TO MEDIUM AND COOK, STIRRING OCCASIONALLY, FOR ABOUT 10 MINUTES OR UNTIL NOODLES ARE AL DENTE (COOK A FEW MINUTES LONGER IF USING VERY WIDE EGG NOODLES). REMOVE FROM HEAT AND STIR IN SOUR CREAM. SERVE GARNISHED WITH PARSLEY. SERVES 6.

ASIAN-STYLE BEEF TACOS WITH SPICY COLESLAW

TACO TUESDAY NEVER TASTED SO GOOD!

1	GARLIC CLOVE, MINCED	1
1	SMALL SHALLOT, MINCED	1
2 TBSP	PACKED BROWN SUGAR	30 ML
1/4 CUP	SOY SAUCE	60 ML
2 TBSP	WATER	30 ML
1	BEEF FLANK STEAK (ABOUT 2 LBS/1 KG)	1
8	7-INCH (18 CM) FLOUR OR CORN TORTILLAS	8

SPICY COLESLAW

2 CUPS	CABBAGE COLESLAW MIX	500 ML
1/2 TSP	SALT	2 ML
1/2 TSP	SUGAR	2 ML
2	GARLIC CLOVES, MINCED	2
3 TBSP	UNSEASONED RICE VINEGAR	45 ML
1 TSP	SESAME OIL	5 ML
1/2 TSP	SRIRACHA	2 ML

IN A SEALABLE PLASTIC BAG OR SHALLOW GLASS DISH, COMBINE GARLIC, SHALLOT, BROWN SUGAR, SOY SAUCE AND WATER. ADD STEAK AND MARINATE FOR 15 MINUTES OR COVER AND REFRIGERATE OVERNIGHT.

COLESLAW: MEANWHILE, PREHEAT BARBECUE GRILL TO MEDIUM-HIGH. IN A LARGE BOWL, TOSS COLESLAW WITH SALT AND SUGAR; LET STAND FOR 10 MINUTES. STIR IN GARLIC, VINEGAR, SESAME OIL AND SRIRACHA; SET ASIDE.

REMOVE STEAK FROM MARINADE, DISCARDING MARINADE. PLACE STEAK ON GREASED GRILL AND GRILL, TURNING ONCE, FOR ABOUT 12 MINUTES FOR MEDIUM-RARE OR TO DESIRED DONENESS. TRANSFER TO A CUTTING BOARD AND TENT WITH FOIL FOR 5 MINUTES BEFORE THINLY SLICING AGAINST THE GRAIN. TUCK STEAK INTO TORTILLAS AND TOP WITH COLESLAW. SERVES 4 TO 6.

TIP: YOU CAN ALSO SERVE UP THE BEEF MIXTURE OVER COOKED RICE OR QUINOA AND SERVE THE COLESLAW ON THE SIDE.

KEEP YOUR FRIENDS CLOSE AND YOUR SNACKS CLOSER.

STEAK NACHOS

THERE ARE PLENTY OF VEGGIES AND TOPPINGS IN THIS RECIPE TO BOOST NACHOS INTO A JUSTIFIABLE MEAL.

1	SWEET POTATO, SHREDDED OR CUT INTO THIN MATCHSTICKS	1
2 TBSP	CANOLA OIL	30 ML
1/2 TSP	SALT	2 ML
1/2 TSP	GARLIC POWDER	2 ML
1/2 TSP	SMOKED PAPRIKA	2 ML
12 OZ	BONELESS FAST-FRY BEEF STEAKS	375 G
3	GREEN ONIONS, SLICED	3
1 CUP	COOKED OR DRAINED RINSED CANNED BLACK BEANS	250 ML
1 CUP	CORN KERNELS (THAWED IF FROZEN)	250 ML
1/4 CUP	BARBECUE SAUCE	60 ML
1	BAG (10 OZ/270 G) TORTILLA CHIPS	1
2 CUPS	SHREDDED MOZZARELLA CHEESE	500 ML
1 CUP	SHREDDED CHEDDAR CHEESE	250 ML
2	PLUM (ROMA) TOMATOES, CHOPPED	2
1/2 CUP	SLICED PITTED DRAINED BLACK OLIVES	125 ML
1/2 CUP	CHOPPED FRESH CILANTRO	125 ML
3 CUPS	SHREDDED LETTUCE	750 ML
	SALSA, SOUR CREAM, GUACAMOLE, SLICED PICKLED JALAPEÑOS	

PREHEAT OVEN TO 400°F (200°C). PLACE SWEET POTATO ON A FOIL-LINED LARGE BAKING SHEET AND DRIZZLE WITH OIL, TOSSING TO COAT EVENLY. SPREAD IN A SINGLE LAYER AND SPRINKLE WITH SALT, GARLIC POWDER AND PAPRIKA. BAKE FOR 20 MINUTES, STIRRING ONCE, UNTIL TENDER-CRISP.

MEANWHILE, HEAT A LIGHTLY OILED NONSTICK PAN OVER MEDIUM-HIGH HEAT. IN BATCHES, COOK STEAKS FOR 2 MINUTES PER SIDE. TRANSFER TO A CUTTING BOARD, LET COOL SLIGHTLY, THEN CUT INTO BITE-SIZE PIECES. PLACE BEEF IN A MEDIUM BOWL AND ADD GREEN ONIONS, BEANS, CORN AND BARBECUE SAUCE, TOSSING TO COAT; SET ASIDE.

SPREAD HALF THE TORTILLA CHIPS IN A SINGLE LAYER ON TOP OF SWEET POTATOES. TOP WITH HALF THE BEEF MIXTURE, THEN HALF EACH OF THE MOZZARELLA AND CHEDDAR. REPEAT LAYERS OF CHIPS, BEEF AND CHEESES. BAKE FOR 10 TO 12 MINUTES OR UNTIL HEATED THROUGH AND CHEESE IS MELTED. SERVE IMMEDIATELY, TOPPED WITH TOMATOES, OLIVES, CILANTRO AND SHREDDED LETTUCE. SERVE SALSA, SOUR CREAM, GUACAMOLE AND JALAPEÑOS ON THE SIDE, AS DESIRED. SERVES 4 TO 6.

TIP: USE YOUR FOOD PROCESSOR TO SHRED THE SWEET POTATOES, FOR SPEEDIER PREP.

TIP: MONTEREY JACK CHEESE CAN BE SUBSTITUTED FOR THE MOZZARELLA CHEESE.

LAYERED MEXICAN BEEF PIE

YOUR FAMILY WILL LOVE THIS FLAVOR-PACKED PIE.
INCREASE THE AMOUNT OF HOT PEPPER FLAKES IF YOU
LIKE A LITTLE EXTRA HEAT!

1 TBSP	CANOLA OIL	15 ML
1	ONION, FINELY CHOPPED	1
1 LB	LEAN GROUND BEEF	500 G
3	GARLIC CLOVES, MINCED	3
1 TBSP	CHILI POWDER	15 ML
2 TSP	GROUND CUMIN	10 ML
1 TSP	BLACK PEPPER	5 ML
1 TSP	SALT	5 ML
1/2 TSP	HOT PEPPER FLAKES	2 ML
3 TBSP	TOMATO PASTE	45 ML
1 CUP	CORN KERNELS (THAWED IF FROZEN)	250 ML
1 CUP	COOKED OR DRAINED RINSED CANNED BLACK OR RED KIDNEY BEANS	250 ML
1/2 CUP	SLICED PITTED DRAINED BLACK OLIVES	125 ML
1/2 CUP	CHOPPED FRESH CILANTRO (OPTIONAL)	125 ML
3	10-INCH (25 CM) FLOUR TORTILLAS	3
3 CUPS	SHREDDED MONTEREY JACK CHEESE	750 ML
	SOUR CREAM (OPTIONAL)	

PREHEAT OVEN TO 400°F (200°C). LIGHTLY GREASE A
10-INCH (25 CM) DEEP-DISH PIE PLATE AND SET ON
A BAKING SHEET. IN A LARGE SKILLET, HEAT OIL OVER
MEDIUM-HIGH HEAT. SAUTÉ ONION FOR 5 MINUTES. STIR
IN BEEF, GARLIC, CHILI POWDER, CUMIN, BLACK PEPPER,
SALT, HOT PEPPER FLAKES AND TOMATO PASTE; COOK,
BREAKING BEEF UP WITH A SPOON, FOR 8 MINUTES OR
UNTIL BEEF IS NO LONGER PINK. ADD CORN, BEANS,

OLIVES AND CILANTRO (IF USING); COOK, STIRRING, FOR 5 MINUTES. PRESS 1 TORTILLA INTO PREPARED PIE PLATE. SPREAD ONE-THIRD OF THE BEEF MIXTURE OVER TORTILLA, THEN SPRINKLE WITH 1 CUP (250 ML) CHEESE. REPEAT LAYERS TWICE MORE. THE PLATE WILL BE QUITE FULL, BUT THE CONTENTS WILL SINK A BIT DURING BAKING. BAKE FOR 20 MINUTES OR UNTIL HEATED THROUGH. SERVE WITH SOUR CREAM, IF DESIRED. SERVES 8.

TIP: A 10-INCH (25 CM) CAST-IRON SKILLET IS ANOTHER OPTION FOR COOKING THE PIE.

TIP: SWAP IN JALAPEÑO JACK CHEESE FOR AN EXTRA KICK OF HEAT AND FLAVOR.

SWEET DREAMS ARE MADE OF CHEESE.
WHO AM I TO DIS A BRIE?

DONAIRS

CHOOSE CONDIMENTS SUCH AS SLICED PICKLED TURNIPS AND WILD PICKLED CUCUMBER FOR A MORE AUTHENTIC FLAVOR — THEY'RE READILY FOUND IN THE MEDITERRANEAN SECTION OF MOST GROCERY STORES. HAVE PLENTY OF NAPKINS ON HAND, AS THIS MEAL IS DELICIOUS, BUT CAN BE A BIT MESSY TO EAT.

DONAIR MEAT

1½ LBS	LEAN GROUND BEEF (OR A MIX OF GROUND BEEF AND TURKEY)	750 G
½ CUP	DRY BREAD CRUMBS	125 ML
1 TBSP	DRIED OREGANO	15 ML
1 TBSP	PAPRIKA	15 ML
1 TBSP	ONION POWDER	15 ML
2 TSP	BLACK PEPPER	10 ML
1 TSP	GARLIC POWDER	5 ML
1 TSP	SALT	5 ML
1	LARGE EGG, LIGHTLY BEATEN	1

DONAIR SAUCE

1	CAN (14 OZ OR 300 ML) SWEETENED CONDENSED MILK	1
3 TBSP	WHITE VINEGAR	45 ML
2 TSP	GARLIC POWDER	10 ML
1 TSP	ONION POWDER	5 ML
6	9- TO 10-INCH (23 TO 25 CM) MEDITERRANEAN-STYLE PITAS	6
1	TOMATO, CHOPPED	1
½	ONION, THINLY SLICED	½
½ CUP	SLICED PICKLES	125 ML
½ CUP	SLICED PITTED OLIVES (OPTIONAL)	125 ML

1½ CUPS   SHREDDED LETTUCE   375 ML
            HOT PEPPER SAUCE

MEAT: PREHEAT OVEN TO 350°F (180°C) AND LINE A 13- BY
9-INCH (33 BY 23 CM) BAKING PAN WITH FOIL. IN THE
BOWL OF A STAND MIXER, COMBINE BEEF, BREAD CRUMBS,
OREGANO, PAPRIKA, ONION POWDER, PEPPER, GARLIC
POWDER, SALT AND EGG; MIX ON LOW SPEED UNTIL
THOROUGHLY COMBINED, ABOUT 8 MINUTES (YOU CAN
ALSO MIX BY HAND; IT JUST TAKES A BIT MORE MUSCLE
POWER). PLACE MEAT MIXTURE IN PREPARED PAN AND
SHAPE INTO A 7- BY 4-INCH (18 BY 10 CM) LOAF. BAKE FOR
1 HOUR OR UNTIL A MEAT THERMOMETER INSERTED IN
THE CENTER REGISTERS AT LEAST 160°F (71°C). REMOVE
FROM OVEN, LET COOL FOR 10 MINUTES, THEN CUT LOAF
INTO THIN STRIPS.

SAUCE: IN A BOWL, WHISK ALL INGREDIENTS TO BLEND.
COVER AND REFRIGERATE UNTIL READY TO USE.

    FILL PITAS WITH MEAT, TOMATO, ONION, PICKLES,
OLIVES (IF USING), LETTUCE, HOT PEPPER SAUCE AND A
DRIZZLE OF DONAIR SAUCE. SERVES 6.

TIP: DONAIR SAUCE KEEPS WELL FOR UP TO 1 WEEK. ANY
EXTRA SAUCE IS PERFECT WITH FALAFELS OR AS A DIPPING
SAUCE FOR PIZZA OR GARLIC BREAD.

TIP: FRESH PITAS ARE FLEXIBLE AND HELP KEEP THE
FILLING IN THE SANDWICH. IF THE PITAS ARE A LITTLE
DRY, STACK THEM, COVER THEM WITH A DAMP DISH
TOWEL AND MICROWAVE FOR ABOUT 30 SECONDS TO
RESTORE LOST MOISTURE.

SOUTHWESTERN ONE-POT BEEF CASSEROLE

FAMILIAR FLAVORS ARE FEATURED IN THIS SIMPLE CASSEROLE THAT SKIPS THE STEP OF COOKING PASTA IN A SEPARATE POT.

1 TBSP	CANOLA OIL	15 ML
1 LB	LEAN GROUND BEEF	500 G
1 CUP	FINELY CHOPPED ONION	250 ML
2	GARLIC CLOVES, MINCED	2
2 CUPS	CORN KERNELS (THAWED IF FROZEN)	500 ML
2 CUPS	DRIED MACARONI PASTA	500 ML
2 TSP	CHILI POWDER	10 ML
1 TSP	GROUND CUMIN	5 ML
2 CUPS	READY-TO-USE BEEF BROTH	500 ML
1 1/2 CUPS	DICED TOMATOES (FRESH OR CANNED)	375 ML
1 CUP	TOMATO SALSA	250 ML
1/2 CUP	CHOPPED FRESH CILANTRO (OPTIONAL)	125 ML
1 1/2 CUPS	SHREDDED MOZZARELLA CHEESE	375 ML

IN A LARGE DUTCH OVEN, HEAT OIL OVER MEDIUM-HIGH HEAT. COOK BEEF AND ONION, STIRRING AND BREAKING BEEF UP WITH A SPOON, FOR 7 MINUTES OR UNTIL BEEF IS NO LONGER PINK. STIR IN GARLIC, CORN, PASTA, CHILI POWDER, CUMIN, BROTH, TOMATOES AND SALSA; BRING TO A BOIL. REDUCE HEAT, COVER AND SIMMER, STIRRING OCCASIONALLY, FOR ABOUT 10 MINUTES OR UNTIL PASTA IS TENDER. STIR IN CILANTRO (IF USING) AND TOP WITH CHEESE; COVER AND COOK FOR 3 MINUTES OR UNTIL CHEESE IS MELTED. SERVES 6.

MINI CHEESEBURGER MEATLOAVES

PERFECT CHEESEBURGER FLAVOR WITHOUT THE BUNS!

2 LBS	LEAN GROUND BEEF	1 KG
1¼ CUPS	SHREDDED SHARP (OLD) CHEDDAR CHEESE, DIVIDED	300 ML
⅓ CUP	ITALIAN-SEASONED DRY BREAD CRUMBS	75 ML
1 TSP	DRIED THYME	5 ML
½ TSP	SALT	2 ML
½ TSP	BLACK PEPPER	2 ML
1	LARGE EGG, LIGHTLY BEATEN	1
2 TBSP	KETCHUP	30 ML
2 TBSP	YELLOW MUSTARD	30 ML
1 TBSP	WORCESTERSHIRE SAUCE	15 ML

PREHEAT OVEN TO 375°F (190°C). IN A LARGE BOWL, USING YOUR HANDS, COMBINE BEEF, ¾ CUP (175 ML) CHEESE, BREAD CRUMBS, THYME, SALT, PEPPER, EGG, KETCHUP, MUSTARD AND WORCESTERSHIRE SAUCE. FORM 1 CUP (250 ML) BEEF MIXTURE INTO AN OVAL LOAF, ABOUT 1½ INCHES (4 CM) THICK, AND PLACE ON A FOIL-LINED RIMMED BAKING SHEET. REPEAT TO MAKE 6 LOAFS, SPACING THEM APART. SPRINKLE EACH WITH REMAINING CHEESE. BAKE FOR ABOUT 35 MINUTES OR UNTIL A MEAT THERMOMETER INSERTED HORIZONTALLY INTO THE CENTER OF A LOAF REGISTERS AT LEAST 160°F (71°C). LET STAND FOR 5 MINUTES BEFORE SERVING. SERVES 6.

VARIATION: ADD ½ CUP (125 ML) CHOPPED COOKED BACON TO THE MEATLOAF MIXTURE.

SWEET AND SMOKY MINI MEATLOAVES

MINI MEATLOAVES COOK UP IN NO TIME AND ALSO FREEZE WELL. MAKE AN EXTRA BATCH FOR A SANITY SAVER ON THOSE EXTRA-BUSY NIGHTS.

1/4 CUP	PACKED BROWN SUGAR	60 ML
2 TSP	SMOKED PAPRIKA, DIVIDED	10 ML
1/2 CUP	KETCHUP	125 ML
2/3 CUP	QUICK-COOKING ROLLED OATS	150 ML
1 TSP	ONION POWDER	5 ML
1 TSP	GARLIC POWDER	5 ML
1 TSP	SALT	5 ML
1/2 TSP	BLACK PEPPER	2 ML
1	LARGE EGG, LIGHTLY BEATEN	1
1/2 CUP	MILK	125 ML
1 LB	LEAN GROUND BEEF	500 G
8 OZ	LEAN GROUND PORK OR TURKEY	250 G

PREHEAT OVEN TO 400°F (200°C). PLACE A 12-CUP MUFFIN PAN ON A RIMMED BAKING SHEET LINED WITH FOIL. IN A SMALL BOWL, COMBINE BROWN SUGAR, 1 TSP (5 ML) PAPRIKA AND KETCHUP; SET ASIDE. IN A LARGE BOWL, STIR TOGETHER OATS, REMAINING PAPRIKA, ONION POWDER, GARLIC POWDER, SALT, PEPPER, EGG AND MILK. ADD BEEF AND PORK; MIX UNTIL WELL COMBINED. DIVIDE MEAT MIXTURE EVENLY AMONG MUFFIN CUPS. BAKE FOR 20 MINUTES. SPREAD KETCHUP MIXTURE OVER EACH MEATLOAF AND BAKE FOR 8 TO 10 MINUTES OR UNTIL A MEAT THERMOMETER INSERTED IN THE CENTER OF A LOAF REGISTERS AT LEAST 165°F (74°C). SERVES 6.

CAULIFLOWER BEEF FRITTERS

THESE ARE ADDICTIVE AND ARE PERFECT FOR EATING OUT OF HAND ON A BUSY NIGHT.

12 OZ	LEAN GROUND BEEF	375 G
4 CUPS	CHOPPED CAULIFLOWER	1 L
3	GARLIC CLOVES, MINCED	3
3/4 CUP	ALL-PURPOSE FLOUR	175 ML
2 TBSP	CHOPPED FRESH CILANTRO	30 ML
1/2 TSP	CURRY POWDER	2 ML
1/2 TSP	SALT	2 ML
1/2 TSP	BLACK PEPPER	2 ML
2	LARGE EGGS, LIGHTLY BEATEN	2
3 TBSP	CANOLA OIL	45 ML

IN A NONSTICK SKILLET, COOK BEEF, BREAKING IT UP WITH A SPOON, FOR 8 MINUTES OR UNTIL NO LONGER PINK; DRAIN AND SET ASIDE. IN A POT OF BOILING SALTED WATER, COOK CAULIFLOWER FOR 10 MINUTES OR UNTIL SOFT; DRAIN WELL AND RETURN TO POT. USING A POTATO MASHER, MASH CAULIFLOWER. STIR IN BEEF, GARLIC, FLOUR, CILANTRO, CURRY POWDER, SALT, PEPPER AND EGGS UNTIL WELL COMBINED. WIPE OUT SKILLET AND HEAT OIL OVER MEDIUM HEAT. SCOOP 1/4 CUP (60 ML) BEEF MIXTURE INTO PAN AND FLATTEN SLIGHTLY WITH A SPATULA. ADD A FEW MORE FRITTERS, WITHOUT OVERCROWDING. COOK, TURNING ONCE, FOR ABOUT 5 MINUTES OR UNTIL GOLDEN BROWN ON BOTH SIDES AND HOT IN THE CENTER. TRANSFER TO A PLATE LINED WITH PAPER TOWEL AND KEEP WARM. REPEAT WITH REMAINING BEEF MIXTURE. SERVES 4 (ABOUT 3 FRITTERS PER PERSON).

GREEK STUFFED PATTIES WITH CUCUMBER YOGURT SAUCE

EAT THESE PATTIES WITH A KNIFE AND FORK, OR POP THEM INTO BUNS AND TOP WITH THE SAUCE FOR A MORE TRADITIONAL BURGER.

CUCUMBER YOGURT SAUCE

1	GARLIC CLOVE, MINCED	1
1/2 CUP	GRATED ENGLISH CUCUMBER, SQUEEZED DRY	125 ML
3/4 CUP	PLAIN BALKAN-STYLE OR GREEK YOGURT	175 ML
1/2 TSP	GRATED LEMON ZEST	2 ML
1 TBSP	LEMON JUICE	15 ML
	SALT TO TASTE	

BURGERS

1 LB	LEAN GROUND BEEF	500 G
3	GARLIC CLOVES, MINCED	3
3 TBSP	CHOPPED FRESH PARSLEY	45 ML
1 1/2 TSP	DRIED OREGANO	7 ML
1/2 TSP	GRATED LEMON ZEST	2 ML
1/4 TSP	BLACK PEPPER	1 ML
4 OZ	FETA CHEESE, CUT INTO 4 EQUAL PIECES	125 G

SAUCE: IN A BOWL, COMBINE ALL INGREDIENTS. COVER AND REFRIGERATE UNTIL READY TO USE.

BURGERS: PREHEAT BARBECUE GRILL TO MEDIUM. IN A LARGE BOWL, USING YOUR HANDS, COMBINE BEEF, GARLIC, PARSLEY, OREGANO, LEMON ZEST AND PEPPER. SHAPE INTO 4 BALLS. MAKE A HOLE WITH YOUR FINGER IN THE CENTER OF EACH BALL AND STUFF WITH A PIECE OF FETA,

THEN CLOSE UP HOLE AND SHAPE INTO A ¾-INCH (2 CM) THICK PATTY; PLACE ON A PLATE. PLACE PATTIES ON GREASED GRILL AND GRILL, TURNING ONCE, FOR ABOUT 13 MINUTES OR UNTIL NO LONGER PINK INSIDE AND A MEAT THERMOMETER INSERTED HORIZONTALLY INTO THE THICKEST PART OF A PATTY, AVOIDING THE CHEESE, REGISTERS 160°F (71°C). SERVE WITH CUCUMBER YOGURT SAUCE. SERVES 4.

TIP: THE PATTIES CAN BE PREPARED UP TO 4 HOURS AHEAD, COVERED AND REFRIGERATED TO PLACE ON THE GRILL WHEN FAMILY AND FRIENDS ARRIVE.

TIP: YOU CAN SUBSTITUTE 1 CUP (250 ML) STORE-BOUGHT TZATZIKI FOR THE CUCUMBER YOGURT SAUCE.

WHY WAS THE CUCUMBER MAD? BECAUSE IT WAS IN A PICKLE!

PATTY MELTS

THIS DINNER WILL MAKE YOU WANT TO DRESS UP
IN '50S ATTIRE AND TURN YOUR KITCHEN INTO A DINER.
A CLASSIC WITH A NEW TWIST!

1 TBSP	CANOLA OIL	15 ML
1	SWEET ONION, THINLY SLICED	1
1/4 TSP	SALT	1 ML
1/4 TSP	BLACK PEPPER	1 ML
1 TBSP	BALSAMIC VINEGAR	15 ML
1 LB	LEAN GROUND BEEF	500 G
2 TBSP	DRY ONION SOUP MIX	30 ML
1 TBSP	WORCESTERSHIRE SAUCE	15 ML
1/4 CUP	LIGHT MAYONNAISE	60 ML
2 TBSP	THOUSAND ISLAND DRESSING	30 ML
4	SLICES LIGHT OR MARBLE RYE BREAD, TOASTED	4
4	SLICES HAVARTI CHEESE	4

IN A LARGE SKILLET, HEAT OIL OVER MEDIUM-HIGH HEAT.
SAUTÉ ONION FOR 10 MINUTES. REDUCE HEAT TO MEDIUM-
LOW AND COOK, STIRRING OCCASIONALLY, FOR 10 MINUTES
OR UNTIL SOFTENED AND GOLDEN. STIR IN SALT, PEPPER
AND VINEGAR. SCRAPE INTO A BOWL.

PREHEAT BROILER. IN A LARGE BOWL, COMBINE BEEF,
SOUP MIX AND WORCESTERSHIRE SAUCE. SHAPE INTO
FOUR 3/4-INCH (2 CM) THICK OVAL PATTIES. RETURN
SKILLET TO MEDIUM HEAT AND COOK PATTIES, TURNING
ONCE, FOR ABOUT 12 MINUTES OR UNTIL NO LONGER
PINK INSIDE AND A MEAT THERMOMETER INSERTED
HORIZONTALLY INTO THE CENTER OF A PATTY REGISTERS

160°F (71°C). IN A SMALL BOWL, STIR TOGETHER MAYONNAISE AND DRESSING; SPREAD OVER TOASTED BREAD. TOP EACH BREAD SLICE WITH 1 PATTY AND ONIONS. LAY CHEESE ON TOP. BROIL FOR 1 MINUTE TO MELT CHEESE. SERVES 4.

TIP: FOR AN ADDED KICK, SUBSTITUTE SPICY HAVARTI OR JALAPEÑO GOUDA CHEESE SLICES FOR THE HAVARTI.

FOOD IS SYMBOLIC OF LOVE WHEN WORDS ARE INADEQUATE.
— ALAN D. WOLFELT

STUFFED VEAL MEATBALLS ON POLENTA

A LITTLE SURPRISE IN EVERY BITE!

MEATBALLS

1 1/2 LBS	GROUND VEAL	750 G
1	GARLIC CLOVE, MINCED	1
3/4 CUP	FRESH BREAD CRUMBS	175 ML
1/4 CUP	GRATED PARMESAN CHEESE	60 ML
3 TBSP	CHOPPED FRESH PARSLEY	45 ML
1/4 TSP	SALT	1 ML
1	LARGE EGG, LIGHTLY BEATEN	1
16	SMALL (ABOUT 1-INCH/2.5 CM) BALLS BOCCONCINI CHEESE	16
3 CUPS	TOMATO PASTA SAUCE, HEATED	750 ML

CREAMY POLENTA

3 CUPS	MILK	750 ML
1 CUP	WATER	250 ML
1 CUP	CORNMEAL	250 ML
1 TSP	SALT	5 ML
1/2 CUP	GRATED PARMESAN CHEESE	125 ML

MEATBALLS: PREHEAT OVEN TO 350°F (180°C). IN A BOWL, COMBINE VEAL, GARLIC, BREAD CRUMBS, PARMESAN, PARSLEY, SALT AND EGG. USING WET HANDS, SHAPE MIXTURE INTO 16 ROUGH BALLS. FLATTEN EACH BALL, TUCK A BOCCONCINI BALL IN THE CENTER, PINCH MEAT TO SEAL AND ROLL INTO A MEATBALL. PLACE ON A PARCHMENT-LINED BAKING SHEET, SPACING THEM APART. BAKE FOR 15 MINUTES. POUR HALF THE PASTA SAUCE INTO A SMALL CASSEROLE DISH. ADD MEATBALLS AND POUR IN

REMAINING SAUCE. COVER AND BAKE FOR 20 MINUTES OR UNTIL SAUCE IS BUBBLY AND MEATBALLS ARE NO LONGER PINK INSIDE.

CREAMY POLENTA: MEANWHILE, IN A LARGE SAUCEPAN, BRING MILK AND WATER TO A SIMMER OVER MEDIUM HEAT. WHISK IN CORNMEAL AND SALT. REDUCE HEAT AND SIMMER, WHISKING, FOR ABOUT 15 MINUTES OR UNTIL THICKENED AND VERY CREAMY. STIR IN CHEESE.

SPOON POLENTA ONTO PLATES, TOP WITH MEATBALLS AND SPOON SAUCE OVER TOP. SERVES 6 TO 8.

THIS MIGHT SOUND CHEESY, BUT I THINK YOU'RE GRATE.

VEAL MARSALA

THIS ITALIAN FAVORITE, PACKED WITH MUSHROOMS, IS PERFECT SERVED WITH RICE OR PASTA.

2 TBSP	ALL-PURPOSE FLOUR	30 ML
1 TSP	SALT, DIVIDED	5 ML
PINCH	BLACK PEPPER	PINCH
1 LB	VEAL CUTLETS	500 G
2 TBSP	BUTTER	30 ML
1 TBSP	CANOLA OIL	15 ML
3	GARLIC CLOVES, MINCED	3
1 LB	MUSHROOMS, SLICED	500 G
1 TSP	CHOPPED FRESH THYME OR OREGANO	5 ML
PINCH	HOT PEPPER FLAKES	PINCH
1/2 CUP	MARSALA OR DRY WHITE WINE	125 ML
1 TBSP	CHOPPED FRESH PARSLEY (OPTIONAL)	15 ML

IN A SHALLOW BOWL, STIR TOGETHER FLOUR, HALF THE SALT AND PEPPER. COAT EACH VEAL CUTLET IN FLOUR AND SET ASIDE ON A PLATE; DISCARD EXCESS FLOUR. IN A LARGE NONSTICK SKILLET, MELT HALF THE BUTTER OVER MEDIUM HEAT. IN BATCHES, BROWN CUTLETS ON BOTH SIDES AND RETURN TO PLATE, ADDING REMAINING BUTTER BETWEEN BATCHES. ADD OIL TO THE SKILLET AND SAUTÉ GARLIC, MUSHROOMS, THYME, HOT PEPPER FLAKES AND REMAINING SALT FOR ABOUT 8 MINUTES OR UNTIL MUSHROOMS ARE GOLDEN BROWN. ADD MARSALA AND PARSLEY; SIMMER FOR 1 MINUTE. RETURN VEAL TO SKILLET, TURNING TO COAT WITH SAUCE, AND COOK UNTIL JUST A HINT OF PINK REMAINS INSIDE. SERVES 4.

LAMB AND PORK

CRISPY LAMB ON HUMMUS

THIS CRISPY, AROMATIC LAMB TOPPING SERVED OVER HUMMUS MAKES A DELICIOUS SHARING MEAL.

LAMB

1 TBSP	CANOLA OIL	15 ML
1/4 CUP	FINELY CHOPPED ONION	60 ML
8 OZ	GROUND LAMB	250 G
1	GARLIC CLOVE, MINCED	1
1 TSP	SALT	5 ML
1 TSP	BLACK PEPPER	5 ML
1 TSP	SMOKED PAPRIKA	5 ML
1/2 TSP	GROUND CUMIN	2 ML
1/2 TSP	DRIED OREGANO	2 ML
1/4 TSP	GROUND CINNAMON	1 ML
1/4 TSP	GROUND ALLSPICE	1 ML

HUMMUS

1	CAN (19 OZ/540 ML) CHICKPEAS, RINSED AND DRAINED (2 CUPS/500 ML)	1
3 TBSP	TAHINI	45 ML
3 TBSP	OLIVE OIL	45 ML
3 TBSP	LEMON JUICE	45 ML
2 TBSP	WATER (APPROX.)	30 ML
2	GARLIC CLOVES, MINCED	2
1/2 TSP	SALT	2 ML
1/2 TSP	BLACK PEPPER	2 ML
1/2 TSP	GROUND CUMIN	2 ML
2	PLUM (ROMA) TOMATOES, CHOPPED	2
2 TBSP	TOASTED PINE NUTS	30 ML
1/4 CUP	CHOPPED FRESH PARSLEY	60 ML
6	7-INCH (18 CM) PITAS, WARMED	6

LAMB: IN A LARGE NONSTICK OR CAST-IRON SKILLET, HEAT OIL OVER MEDIUM-HIGH HEAT. SAUTÉ ONION FOR ABOUT 3 MINUTES OR UNTIL SOFTENED. ADD LAMB, GARLIC, SALT, PEPPER, PAPRIKA, CUMIN, OREGANO, CINNAMON AND ALLSPICE; COOK, STIRRING AND BREAKING LAMB UP WITH A SPOON, FOR 15 MINUTES OR UNTIL LAMB IS BROWNED AND CRISPY.

HUMMUS: MEANWHILE, IN A FOOD PROCESSOR, PROCESS ALL HUMMUS INGREDIENTS UNTIL SMOOTH. SCRAPE DOWN THE SIDES OF THE BOWL TO MAKE SURE THE INGREDIENTS ARE WELL BLENDED. IF HUMMUS IS TOO THICK, ADD MORE WATER, A TABLESPOONFUL (15 ML) AT A TIME.

SPREAD HUMMUS ON A PLATTER TO SHARE, OR ON 6 INDIVIDUAL PLATES, THEN TOP WITH LAMB, TOMATOES, PINE NUTS AND PARSLEY. SERVE WITH WARM PITAS. SERVES 6.

TIP: THE HUMMUS KEEPS FOR 4 DAYS IN AN AIRTIGHT CONTAINER IN THE REFRIGERATOR.

TIP: IF YOU'RE PINCHED FOR TIME IN MAKING THIS RECIPE, 2 CUPS (500 ML) PURCHASED HUMMUS IS A GREAT OPTION.

TIP: SPRINKLE WITH POMEGRANATE SEEDS FOR A BEAUTIFUL AND FLAVORFUL GARNISH.

LAMB MEATBALLS WITH LEMONY GARLIC POTATOES

HERE, THE POTATOES ROAST UNDERNEATH THE TENDER LAMB MEATBALLS, WHERE THEY HAVE A CHANCE TO ABSORB THE FLAVORFUL JUICES.

POTATOES

5	GARLIC CLOVES, CHOPPED	5
4	POTATOES, CUT INTO I-INCH (2.5 CM) CUBES	4
2 TSP	DRIED OREGANO	10 ML
1/2 TSP	SALT	2 ML
1/2 TSP	BLACK PEPPER	2 ML
1/4 CUP	WATER	60 ML
1/4 CUP	LEMON JUICE (SEE TIP)	60 ML
2 TBSP	CANOLA OIL	30 ML

LAMB MEATBALLS

2	GARLIC CLOVES, MINCED	2
1/2 CUP	DRY BREAD CRUMBS	125 ML
4 TBSP	CHOPPED FRESH PARSLEY, DIVIDED	60 ML
I TSP	GRATED LEMON ZEST	5 ML
I TSP	ONION POWDER	5 ML
1/2 TSP	DRIED ROSEMARY, CRUMBLED	2 ML
1/2 TSP	SALT	2 ML
1/2 TSP	BLACK PEPPER	2 ML
1/2 TSP	GROUND FENNEL	2 ML
I	LARGE EGG, LIGHTLY BEATEN	I
2 TBSP	MILK	30 ML
I LB	GROUND LAMB	500 G
1/4 CUP	CRUMBLED FETA CHEESE	60 ML
	PLAIN YOGURT (OPTIONAL)	

POTATOES: PREHEAT OVEN TO 400°F (200°C). IN A LARGE BOWL, COMBINE GARLIC, POTATOES, OREGANO, SALT, PEPPER, WATER, LEMON JUICE AND OIL. SPREAD IN A SINGLE LAYER ON A FOIL-LINED LARGE RIMMED BAKING SHEET. COVER WITH FOIL AND BAKE FOR 30 MINUTES, STIRRING HALFWAY THROUGH.

MEATBALLS: MEANWHILE, IN THE SAME LARGE BOWL, COMBINE GARLIC, BREAD CRUMBS, 2 TBSP (30 ML) PARSLEY, LEMON ZEST, ONION POWDER, ROSEMARY, SALT, PEPPER, FENNEL, EGG AND MILK. ADD LAMB AND FETA, MIXING UNTIL WELL COMBINED. FORM INTO 1½-INCH (4 CM) MEATBALLS.

REMOVE POTATOES FROM OVEN, CAREFULLY REMOVE FOIL AND PLACE MEATBALLS ON TOP OF POTATOES. BAKE, UNCOVERED, FOR 25 MINUTES OR UNTIL MEATBALLS ARE NO LONGER PINK INSIDE AND POTATOES ARE TENDER. SPRINKLE REMAINING PARSLEY ON TOP. SERVE WITH YOGURT ON THE SIDE, IF DESIRED. SERVES 4.

TIP: BE SURE TO ZEST THE LEMON FOR THE MEATBALLS BEFORE YOU JUICE IT FOR THE POTATOES.

SLOW COOKER PORK LOIN WITH APPLES

WHEN YOU WANT TO PUT YOUR SLOW COOKER TO USE, THIS SUPPER WILL BE A WINNER, ESPECIALLY WHEN SERVED UP WITH MASHED POTATOES.

I	BONELESS CENTER-CUT PORK LOIN ROAST (ABOUT 2 LBS/I KG)	I
I TBSP	CAJUN SEASONING	15 ML
I TBSP	CANOLA OIL	15 ML
2	TART COOKING APPLES, SLICED	2
I	LARGE SWEET ONION, SLICED	I
I	LARGE CARROT, THINLY SLICED	I
I CUP	HARD APPLE CIDER	250 ML

RUB PORK LOIN WITH CAJUN SEASONING. IN A SKILLET, HEAT OIL OVER MEDIUM-HIGH HEAT. BROWN PORK ALL OVER. PLACE IN A MINIMUM 4-QUART SLOW COOKER. RETURN SKILLET TO MEDIUM HEAT AND SAUTÉ APPLES, ONION AND CARROT FOR 3 MINUTES. ADD TO SLOW COOKER. ADD CIDER TO SKILLET AND BRING TO A BOIL, SCRAPING UP BROWN BITS STUCK TO PAN. POUR INTO SLOW COOKER. COVER AND COOK ON LOW FOR 4 HOURS OR ON HIGH FOR 2 HOURS, UNTIL NO LONGER PINK INSIDE. SLICE ROAST AND SERVE WITH SAUCE. SERVES 4.

TIP: SELECT TART APPLES SUCH AS CRISPIN (MUTSU), NORTHERN SPY, GRANNY SMITH, CORTLAND OR GOLDEN DELICIOUS APPLES TO COOK WITH, FOR GREAT FLAVOR AND TEXTURE.

TIP: SUBSTITUTE REGULAR UNSWEETENED APPLE CIDER FOR A NONALCOHOLIC OPTION.

PORK MEDALLIONS WITH POLENTA AND GREENS

SHEET-PAN DINNERS ARE SUCH AN EASY WAY TO COOK A COMPLETE MEAL, WITH ONLY A FEW INGREDIENTS.

I	LARGE PORK TENDERLOIN (ABOUT 1½ LBS/750 G)	I
½ CUP	PANKO	125 ML
I TSP	DRIED THYME	5 ML
½ TSP	SALT, DIVIDED	2 ML
½ TSP	BLACK PEPPER, DIVIDED	2 ML
I	BUNCH (ABOUT I LB/500 G) RAPINI, ENDS TRIMMED	I
½	2-LB (I KG) LOG PREPARED POLENTA, CUT INTO I-INCH (2.5 CM) SLICES	½
3 TBSP	EXTRA VIRGIN OLIVE OIL	45 ML
2 TBSP	GRATED PARMESAN CHEESE	30 ML

PREHEAT OVEN TO 400°F (200°C). SLICE TENDERLOIN INTO I-INCH (2.5 CM) MEDALLIONS. IN A SHALLOW DISH, COMBINE PANKO, THYME AND HALF EACH OF THE SALT AND PEPPER. DREDGE PORK MEDALLIONS IN PANKO MIXTURE, TURNING TO COAT BOTH SIDES; SET ASIDE. IN A LARGE BOWL, TOSS RAPINI AND POLENTA WITH OIL AND REMAINING SALT AND PEPPER. SPREAD OVER A PARCHMENT-LINED RIMMED BAKING SHEET AND SPRINKLE WITH CHEESE. TOP WITH PORK MEDALLIONS AND ANY REMAINING CRUMB MIXTURE. ROAST FOR ABOUT 20 MINUTES OR UNTIL JUST A HINT OF PINK REMAINS IN PORK AND RAPINI IS TENDER-CRISP. SERVES 4.

APRICOT CRANBERRY
STUFFED PORK TENDERLOIN

*FRUIT AND PORK MARRY PERFECTLY FOR DINNER,
AND PORK TENDERLOIN IS EASY TO STUFF, TOO.
SERVE THIS YUMMY DISH WITH STEAMED
GREEN BEANS OR ASPARAGUS FOR ADDED COLOR.*

1 TBSP	CANOLA OIL	15 ML
2	GARLIC CLOVES, MINCED	2
1	SHALLOT, DICED	1
2 TSP	DRIED SAVORY OR SAGE	10 ML
3/4 CUP	FRESH BREAD CRUMBS	175 ML
1/3 CUP	DICED DRIED APRICOTS	75 ML
2 TBSP	CHOPPED FRESH PARSLEY	30 ML
1/4 CUP	CRANBERRY SAUCE	60 ML
1	PORK TENDERLOIN (ABOUT 1 1/4 LBS/625 G)	1
1/2 TSP	SALT	2 ML
1/2 TSP	BLACK PEPPER	2 ML
4	SLICES BACON	4

PREHEAT OVEN TO 400°F (200°C). IN A NONSTICK SKILLET,
HEAT OIL OVER MEDIUM HEAT. SAUTÉ GARLIC, SHALLOT
AND SAVORY FOR 4 MINUTES OR UNTIL SHALLOT IS
SOFTENED. REMOVE FROM HEAT AND STIR IN BREAD
CRUMBS, APRICOTS, PARSLEY AND CRANBERRY SAUCE.
CUT PORK TENDERLOIN IN HALF LENGTHWISE, ALMOST
BUT NOT ALL THE WAY THROUGH, AND OPEN UP LIKE
A BOOK. STARTING AT THE CENTER, MAKE A SIMILAR
CUT ON BOTH SIDES OF TENDERLOIN TO OPEN IT UP
FOR STUFFING. SPRINKLE PORK WITH SALT AND PEPPER.

SPREAD STUFFING OVER TENDERLOIN AND ROLL UP LIKE A JELLY ROLL TO SEAL. WRAP TENDERLOIN WITH BACON AND PLACE ON SMALL FOIL-LINED RIMMED BAKING SHEET. ROAST FOR ABOUT 30 MINUTES OR UNTIL A MEAT THERMOMETER INSERTED IN THE CENTER OF THE ROAST REGISTERS 145°F (63°C) FOR MEDIUM-RARE OR TO DESIRED DONENESS. SERVES 3 TO 4.

TIP: FOR FRESH BREAD CRUMBS, BUZZ A SLICE OF BREAD OR A BUN IN THE FOOD PROCESSOR.

TIP: DOUBLE-SMOKED SLICED BACON HAS A DEEPER SMOKINESS AND IS AN EASY SUBSTITUTE IN THIS RECIPE.

GUESS WHAT'S ON TONIGHT'S DINNER MENU? ME-N-U.

PEPPERED SKILLET PORK CHOPS WITH MUSHROOM SAUCE

OUR FAMILIES ENJOY PORK CHOPS, SO WE SPIKED SOME UP WITH PEPPER AND MUSHROOM SAUCE.

1 TSP	CRUSHED BLACK PEPPERCORNS	5 ML
4	BONE-IN PORK LOIN CHOPS, ABOUT $\frac{1}{2}$ INCH (1 CM) THICK	4
$\frac{1}{2}$ TSP	SALT	2 ML
2 TBSP	BUTTER	30 ML
1 TBSP	CANOLA OIL	15 ML
8 OZ	MUSHROOMS, SLICED	250 G
$\frac{1}{2}$ TSP	DRIED THYME	2 ML
1 CUP	HEAVY OR WHIPPING (35%) CREAM	250 ML

RUB PEPPERCORNS INTO PORK CHOPS AND SPRINKLE WITH SALT. IN A LARGE SKILLET, HEAT BUTTER AND OIL OVER MEDIUM-HIGH HEAT. BROWN PORK CHOPS ON BOTH SIDES AND TRANSFER TO A PLATE. ADD MUSHROOMS AND THYME TO SKILLET AND SAUTÉ FOR ABOUT 8 MINUTES OR UNTIL MUSHROOMS ARE GOLDEN AND LIQUID IS EVAPORATED. ADD CREAM, REDUCE HEAT AND SIMMER, STIRRING OCCASIONALLY, FOR 4 MINUTES OR UNTIL SLIGHTLY THICKENED. RETURN PORK CHOPS TO SKILLET, ALONG WITH ANY ACCUMULATED JUICES, AND COOK, TURNING ONCE, FOR ABOUT 5 MINUTES OR UNTIL JUST A HINT OF PINK REMAINS IN PORK. SERVES 4.

PEPPER AND PEACH PORK CHOPS

IN-SEASON PEACHES ARE JUICY AND DELICIOUS IN THIS RECIPE, BUT YOU CAN STILL MAKE IT OUT OF SEASON, USING TASTY CANNED PEACH HALVES AS A SUBSTITUTE.

4	BONE-IN PORK LOIN CHOPS, ABOUT $\frac{1}{2}$ INCH (1 CM) THICK	4
2 TSP	CHOPPED FRESH THYME	10 ML
$\frac{1}{4}$ TSP	SALT	1 ML
$\frac{1}{4}$ TSP	BLACK PEPPER	1 ML
1 TBSP	CANOLA OIL	15 ML
1	SHALLOT, THINLY SLICED	1
1	JALAPEÑO PEPPER, SEEDED AND MINCED	1
1	GARLIC CLOVE, MINCED	1
3	RIPE PEACHES, SLICED	3
$\frac{1}{3}$ CUP	DRY WHITE WINE	75 ML
2	GREEN ONIONS, CHOPPED	2

SPRINKLE BOTH SIDES OF PORK CHOPS WITH THYME, SALT AND PEPPER. IN A LARGE SKILLET, HEAT OIL OVER MEDIUM-HIGH HEAT. BROWN PORK CHOPS ON BOTH SIDES AND TRANSFER TO A PLATE. RETURN SKILLET TO MEDIUM HEAT AND SAUTÉ SHALLOT, JALAPEÑO AND GARLIC FOR 3 MINUTES TO SOFTEN. ADD PEACHES AND WINE; BRING TO A SIMMER. SIMMER FOR 5 MINUTES OR UNTIL PEACHES ARE STARTING TO SOFTEN. NESTLE PORK CHOPS INTO PEACH MIXTURE AND SIMMER FOR 5 MINUTES, TURNING A FEW TIMES, UNTIL JUST A HINT OF PINK REMAINS IN PORK. SERVE SPRINKLED WITH GREEN ONIONS. SERVES 4.

TIP: SUBSTITUTE A 14-OZ (398 ML) CAN OF PEACH HALVES, DRAINED, FOR THE FRESH PEACHES.

— PORK AND PEPPER RISOTTO —

EMILY'S SON MATTHEW ENJOYS MAKING RISOTTO, AND
HE STEPPED IT UP A NOTCH HERE BY ADDING PORK.

8	FAST-FRY BONELESS PORK LOIN CHOPS, CUT INTO STRIPS	8
1	LARGE GARLIC CLOVE, MINCED	1
1 TSP	DRIED ITALIAN SEASONING	5 ML
1/4 TSP	SALT	1 ML
1/4 TSP	BLACK PEPPER	1 ML
2 TBSP	CANOLA OIL, DIVIDED	30 ML
1	ONION, CHOPPED	1
1	LARGE RED BELL PEPPER, CHOPPED	1
1 1/2 CUPS	ARBORIO RICE	375 ML
5 CUPS	READY-TO-USE CHICKEN OR VEGETABLE BROTH	1.25 L
1/2 CUP	GRATED PARMESAN CHEESE	125 ML
2 TBSP	CHOPPED FRESH BASIL	30 ML

IN A LARGE BOWL, TOSS PORK WITH GARLIC, ITALIAN
SEASONING, SALT AND PEPPER. IN A LARGE, SHALLOW
SAUCEPAN, HEAT HALF THE OIL OVER MEDIUM-HIGH HEAT.
BROWN PORK AND TRANSFER TO A PLATE. ADD REMAINING
OIL TO PAN AND SAUTÉ ONION AND RED PEPPER FOR
3 MINUTES TO SOFTEN. STIR IN RICE UNTIL WELL COATED.
REDUCE HEAT TO MEDIUM AND LADLE IN BROTH, 1/2 CUP
(125 ML) AT A TIME, STIRRING UNTIL EACH ADDITION IS
ABSORBED BEFORE ADDING THE NEXT, AND COOK FOR
ABOUT 15 MINUTES OR UNTIL RICE IS AL DENTE. RETURN
PORK AND ANY ACCUMULATED JUICES TO THE PAN,
ALONG WITH CHEESE, BASIL AND ANY REMAINING BROTH,
STIRRING UNTIL COMBINED AND CREAMY. SERVES 4 TO 6.

KIM'S LEMONGRASS PORK LETTUCE WRAPS

SYLVIA'S FRIEND KIM SAYS THIS IS A THUMBS-UP FAMILY FAVORITE. SERVE IT WITH HOT COOKED RICE.

1½ LBS	LEAN GROUND PORK	750 G
3 TBSP	LEMONGRASS PASTE OR MINCED LEMONGRASS	45 ML
1½ TSP	GRATED FRESH GINGER	7 ML
4	GREEN ONIONS, SLICED	4
3	GARLIC CLOVES, MINCED	3
1 CUP	DICED RED BELL PEPPER	250 ML
1 CUP	CABBAGE COLESLAW MIX	250 ML
2 TBSP	PACKED BROWN SUGAR	30 ML
¾ CUP	HOISIN SAUCE	175 ML
1 TBSP	RICE OR WHITE VINEGAR	15 ML
1 TBSP	SESAME OIL	15 ML
2 TSP	SRIRACHA	10 ML
	ROMAINE OR BUTTER LETTUCE LEAVES	
1 CUP	FRIED CHOW MEIN NOODLES	250 ML

IN A LARGE SKILLET OVER MEDIUM-HIGH HEAT, COOK PORK, LEMONGRASS PASTE AND GINGER FOR 7 MINUTES, BREAKING PORK UP WITH A SPOON, UNTIL PORK IS NO LONGER PINK. ADD GREEN ONIONS, GARLIC, RED PEPPER, COLESLAW MIX, BROWN SUGAR, HOISIN, VINEGAR, SESAME OIL AND SRIRACHA; COOK, STIRRING, FOR 5 MINUTES OR UNTIL SLIGHTLY THICKENED. SPOON FILLING INTO CENTER OF INDIVIDUAL LETTUCE LEAVES; SPRINKLE WITH CHOW MEIN NOODLES AND WRAP LEAVES AROUND FILLING TO ENCLOSE. SERVES 4 TO 5.

TIP: GROUND BEEF OR CHICKEN MAY BE USED INSTEAD.

CHIPOTLE PORK STUFFED SWEET POTATOES

TRANSFORM A BAKED SWEET POTATO INTO A MEAL WITH THIS HEARTY TOPPING. ANY LEFTOVERS ARE GREAT REHEATED THE NEXT DAY.

4	SMALL SWEET POTATOES (EACH ABOUT 5 OZ/150 G)	4
1 TBSP	CANOLA OIL	15 ML
8 OZ	BONELESS PORK SHOULDER STEAK, CUT INTO SMALL CUBES	250 G
2	GREEN ONIONS, SLICED	2
1	GARLIC CLOVE, MINCED	1
1/2 CUP	CHOPPED FRESH CILANTRO	125 ML
2 TSP	CHIPOTLE CHILE POWDER	10 ML
1/2 TSP	GROUND CUMIN	2 ML
1/2 TSP	SALT	2 ML
1	CAN (19 OZ/540 ML) BLACK BEANS, RINSED AND DRAINED (2 CUPS/500 ML)	1
1 CUP	CORN KERNELS (THAWED IF FROZEN)	250 ML
1/4 CUP	WATER	60 ML
2 TBSP	BARBECUE SAUCE	30 ML
2 TBSP	SALSA	30 ML
1	LIME, CUT INTO WEDGES	1
1/4 CUP	SOUR CREAM	60 ML
	HOT PEPPER SAUCE (OPTIONAL)	

SCRUB POTATOES, THEN PRICK ALL OVER WITH A FORK. PLACE ON A MICROWAVE-SAFE PLATE AND MICROWAVE ON HIGH FOR 12 TO 14 MINUTES, TURNING HALFWAY THROUGH, UNTIL FORK-TENDER. SET ASIDE UNTIL COOL ENOUGH TO HANDLE.

MEANWHILE, IN A SKILLET, HEAT OIL OVER MEDIUM-HIGH HEAT. ADD PORK AND COOK, STIRRING, FOR 4 MINUTES OR UNTIL STARTING TO BROWN. ADD GREEN ONIONS, GARLIC, CILANTRO, CHILE POWDER, CUMIN, SALT, BEANS, CORN, WATER, BARBECUE SAUCE AND SALSA; COOK, STIRRING, FOR ABOUT 5 MINUTES OR UNTIL HEATED THROUGH.

USING A KNIFE, CUT AN X ON THE TOP OF EACH POTATO AND SQUEEZE GENTLY TO OPEN. SPOON PORK MIXTURE ON TOP. SERVE WITH LIME WEDGES, SOUR CREAM AND HOT PEPPER SAUCE (IF USING). SERVES 4.

TIP: THE POTATOES CAN ALSO BE COOKED IN A 425°F (220°C) OVEN. SCRUB POTATOES AND PRICK ALL OVER WITH A FORK TO ALLOW STEAM TO ESCAPE. WRAP EACH POTATO WITH FOIL, THEN PLACE ON A BAKING SHEET. BAKE FOR 55 TO 65 MINUTES OR UNTIL POTATO FEELS VERY SOFT WHEN SQUEEZED.

CAESAR PORK BURGERS

PUT YOUR FAVORITE SALAD IN A BURGER!

I CUP	GARLIC-AND-PARMESAN-FLAVORED CROUTONS	250 ML
I LB	GROUND PORK	500 G
4	SLICES BACON, COOKED CRISP AND CHOPPED	4
I	SMALL SHALLOT, MINCED	I
3 TBSP	GRATED PARMESAN CHEESE	45 ML
6 TBSP	CAESAR DRESSING, DIVIDED	90 ML
$1/2$ TSP	WORCESTERSHIRE SAUCE	2 ML
4	HAMBURGER BUNS, SPLIT	4
	CHOPPED ROMAINE LETTUCE	
	COOKED BACON SLICES	
	SHAVED PARMESAN CHEESE	

PREHEAT BARBECUE GRILL TO MEDIUM. PLACE CROUTONS IN A SMALL SEALABLE PLASTIC BAG, SEAL AND CRUSH WITH A ROLLING PIN, LEAVING SOME LARGER PIECES. POUR INTO A LARGE BOWL. ADD PORK, BACON, SHALLOT, CHEESE, 2 TBSP (30 ML) DRESSING AND WORCESTERSHIRE SAUCE; MIX WITH YOUR HANDS UNTIL COMBINED. SHAPE INTO FOUR $1/2$-INCH (I CM) THICK PATTIES. PLACE PATTIES ON GREASED GRILL AND GRILL FOR ABOUT 5 MINUTES PER SIDE OR UNTIL NO LONGER PINK INSIDE AND A MEAT THERMOMETER INSERTED HORIZONTALLY INTO THE CENTER OF A PATTY REGISTERS 160°F (71°C). SPREAD REMAINING DRESSING OVER CUT SIDES OF BUNS. PLACE LETTUCE ON BOTTOM HALVES OF BUNS AND TOP EACH WITH A PATTY. TOP WITH BACON SLICES AND CHEESE. COVER WITH TOP HALVES OF BUNS. SERVES 4.

Curried Turkey Pot Pies (page 192)

Crab Cakes with Greens and Lemon Garlic Mayonnaise (page 212)

Thai Shrimp Stir-Fry (page 218)

HAWAIIAN FRIED RICE

THIS IS THE PERFECT WAY TO USE UP SOME LEFTOVERS AND ENJOY A WHOLE NEW MEAL.

2 TBSP	CANOLA OIL, DIVIDED	30 ML
2	LARGE EGGS, LIGHTLY BEATEN	2
2	GARLIC CLOVES, MINCED	2
1	SMALL ONION, DICED	1
1	CELERY STALK, DICED	1
1	CARROT, DICED	1
1 CUP	DICED COOKED HAM (LEFTOVER OR DELI)	250 ML
4 CUPS	COOKED RICE (SEE TIP)	1 L
3 TBSP	SOY SAUCE	45 ML
3 TBSP	OYSTER SAUCE	45 ML
1 CUP	DICED PINEAPPLE	250 ML
1/2 CUP	FROZEN OR FRESH GREEN PEAS	125 ML

IN A LARGE NONSTICK SKILLET OR WOK, HEAT HALF THE OIL OVER MEDIUM-HIGH HEAT. SCRAMBLE EGGS AND TRANSFER TO A PLATE. ADD REMAINING OIL TO SKILLET AND STIR-FRY GARLIC, ONION, CELERY AND CARROT FOR 2 MINUTES. ADD HAM AND STIR-FRY TO COAT. ADD RICE AND STIR-FRY FOR 2 MINUTES OR UNTIL STARTING TO GET SOME COLOR. STIR IN SOY SAUCE AND OYSTER SAUCE. ADD PINEAPPLE, PEAS AND SCRAMBLED EGGS; COOK, STIRRING, FOR ABOUT 5 MINUTES OR UNTIL HEATED THROUGH. SERVES 4.

TIP: USE ANY LEFTOVER RICE YOU HAVE ON HAND FOR THIS RECIPE. IF YOU DON'T HAVE ANY LEFTOVER RICE, COOK UP ABOUT 1 1/4 CUPS (300 ML) UNCOOKED RICE TO GET THE 4 CUPS (1 L) COOKED RICE YOU NEED HERE.

EASY SLOW COOKER SAUSAGE AND SPAGHETTI SQUASH RAGOÛT

SLOW COOKING THE SQUASH IN THE SAUCE MAKES THE COOKED FLESH REALLY EASY TO SCRAPE OUT. PASTA FANS CAN STRETCH THIS DISH TO SERVE A CROWD BY TOSSING IT WITH HOT COOKED PASTA.

I LB	SAUSAGE (BULK OR CASINGS REMOVED)	500 G
4	GARLIC CLOVES, CHOPPED	4
I	LARGE ONION, CHOPPED	I
I	LARGE CARROT, CHOPPED	I
I TBSP	DRIED ITALIAN SEASONING	I5 ML
I	CAN (28 OZ/796 ML) DICED TOMATOES, WITH JUICE	I
I	CAN (5$\frac{1}{2}$ OZ/I56 ML) TOMATO PASTE	I
$\frac{1}{2}$ CUP	READY-TO-USE CHICKEN BROTH	I25 ML
I	SPAGHETTI SQUASH (ABOUT 2 LBS/I KG)	I
	CHOPPED FRESH BASIL	
	GRATED PARMESAN CHEESE	

IN A NONSTICK SKILLET OVER MEDIUM HEAT, COOK SAUSAGE, GARLIC, ONION, CARROT AND ITALIAN SEASONING, BREAKING UP SAUSAGE WITH A SPOON, FOR ABOUT 8 MINUTES OR UNTIL SAUSAGE IS NO LONGER PINK. TRANSFER TO A 4- TO 6-QUART SLOW COOKER. STIR IN TOMATOES WITH JUICE, TOMATO PASTE AND BROTH. CUT SPAGHETTI SQUASH IN HALF CROSSWISE AND SCRAPE OUT SEEDS. PLACE SQUASH, CUT SIDE DOWN, IN SAUCE MIXTURE. COVER AND COOK ON HIGH FOR 4 HOURS OR ON LOW FOR 8 HOURS, UNTIL SQUASH IS FORK-TENDER. REMOVE SQUASH AND SCRAPE OUT FLESH

WITH A FORK, DISCARDING SKIN. ADD SQUASH FLESH TO SAUCE, STIRRING WELL. SERVE SPRINKLED WITH BASIL AND PARMESAN. SERVES 4 TO 6.

PRESSURE COOKER VARIATION: PREPARE THIS RECIPE FASTER IN AN ELECTRIC PRESSURE COOKER. SAUTÉ THE SAUSAGE AND VEGETABLES USING THE BROWNING FUNCTION, ADD THE TOMATOES, TOMATO PASTE, BROTH AND SQUASH, THEN COOK UNDER HIGH PRESSURE FOR 15 MINUTES (IF YOUR SQUASH IS A BIT BIGGER, ADD ANOTHER 5 MINUTES).

AGE AND GLASSES OF WINE SHOULD NEVER BE COUNTED.
— ITALIAN PROVERB

SAUSAGE AND PEROGY BAKE

SOME RECIPES ARE BELOVED FOR THEIR CONVENIENCE AND SIMPLICITY, AND THIS IS ONE OF THEM. IT'S A PERFECT WAY TO GET THE KIDS INVOLVED IN MEAL PREPARATION. SERVE WITH COOKED VEGGIES OR A SIDE SALAD.

	CANOLA OIL	
1	LARGE ONION, THINLY SLICED	1
24	FROZEN PEROGIES	24
3 CUPS	SLICED COOKED SMOKED SAUSAGE	750 ML
8 OZ	BRICK-STYLE CREAM CHEESE, SOFTENED	250 G
1 1/2 CUPS	SHREDDED CHEDDAR CHEESE	375 ML
1/2 TSP	BLACK PEPPER	2 ML
3/4 CUP	READY-TO-USE CHICKEN BROTH	175 ML
1/2 CUP	MILK	125 ML
2	GREEN ONIONS, SLICED	2

PREHEAT OVEN TO 375°F (190°C) AND LIGHTLY OIL A 13- BY 9-INCH (33 BY 23 CM) GLASS BAKING DISH. IN A SKILLET, HEAT 1 TBSP (15 ML) OIL OVER MEDIUM-HIGH HEAT. COOK ONION, STIRRING OCCASIONALLY, FOR ABOUT 10 MINUTES OR UNTIL GOLDEN. SPREAD ONION IN PREPARED BAKING DISH. PLACE PEROGIES AND SAUSAGE ON TOP IN A SINGLE LAYER. IN A MEDIUM BOWL, COMBINE CREAM CHEESE, CHEDDAR, PEPPER, BROTH AND MILK; POUR OVER CASSEROLE. COVER WITH FOIL AND BAKE FOR 30 MINUTES. REMOVE FOIL, SPRINKLE CASSEROLE WITH GREEN ONIONS AND BAKE FOR 5 MINUTES. SERVES 6 TO 8.

TIP: MOZZARELLA OR A MOZZARELLA/CHEDDAR CHEESE BLEND CAN BE SUBSTITUTED FOR THE CHEDDAR CHEESE.

CHORIZO AND CHEESE STRATA

EGGS AREN'T JUST FOR BREAKFAST, AND YOU CAN
USE UP DAY-OLD BREAD IN THIS SAVORY CASSEROLE.

1/4 CUP	CANOLA OIL	60 ML
1/2	ONION, FINELY CHOPPED	1/2
8 OZ	DRIED CHORIZO SAUSAGES (SEE TIP, PAGE 105), CHOPPED	250 G
1	RED OR YELLOW BELL PEPPER, CHOPPED	1
1	GARLIC CLOVE, MINCED	1
3	SLICES DAY-OLD BREAD, CUBED (ABOUT 3 CUPS/750 ML)	3
3	LARGE EGGS	3
3/4 CUP	MILK	175 ML
1/2 CUP	SHREDDED MANCHEGO CHEESE	125 ML
1/2 TSP	SALT	2 ML
1/2 TSP	BLACK PEPPER	2 ML
1/2 TSP	DRIED OREGANO	2 ML

PREHEAT OVEN TO 425°F (220°C). IN A 10-INCH (25 CM)
OVENPROOF SKILLET, HEAT OIL OVER MEDIUM-HIGH HEAT.
SAUTÉ ONION FOR 5 MINUTES. ADD CHORIZO AND SAUTÉ
FOR 3 MINUTES. ADD RED PEPPER AND GARLIC; SAUTÉ FOR
3 MINUTES. REMOVE FROM HEAT AND STIR IN BREAD
CUBES. IN A MEDIUM BOWL, WHISK TOGETHER EGGS, MILK,
CHEESE, SALT, PEPPER AND OREGANO; POUR OVER BREAD
MIXTURE, PRESSING DOWN GENTLY SO THE BREAD GETS
SOAKED WITH EGG. LET STAND FOR 5 MINUTES. BAKE FOR
15 MINUTES OR UNTIL EDGES BEGIN TO PULL AWAY FROM
SIDES OF PAN. SERVES 4.

TIP: MANCHEGO CAN BE REPLACED WITH PARMESAN,
ROMANO OR ASIAGO CHEESE.

SAUSAGE PANCAKES WITH VEGGIE SLAW

BREAKFAST FOR DINNER, WITH SAUSAGE RIGHT IN THE PANCAKE! THE CRUNCHY SLAW ADDS A CONTRAST THE FAMILY WILL LOVE.

VEGGIE SLAW

1	BAG (12 OZ/340 G) BROCCOLI SLAW	1
2 TSP	SUGAR	10 ML
1/2 TSP	CELERY SEEDS	2 ML
1/2 TSP	SALT	2 ML
1/4 CUP	MAYONNAISE	60 ML
2 TBSP	APPLE CIDER VINEGAR	30 ML

SAUSAGE PANCAKES

8 OZ	SAUSAGE (BULK OR CASINGS REMOVED)	250 G
3/4 CUP	ALL-PURPOSE FLOUR	175 ML
1/3 CUP	CORNMEAL	75 ML
1 TBSP	SUGAR	15 ML
2 TSP	BAKING POWDER	10 ML
1/2 TSP	DRIED OREGANO	2 ML
1/4 TSP	SALT	1 ML
1	LARGE EGG	1
1 CUP	MILK	250 ML
2 TBSP	CANOLA OIL	30 ML
	NONSTICK COOKING SPRAY	

SLAW: IN A LARGE BOWL, TOSS TOGETHER ALL INGREDIENTS; SET ASIDE.

PANCAKES: IN A NONSTICK SKILLET, COOK SAUSAGE OVER MEDIUM-HIGH HEAT, BREAKING IT UP WITH A SPOON, FOR ABOUT 8 MINUTES OR UNTIL NO LONGER PINK. DRAIN AND

SET ASIDE. IN A LARGE BOWL, WHISK TOGETHER FLOUR, CORNMEAL, SUGAR, BAKING POWDER, OREGANO AND SALT. IN A SMALL BOWL, WHISK TOGETHER EGG, MILK AND OIL; POUR OVER FLOUR MIXTURE AND STIR A COUPLE OF TIMES. ADD SAUSAGE AND STIR UNTIL WELL COMBINED. WIPE OUT SKILLET, SPRAY WITH COOKING SPRAY AND HEAT OVER MEDIUM HEAT. LADLE IN ABOUT $\frac{1}{4}$ CUP (60 ML) BATTER PER PANCAKE. COOK FOR ABOUT 2 MINUTES OR UNTIL BUBBLES APPEAR ON TOP. FLIP PANCAKE AND COOK FOR I MINUTE OR UNTIL GOLDEN. TRANSFER PANCAKE TO A PLATE AND KEEP WARM. REPEAT WITH REMAINING BATTER, SPRAYING SKILLET AS NEEDED BETWEEN PANCAKES. SERVE PANCAKES WITH VEGGIE SLAW ON TOP. SERVES 4.

VARIATION: FOR SOME ADDED GOOEYNESS, ADD $\frac{1}{2}$ CUP (125 ML) SHREDDED CHEDDAR CHEESE TO THE BATTER WITH THE SAUSAGE.

AN APPLE A DAY KEEPS ANYONE AWAY
IF THROWN HARD ENOUGH.

POTATO CHORIZO TACOS

THESE TACOS ARE SURPRISINGLY ADDICTIVE!

3	POTATOES (ABOUT 12 OZ/375 G TOTAL), PEELED AND DICED	3
1/2 CUP	READY-TO-USE VEGETABLE BROTH	125 ML
1/2 TSP	SMOKED PAPRIKA	2 ML
1 TBSP	CANOLA OIL	15 ML
3	GARLIC CLOVES, MINCED	3
1	ONION, CHOPPED	1
1 CUP	DICED DRIED SPICY CHORIZO SAUSAGES (SEE TIP, PAGE 105)	250 ML
2 TBSP	CHOPPED FRESH CILANTRO	30 ML
1/2 CUP	SALSA	125 ML
8	HARD TACO SHELLS	8
1	TOMATO, CHOPPED	1
1	AVOCADO, CHOPPED	1
	SOUR CREAM AND CHOPPED LETTUCE (OPTIONAL)	

IN A SKILLET, COMBINE POTATOES, BROTH AND PAPRIKA. BRING TO A SIMMER OVER MEDIUM HEAT. REDUCE HEAT, COVER AND SIMMER FOR 8 MINUTES OR UNTIL POTATOES ARE TENDER. TRANSFER TO A BOWL. RETURN SKILLET TO MEDIUM HEAT AND ADD OIL. COOK GARLIC, ONION AND SAUSAGE, STIRRING, FOR 5 MINUTES OR UNTIL ONION IS SOFTENED. STIR IN POTATOES AND ANY REMAINING LIQUID; COOK, STIRRING, FOR 5 MINUTES OR UNTIL STARTING TO BECOME GOLDEN. STIR IN CILANTRO AND SALSA; COOK UNTIL WARMED THROUGH. SPOON POTATO MIXTURE INTO TACO SHELLS AND TOP WITH TOMATO AND AVOCADO. IF DESIRED, ADD SOUR CREAM AND LETTUCE. SERVES 4.

CHICKEN AND TURKEY

ROAST CHICKEN, POTATOES AND CHICKPEAS

CHICKEN, POTATOES AND AROMATICS COME TOGETHER FOR A FLAVORFUL MEAL. CUTTING THE POTATOES INTO SMALL CUBES SPEEDS UP THE COOKING PROCESS.

5	GARLIC CLOVES, HALVED	5
1 TBSP	SMOKED PAPRIKA	15 ML
1 TSP	GROUND CUMIN	5 ML
1 TSP	GROUND CORIANDER	5 ML
1 TSP	SALT	5 ML
1 TSP	BLACK PEPPER	5 ML
2 TBSP	CANOLA OIL	30 ML
8	BONE-IN SKIN-ON CHICKEN THIGHS OR DRUMSTICKS	8
1½ LBS	WAXY POTATOES (SEE TIP, PAGE 81), CUT INTO 1-INCH (2.5 CM) CUBES	750 G
1	ONION, THINLY SLICED	1
1	CAN (19 OZ/540 ML) CHICKPEAS, RINSED AND DRAINED (2 CUPS/500 ML)	1
1	LEMON, CUT INTO WEDGES	1

PREHEAT OVEN TO 425°F (220°C). IN A LARGE BOWL, COMBINE GARLIC, PAPRIKA, CUMIN, CORIANDER, SALT, PEPPER AND OIL. ADD CHICKEN, POTATOES, ONION AND CHICKPEAS, STIRRING TO COAT EVENLY. TRANSFER TO A FOIL-LINED LARGE RIMMED BAKING SHEET, ARRANGING CHICKEN, SKIN SIDE UP, ON TOP OF VEGETABLES. SQUEEZE LEMON JUICE OVER TOP AND PLACE LEMON WEDGES ON BAKING SHEET. BAKE FOR 30 TO 35 MINUTES OR UNTIL POTATOES ARE TENDER AND A MEAT THERMOMETER

INSERTED IN THE THICKEST PART OF A CHICKEN PIECE REGISTERS 165°F (74°C). SERVES 4.

TIP: IF YOUR BAKING SHEET IS TOO CROWDED OR FULL, DIVIDE THE MIXTURE BETWEEN TWO LARGE BAKING SHEETS FOR FASTER, EVEN COOKING. YOU WANT THE FOOD TO BAKE, NOT STEAM. SWITCH THE POSITIONS OF THE BAKING SHEETS ON THE OVEN RACKS HALFWAY THROUGH THE COOKING TIME.

TIP: TO GET DINNER ON THE TABLE EVEN FASTER, PREPARE THE POTATO AND CHICKPEA MIXTURE THE NIGHT BEFORE, OMITTING THE CHICKEN. COVER AND REFRIGERATE THE MIXTURE IN THE LARGE BOWL. WHEN YOU'RE READY TO BAKE, PREHEAT THE OVEN AND ADD THE CHICKEN TO THE MIXTURE, STIRRING TO COAT EVENLY. TRANSFER THE MIXTURE TO THE PREPARED BAKING SHEET AND BAKE AS DIRECTED.

SHEET PAN CHICKEN, CHORIZO, BRUSSELS SPROUTS AND POTATOES

DON'T YOU LOVE IT WHEN YOU CAN COOK YOUR ENTIRE MEAL ON ONE PAN?

2 TSP	DRIED OREGANO	10 ML
1 TSP	GARLIC POWDER	5 ML
1 TSP	BLACK PEPPER	5 ML
1/2 TSP	SALT	2 ML
2 TBSP	CANOLA OIL	30 ML
8	BONE-IN SKIN-ON CHICKEN THIGHS	8
8 OZ	DRIED CHORIZO SAUSAGES (SEE TIP, PAGE 105), SLICED	250 G
1 LB	BRUSSELS SPROUTS, HALVED	500 G
8 OZ	WAXY POTATOES (SEE TIP, PAGE 81), CUT INTO 1-INCH (2.5 CM) CUBES	250 G
1	RED ONION, SLICED	1

PREHEAT OVEN TO 425°F (220°C). IN A LARGE BOWL, COMBINE OREGANO, GARLIC POWDER, PEPPER, SALT AND OIL. ADD CHICKEN, CHORIZO, BRUSSELS SPROUTS, POTATOES AND ONION, STIRRING TO COAT EVENLY. SPREAD IN A SINGLE LAYER ON A FOIL-LINED LARGE RIMMED BAKING SHEET, ARRANGING CHICKEN, SKIN SIDE UP, ON TOP OF VEGETABLES. BAKE FOR 30 TO 35 MINUTES OR UNTIL VEGETABLES ARE TENDER AND A MEAT THERMOMETER INSERTED IN THE THICKEST PART OF A CHICKEN THIGH REGISTERS 165°F (74°C). SERVES 4.

TIP: IF YOUR BAKING SHEET IS OVERCROWDED, THEN USE TWO BAKING SHEETS AND SWITCH THE POSITIONS OF THE BAKING SHEETS ON THE OVEN RACKS HALFWAY THROUGH THE COOKING TIME.

CHICKEN THIGHS WITH APPLE, BACON AND SPROUTS

EMILY'S FRIEND SHAN'S BOYS LOVE THIS COMBINATION SO MUCH, THEY ALWAYS ASK FOR SECOND HELPINGS. IT'S A GREAT WAY TO GET KIDS TO EAT BRUSSELS SPROUTS.

6	SLICES BACON, CHOPPED	6
1 LB	BONELESS SKINLESS CHICKEN THIGHS, CHOPPED	500 G
2 TSP	CHOPPED FRESH THYME	10 ML
1 LB	BRUSSELS SPROUTS, HALVED	500 G
1/3 CUP	APPLE JUICE	75 ML
PINCH	SALT	PINCH
PINCH	BLACK PEPPER	PINCH
1	RED-SKINNED APPLE, CHOPPED	1

IN A LARGE SKILLET OVER MEDIUM-HIGH HEAT, COOK BACON, STIRRING, UNTIL CRISPY. USING A SLOTTED SPOON, TRANSFER BACON TO A PLATE LINED WITH PAPER TOWEL. ADD CHICKEN AND THYME TO BACON FAT IN SKILLET AND COOK, STIRRING, FOR ABOUT 5 MINUTES, UNTIL CHICKEN IS BROWNED ON ALL SIDES. USING A SLOTTED SPOON, TRANSFER TO PLATE WITH BACON. ADD BRUSSELS SPROUTS, APPLE JUICE, SALT AND PEPPER TO SKILLET; REDUCE HEAT, COVER AND SIMMER FOR ABOUT 8 MINUTES OR UNTIL SPROUTS ARE TENDER-CRISP. RETURN CHICKEN AND BACON TO SKILLET AND STIR IN APPLE. COOK, STIRRING, FOR ABOUT 5 MINUTES OR UNTIL JUICES RUN CLEAR WHEN CHICKEN IS PIERCED. SERVES 4.

TIP: NEED SOME HEAT? ADD A PINCH OF HOT PEPPER FLAKES WITH THE APPLE JUICE.

PAN-ROASTED PERUVIAN CHICKEN WITH CAULIFLOWER AND GREEN SAUCE

THIS FLAVORFUL MEAL IS A BIG HIT WITH SYLVIA'S FAMILY. THE FRESH ZESTY GREEN SAUCE WILL MAKE YOU WANT TO LICK THE PLATE CLEAN! SERVE WITH HOT COOKED RICE.

GREEN SAUCE

2	GARLIC CLOVES	2
1/2	JALAPEÑO PEPPER, SEEDS AND RIBS REMOVED	1/2
1/2 CUP	LIGHTLY PACKED FRESH CILANTRO	125 ML
1/2 CUP	LIGHTLY PACKED FRESH PARSLEY	125 ML
1/2 TSP	BLACK PEPPER	2 ML
1/2 TSP	SALT	2 ML
1/2 CUP	CANOLA OIL	125 ML
2 TBSP	MAYONNAISE	30 ML
1 TBSP	LIME JUICE	15 ML

PERUVIAN CHICKEN AND CAULIFLOWER

4	GARLIC CLOVES, MINCED	4
2 TBSP	PAPRIKA	30 ML
1 TBSP	GROUND CUMIN	15 ML
1 TSP	BLACK PEPPER	5 ML
2 TBSP	SOY SAUCE	30 ML
2 TBSP	CANOLA OIL	30 ML
2 TBSP	WHITE VINEGAR	30 ML
10	BONE-IN SKIN-ON CHICKEN THIGHS	10
1	HEAD CAULIFLOWER, CUT INTO FLORETS (ABOUT 4 CUPS/1 L)	1

SAUCE: IN A BLENDER OR FOOD PROCESSOR, BLEND ALL INGREDIENTS UNTIL SMOOTH. COVER AND REFRIGERATE UNTIL READY TO USE.

CHICKEN AND CAULIFLOWER: PREHEAT OVEN TO 400°F (200°C). IN A LARGE BOWL, COMBINE GARLIC, PAPRIKA, CUMIN, PEPPER, SOY SAUCE, OIL AND VINEGAR. ADD CHICKEN AND CAULIFLOWER, STIRRING TO COAT EVENLY. SPREAD CAULIFLOWER IN A SINGLE LAYER ON A FOIL-LINED LARGE RIMMED BAKING SHEET AND PLACE CHICKEN ON TOP, SKIN SIDE UP. BAKE FOR 30 TO 35 MINUTES OR UNTIL CAULIFLOWER IS TENDER AND A MEAT THERMOMETER INSERTED IN THE THICKEST PART OF A CHICKEN THIGH REGISTERS 165°F (74°C). SERVE DRIZZLED WITH GREEN SAUCE. SERVES 5.

TIP: PRECHOPPED CAULIFLOWER IS A TIME-SAVER.

SPICY HOISIN CHICKEN AND GREEN BEANS

THIS JUICY, ASIAN-STYLE CHICKEN HAS A HINT OF HEAT. SERVE WITH HOT COOKED RICE TO SOAK UP THE FLAVORFUL SAUCE.

1 TBSP	PACKED BROWN SUGAR	15 ML
1 TBSP	CORNSTARCH	15 ML
2 TSP	GRATED FRESH GINGER	10 ML
1 TSP	HOT PEPPER FLAKES	5 ML
1 CUP	READY-TO-USE CHICKEN BROTH	250 ML
1/4 CUP	HOISIN SAUCE	60 ML
3 TBSP	SOY SAUCE	45 ML
1 TSP	WHITE VINEGAR	5 ML
1 TSP	SESAME OIL	5 ML
2 TBSP	CANOLA OIL, DIVIDED	30 ML
1/2	ONION, THINLY SLICED	1/2
1 LB	BONELESS SKINLESS CHICKEN THIGHS, CUT INTO THIN STRIPS	500 G
3	GARLIC CLOVES, THINLY SLICED	3
12 OZ	GREEN BEANS, HALVED LENGTHWISE	375 G
2	GREEN ONIONS, THINLY SLICED	2
1 TBSP	TOASTED SESAME SEEDS (SEE TIP)	15 ML

IN A SMALL BOWL, COMBINE BROWN SUGAR, CORNSTARCH, GINGER, HOT PEPPER FLAKES, BROTH, HOISIN SAUCE, SOY SAUCE, VINEGAR AND SESAME OIL; SET ASIDE. IN A LARGE SKILLET, HEAT 1 TBSP (15 ML) CANOLA OIL OVER MEDIUM-HIGH HEAT. SAUTÉ ONION FOR 3 MINUTES. ADD CHICKEN AND COOK, STIRRING OCCASIONALLY, FOR 3 MINUTES. TRANSFER CHICKEN AND ONION TO A PLATE. ADD REMAINING CANOLA OIL TO SKILLET AND SAUTÉ

GARLIC FOR 30 SECONDS. ADD GREEN BEANS AND BROTH MIXTURE; COVER AND COOK FOR 3 MINUTES. RETURN CHICKEN AND ONION TO SKILLET, ALONG WITH ANY ACCUMULATED JUICES. STIR IN GREEN ONIONS, REDUCE HEAT AND SIMMER, UNCOVERED, FOR 3 TO 5 MINUTES OR UNTIL BEANS ARE TENDER-CRISP AND JUICES RUN CLEAR WHEN CHICKEN IS PIERCED. SERVE SPRINKLED WITH SESAME SEEDS. SERVES 4.

TIP: TOAST SESAME SEEDS IN A SMALL SKILLET OVER MEDIUM HEAT FOR ABOUT 2 MINUTES OR UNTIL GOLDEN BROWN.

CURRY LIME CHICKEN SKEWERS WITH PEPPERS AND ZUCCHINI

THESE FRAGRANT GRILLED SKEWERS CAN ALSO BE SERVED AS AN APPETIZER. AS AN ENTRÉE, SERVE THEM WITH STEAMED RICE.

3	GARLIC CLOVES, MINCED	3
2 TBSP	PACKED BROWN SUGAR	30 ML
3/4 CUP	COCONUT MILK	175 ML
3 TBSP	FISH SAUCE	45 ML
2 TSP	GRATED LIME ZEST	10 ML
2 TBSP	LIME JUICE	30 ML
1 TBSP	THAI RED OR GREEN CURRY PASTE	15 ML
1 1/2 LBS	BONELESS SKINLESS CHICKEN THIGHS, CUT INTO 1 1/2-INCH (4 CM) PIECES	750 G
2	RED OR YELLOW BELL PEPPERS, CUT INTO 1 1/2-INCH (4 CM) PIECES	2
1	ZUCCHINI, CUT INTO 1 1/2-INCH (4 CM) CHUNKS	1
1/2	ONION, CUT INTO 1 1/2-INCH (4 CM) PIECES	1/2
	METAL OR BAMBOO SKEWERS	

IN A LARGE BOWL, STIR TOGETHER GARLIC, BROWN SUGAR, COCONUT MILK, FISH SAUCE, LIME ZEST, LIME JUICE AND CURRY PASTE UNTIL WELL COMBINED. RESERVE 1/4 CUP (60 ML) MARINADE FOR BASTING. TO THE LARGE BOWL, ADD CHICKEN, PEPPERS, ZUCCHINI AND ONION, STIRRING TO COMBINE. COVER AND REFRIGERATE FOR 30 MINUTES.

MEANWHILE, IF USING BAMBOO SKEWERS, SOAK IN WATER FOR 30 MINUTES. PREHEAT BARBECUE GRILL TO HIGH. REMOVE CHICKEN AND VEGETABLES FROM

MARINADE, DISCARDING MARINADE, AND THREAD ONTO SKEWERS. GRILL SKEWERS FOR 4 MINUTES. BASTE WITH RESERVED MARINADE, TURN SKEWERS OVER AND COOK FOR 3 TO 4 MINUTES OR UNTIL JUICES RUN CLEAR WHEN CHICKEN IS PIERCED. SERVES 6.

TIP: PREPARED THAI RED OR GREEN CURRY PASTE IS READILY AVAILABLE IN THE ASIAN FOODS SECTION OF MOST GROCERY STORES.

TIP: THIS RECIPE IS A GREAT MAKE AHEAD. PREPARE THE SKEWERS THE NIGHT BEFORE, COVER AND REFRIGERATE.

IS IT JUST ME, OR DO BUFFALO WINGS TASTE LIKE CHICKEN?

QUICK STOVETOP CHICKEN STEW

CHOOSE CHICKEN THIGHS FOR A QUICK WEEKNIGHT MEAL TO SERVE OVER PASTA OR RICE.

1½ LBS	BONELESS SKINLESS CHICKEN THIGHS, CUT INTO 1-INCH (2.5 CM) PIECES	750 G
2	GARLIC CLOVES, MINCED	2
2 TBSP	ALL-PURPOSE FLOUR	30 ML
1 TBSP	DRIED ITALIAN SEASONING	15 ML
½ TSP	SALT, DIVIDED	2 ML
½ TSP	BLACK PEPPER, DIVIDED	2 ML
2 TBSP	CANOLA OIL	30 ML
1	LARGE ONION, CHOPPED	1
1	LARGE CARROT, CHOPPED	1
1	CAN (5½ OZ/156 ML) TOMATO PASTE	1
2 CUPS	READY-TO-USE CHICKEN BROTH	500 ML
1 TBSP	CHOPPED FRESH PARSLEY	15 ML

IN A LARGE BOWL, TOSS CHICKEN WITH GARLIC, FLOUR, ITALIAN SEASONING AND HALF EACH OF THE SALT AND PEPPER. IN A LARGE SAUCEPAN, HEAT HALF THE OIL OVER MEDIUM-HIGH HEAT. IN BATCHES, BROWN CHICKEN AND TRANSFER TO A PLATE, ADDING REMAINING OIL BETWEEN BATCHES. ADD ONION AND CARROT TO SKILLET AND SAUTÉ FOR 3 MINUTES. STIR IN TOMATO PASTE, BROTH AND REMAINING SALT AND PEPPER. RETURN CHICKEN TO SKILLET, ALONG WITH ANY ACCUMULATED JUICES, AND BRING TO A SIMMER. SPRINKLE WITH PARSLEY, REDUCE HEAT, COVER AND SIMMER FOR ABOUT 15 MINUTES OR UNTIL CHICKEN IS STARTING TO FALL APART. SERVES 6.

CHICKEN WITH MUSHROOM GRAVY

MANY PEOPLE USE A CAN OF SOUP TO MAKE THIS DINNERTIME FAVORITE, BUT IT'S JUST AS EASY TO MAKE YOUR OWN SAUCE, WITH LOTS OF MUSHROOMS.

I TSP	DRIED ITALIAN SEASONING	5 ML
1/2 TSP	DRIED BASIL	2 ML
1/4 TSP	BLACK PEPPER	I ML
2	BONELESS SKINLESS CHICKEN BREASTS, CUT IN HALF HORIZONTALLY	2
I TBSP	CANOLA OIL	15 ML
I	LARGE ONION, THINLY SLICED	I
I LB	CREMINI MUSHROOMS, SLICED	500 G
I TBSP	CHOPPED FRESH THYME (OR I TSP/5 ML DRIED)	15 ML
I TBSP	ALL-PURPOSE FLOUR	15 ML
1 1/2 CUPS	READY-TO-USE CHICKEN BROTH	375 ML

IN A SMALL BOWL, COMBINE ITALIAN SEASONING, BASIL AND PEPPER; SPRINKLE EVENLY OVER BOTH SIDES OF CHICKEN. IN A LARGE NONSTICK SKILLET, HEAT OIL OVER MEDIUM-HIGH HEAT. IN BATCHES AS NECESSARY, BROWN CHICKEN ON BOTH SIDES AND TRANSFER TO A PLATE. ADD ONION, MUSHROOMS AND THYME TO SKILLET AND SAUTÉ FOR ABOUT 10 MINUTES OR UNTIL SOFTENED AND GOLDEN. SPRINKLE WITH FLOUR AND COOK, STIRRING, FOR 30 SECONDS. STIR IN BROTH AND BRING TO A BOIL, STIRRING. RETURN CHICKEN TO SKILLET, ALONG WITH ANY ACCUMULATED JUICES; REDUCE HEAT AND SIMMER, TURNING CHICKEN OCCASIONALLY, FOR ABOUT 5 MINUTES OR UNTIL CHICKEN IS NO LONGER PINK INSIDE. SERVES 4.

QUICK CHICKEN CUTLETS

THIS QUICK BREADING METHOD CREATES CUTLETS THAT ARE PERFECT FOR A FAMILY MEAL WHEN TOPPED OFF WITH YOUR FAVORITE VEGETABLES OR PASTA SAUCE. THEY'RE ALSO GREAT SERVED IN A BUN FOR DINNER OR LUNCH THE NEXT DAY.

1/2 CUP	ITALIAN-SEASONED DRY BREAD CRUMBS	125 ML
2 TBSP	GRATED PARMESAN CHEESE	30 ML
1 TSP	DRIED OREGANO	5 ML
PINCH	SALT	PINCH
PINCH	BLACK PEPPER	PINCH
1 LB	CHICKEN BREAST CUTLETS	500 G
1/4 CUP	EXTRA VIRGIN OLIVE OIL	60 ML

IN A SHALLOW DISH, COMBINE BREAD CRUMBS, CHEESE, OREGANO, SALT AND PEPPER. DREDGE EACH CUTLET IN CRUMB MIXTURE, COATING EVENLY; DISCARD ANY EXCESS CRUMB MIXTURE. IN A LARGE NONSTICK SKILLET, HEAT HALF THE OIL OVER MEDIUM-HIGH HEAT. IN BATCHES, COOK CUTLETS, TURNING ONCE, FOR ABOUT 5 MINUTES OR UNTIL GOLDEN BROWN AND NO LONGER PINK INSIDE, ADDING REMAINING OIL BETWEEN BATCHES. TRANSFER CHICKEN TO A PLATE LINED WITH PAPER TOWEL AND KEEP WARM. SERVES 4.

TURKEY VARIATION: REPLACE THE CHICKEN WITH TURKEY CUTLETS AND COOK AS ABOVE.

VEAL OR PORK VARIATION: REPLACE THE CHICKEN WITH VEAL SCALOPPINE OR PORK CUTLETS AND COOK UNTIL JUST A HINT OF PINK REMAINS INSIDE.

CRUNCHY CHICKEN FINGERS
WITH SRIRACHA DIPPING SAUCE

TENDER AND JUICY, WITH A CRISP COATING, THESE
CHICKEN FINGERS ARE ALWAYS A CROWD PLEASER.
SERVE WITH A SALAD AND CRUSTY BUNS.

1 1/2 LBS	BONELESS SKINLESS CHICKEN BREASTS, CUT INTO 1 1/2-INCH (4 CM) STRIPS	750 G
1 CUP	MAYONNAISE, DIVIDED	250 ML
1 TSP	PAPRIKA	5 ML
1/2 TSP	SALT	2 ML
1/2 TSP	BLACK PEPPER	2 ML
1 TSP	GARLIC POWDER, DIVIDED	5 ML
2 CUPS	CRUSHED CORN FLAKES CEREAL	500 ML
1 TBSP	CANOLA OIL	15 ML
2 TBSP	SRIRACHA	30 ML
1 TBSP	LIQUID HONEY	15 ML

PREHEAT OVEN TO 425°F (220°C). IN A MEDIUM BOWL,
COMBINE CHICKEN, 1/2 CUP (125 ML) MAYONNAISE, PAPRIKA,
SALT, PEPPER AND 1/2 TSP (2 ML) GARLIC POWDER,
STIRRING TO COAT CHICKEN. PLACE CEREAL IN A SHALLOW
BOWL. DIP EACH PIECE OF CHICKEN IN CEREAL, PRESSING
TO COAT. PLACE CHICKEN ON A PARCHMENT-LINED RIMMED
BAKING SHEET AND DRIZZLE WITH OIL. DISCARD EXCESS
CEREAL. BAKE FOR 12 TO 15 MINUTES OR UNTIL CHICKEN
IS CRISP AND NO LONGER PINK INSIDE.

MEANWHILE, IN A SMALL BOWL, COMBINE REMAINING
MAYONNAISE, SRIRACHA, HONEY AND REMAINING GARLIC
POWDER. SERVE CHICKEN WITH SAUCE. SERVES 6.

BUFFALO CHICKEN QUESADILLA PIE

SYLVIA'S FAMILY ENJOYS THIS PIE ON THE HOTTER SIDE.
IF YOU PREFER A MILDER FLAVOR, CUT BACK ON
THE HOT SAUCE. SERVE WITH ADDITIONAL
HOT PEPPER SAUCE AND SOUR CREAM, IF DESIRED.

2	GREEN ONIONS, SLICED	2
1/4 CUP	FINELY CHOPPED ONION	60 ML
3 CUPS	CHOPPED COOKED CHICKEN	750 ML
2 CUPS	SHREDDED MOZZARELLA CHEESE	500 ML
3 TBSP	ALL-PURPOSE FLOUR	45 ML
1 TBSP	SMOKED PAPRIKA	15 ML
2 TSP	GARLIC POWDER	10 ML
2	LARGE EGGS, LIGHTLY BEATEN	2
1/2 CUP	SOUR CREAM	125 ML
1/4 to 1/3 CUP	HOT PEPPER SAUCE (SUCH AS FRANK'S REDHOT)	60 to 75 ML
3	10-INCH (25 CM) FLOUR TORTILLAS	3
1 CUP	SHREDDED CHEDDAR CHEESE	250 ML

PREHEAT OVEN TO 400°F (200°C) AND LIGHTLY GREASE A
10-INCH (25 CM) DEEP-DISH PIE PLATE. IN A MEDIUM BOWL,
COMBINE GREEN ONIONS, ONION, CHICKEN, MOZZARELLA,
FLOUR, PAPRIKA, GARLIC POWDER, EGGS, SOUR CREAM
AND HOT PEPPER SAUCE TO TASTE. PRESS 1 TORTILLA
INTO PREPARED PIE PLATE AND SPREAD ONE-THIRD OF
THE CHICKEN MIXTURE OVER TOP. REPEAT LAYERS TWICE
MORE. SPRINKLE WITH CHEDDAR. BAKE FOR 35 MINUTES,
THEN BROIL FOR 1 TO 2 MINUTES OR UNTIL CHEESE IS
LIGHTLY BROWNED. LET COOL FOR 5 MINUTES BEFORE
CUTTING INTO WEDGES. SERVES 8.

CHICKEN, SPINACH AND SWEET POTATO HASH

SIMPLE SUPPERS THAT ARE HEALTHY AND COLORFUL ARE ALWAYS A HIT FOR THE FAMILY.

1	LARGE SWEET POTATO, PEELED AND DICED (ABOUT 8 OZ/250 G)	1
3 TBSP	WATER	45 ML
2 TBSP	CANOLA OIL	30 ML
1 LB	GROUND CHICKEN	500 G
1	ONION, DICED	1
1	RED BELL PEPPER, DICED	1
1 TSP	DRIED THYME	5 ML
1/2 TSP	SALT	2 ML
1/2 TSP	BLACK PEPPER	2 ML
PINCH	HOT PEPPER FLAKES	PINCH
1	PACKAGE (5 OZ/142 G) BABY SPINACH (ABOUT 5 CUPS/1.25 L)	1

PLACE SWEET POTATO AND WATER IN A MICROWAVE-SAFE BOWL. COVER WITH PLASTIC WRAP AND MICROWAVE ON HIGH FOR 4 MINUTES OR UNTIL TENDER. DRAIN, IF NECESSARY. IN A LARGE NONSTICK SKILLET, HEAT OIL OVER MEDIUM-HIGH HEAT. COOK CHICKEN, ONION, RED PEPPER, THYME, SALT, BLACK PEPPER AND HOT PEPPER FLAKES, STIRRING AND BREAKING CHICKEN UP WITH A SPOON, UNTIL CHICKEN IS NO LONGER PINK. STIR IN SWEET POTATO AND SPINACH; COOK, STIRRING, UNTIL WARMED THROUGH AND SPINACH IS WILTED. SERVES 4.

VARIATION: OMIT THE THYME AND ADD 2 GARLIC CLOVES, MINCED, AND 2 TBSP (30 ML) HOISIN SAUCE WITH THE SPINACH.

TINA'S HARISSA CHICKEN BURGERS

EMILY'S SISTER TINA HAS LONG DAYS AND STILL WANTS TO MAKE DINNER AT HOME AFTER WORK. THESE BURGERS ARE A GO-TO RECIPE THAT SHE CAN RELY ON FOR A QUICK, TASTY MEAL.

1 LB	GROUND CHICKEN	500 G
1 TSP	FINELY CHOPPED FRESH ROSEMARY	5 ML
1/2 TSP	SALT	2 ML
1/2 TSP	BLACK PEPPER	2 ML
2 TBSP	EXTRA VIRGIN OLIVE OIL, DIVIDED	30 ML
1 TBSP	HARISSA PASTE	15 ML
4	THICK SLICES CRUSTY BREAD	4
1	TOMATO, SLICED	1

IN A BOWL, COMBINE CHICKEN, ROSEMARY, SALT, PEPPER, HALF THE OIL AND HARISSA PASTE. SHAPE INTO FOUR 1/4-INCH (0.5 CM) THICK PATTIES. IN A LARGE NONSTICK SKILLET, HEAT REMAINING OIL OVER MEDIUM-HIGH HEAT. IN BATCHES AS NECESSARY, COOK PATTIES, TURNING ONCE, FOR ABOUT 8 MINUTES OR UNTIL NO LONGER PINK INSIDE AND A MEAT THERMOMETER INSERTED HORIZONTALLY INTO THE CENTER OF A PATTY REGISTERS 165°F (74°C). SERVE WITH BREAD AND TOMATO. SERVES 4.

VARIATION: ADD 2 TSP (10 ML) CHOPPED FRESH MINT WITH THE ROSEMARY.

BREADED CHICKEN WINGS

CHICKEN WINGS ARE SUCH A KID FAVORITE FOR DINNER, AND THEY ARE SUPER-FUN FOR THE WHOLE FAMILY. THIS EASY BREADING ADDS SOME CRUNCH!

2 LBS	CHICKEN WINGS, SPLIT	1 KG
2 TBSP	CANOLA OIL	30 ML
1/2 CUP	ITALIAN-SEASONED DRY BREAD CRUMBS	125 ML
3 TBSP	GRATED PARMESAN CHEESE	45 ML
1 TSP	DRIED ITALIAN SEASONING	5 ML
1/4 TSP	HOT PEPPER FLAKES	1 ML
1/4 TSP	SALT	1 ML
1/4 TSP	BLACK PEPPER	1 ML

PREHEAT OVEN TO 400°F (200°C), WITH RACK SET IN BOTTOM THIRD. IN A LARGE BOWL, TOSS CHICKEN WINGS WITH OIL, COATING EVENLY. IN A SMALL BOWL, COMBINE BREAD CRUMBS, PARMESAN, ITALIAN SEASONING, HOT PEPPER FLAKES, SALT AND BLACK PEPPER. SPRINKLE OVER CHICKEN AND TOSS TO COAT WELL. SPREAD DRUMETTES IN A SINGLE LAYER ON A PARCHMENT-LINED BAKING SHEET; DISCARD ANY EXCESS CRUMB MIXTURE. BAKE FOR ABOUT 30 MINUTES OR UNTIL JUICES RUN CLEAR WHEN CHICKEN IS PIERCED. SERVES 4.

TIP: SERVE A HOT PASTA OR PIZZA SAUCE TO DIP THE WINGS IN, FOR A GREAT CHICKEN PARMESAN TASTE.

SOY GINGER CHICKEN WINGS

"FINGER-LICKING GOOD, MOM!" WAS THE REACTION THESE WINGS RECEIVED AT EMILY'S HOUSE WHEN SHE SERVED THEM UP FOR DINNER.

1 TBSP	CANOLA OIL	15 ML
4	GARLIC CLOVES, MINCED	4
2 TSP	MINCED FRESH GINGER	10 ML
3 TBSP	SUGAR	45 ML
1/4 CUP	SOY SAUCE	60 ML
2 LBS	CHICKEN WINGS, SPLIT	1 KG
1/4 TSP	HOT PEPPER FLAKES	1 ML
2 TBSP	LIQUID HONEY	30 ML

IN A LARGE, WIDE, SHALLOW NONSTICK SKILLET, HEAT OIL OVER MEDIUM HEAT. SAUTÉ GARLIC AND GINGER FOR 1 MINUTE. ADD SUGAR AND SOY SAUCE; BRING TO A SIMMER. GENTLY STIR IN CHICKEN WINGS UNTIL WELL COATED; RETURN TO A SIMMER. REDUCE HEAT, COVER AND SIMMER, STIRRING OCCASIONALLY, FOR 15 MINUTES. STIR IN HOT PEPPER FLAKES AND HONEY; SIMMER, UNCOVERED, STIRRING OFTEN, FOR ABOUT 8 MINUTES OR UNTIL CHICKEN IS WELL GLAZED AND JUICES RUN CLEAR WHEN CHICKEN IS PIERCED. SERVES 4.

WHEN I MAKE CHICKEN WINGS, THEY FLY OUT OF MY KITCHEN.

APPLE BUTTER-BASTED TURKEY BREAST

*TURKEY IS NOT JUST FOR SPECIAL OCCASIONS —
YOU CAN ENJOY THIS SKILLET DINNER, WITH
MASHED POTATOES TO SOP UP ALL THE SAUCE,
FOR A WEEKNIGHT SUPPER.*

1	BONELESS SKINLESS TURKEY BREAST (ABOUT 1 LB/500 G)	1
1 TBSP	CANOLA OIL	15 ML
1/2 TSP	DRIED SAGE	2 ML
1/2 TSP	DRIED THYME	2 ML
1/4 TSP	SALT	1 ML
1/4 TSP	BLACK PEPPER	1 ML
1	RED ONION, SLICED	1
2 TBSP	APPLE CIDER VINEGAR	30 ML
1/2 CUP	APPLE BUTTER	125 ML

RUB TURKEY ALL OVER WITH OIL AND SPRINKLE WITH
SAGE, THYME, SALT AND PEPPER. HEAT A LARGE SKILLET
OR GRILL PAN OVER MEDIUM-HIGH HEAT. BROWN TURKEY
ON BOTH SIDES AND TRANSFER TO A PLATE. REDUCE
HEAT TO MEDIUM, ADD ONION AND VINEGAR TO SKILLET
AND COOK, STIRRING, FOR 4 MINUTES OR UNTIL ONION
IS SLIGHTLY SOFTENED. SPREAD SOME OF THE APPLE
BUTTER OVER BOTH SIDES OF TURKEY AND RETURN TO
SKILLET, ALONG WITH ANY ACCUMULATED JUICES. REDUCE
HEAT TO MEDIUM-LOW AND ADD REMAINING APPLE BUTTER.
COOK, TURNING TURKEY A FEW TIMES, FOR ABOUT
10 MINUTES OR UNTIL A MEAT THERMOMETER INSERTED
IN THE THICKEST PART OF THE TURKEY REGISTERS
165°F (74°C). SERVES 4.

CURRIED TURKEY POT PIES

POT PIES ARE ALWAYS A WELCOME COMFORT FOOD MEAL, AND STORE-BOUGHT PUFF PASTRY IS A CONVENIENT AND DELICIOUS WAY TO GET SUPPER ON THE TABLE FUSS-FREE.

	CANOLA OIL	
1 CUP	DICED ONION	250 ML
1 CUP	DICED CELERY	250 ML
1 CUP	DICED SWEET POTATO	250 ML
1/2	PACKAGE (1 LB/454 G) FROZEN PUFF PASTRY, THAWED	1/2
1/4 CUP	ALL-PURPOSE FLOUR	60 ML
2 1/2 TSP	CURRY POWDER	12 ML
1 TSP	GARLIC POWDER	5 ML
1 1/2 CUPS	READY-TO-USE CHICKEN BROTH	375 ML
2 CUPS	CHOPPED COOKED TURKEY	500 ML
1 CUP	FROZEN GREEN PEAS, THAWED	250 ML
1/2 CUP	CHOPPED FRESH CILANTRO	125 ML
1 CUP	HALF-AND-HALF (10%) CREAM	250 ML
1/2 TSP	SALT	2 ML
1/2 TSP	BLACK PEPPER	2 ML
1	LARGE EGG, LIGHTLY BEATEN	1

PREHEAT OVEN TO 425°F (220°C) AND LIGHTLY OIL SIX 1-CUP (250 ML) RAMEKINS. IN A LARGE POT, HEAT 3 TBSP (45 ML) OIL OVER MEDIUM-HIGH HEAT. ADD ONION, CELERY AND SWEET POTATO; COVER AND COOK, STIRRING OCCASIONALLY, FOR 10 MINUTES OR UNTIL TENDER.

MEANWHILE, ON A LIGHTLY FLOURED WORK SURFACE, ROLL OUT PASTRY INTO A 12- BY 8-INCH (30 BY 20 CM)

RECTANGLE. CUT INTO SIX 4-INCH (IO CM) SQUARES;
COVER AND REFRIGERATE UNTIL READY TO USE.

SPRINKLE FLOUR, CURRY POWDER AND GARLIC POWDER
OVER VEGETABLES, STIR AND COOK FOR I MINUTE.
GRADUALLY STIR IN BROTH AND BRING TO A BOIL. STIR IN
TURKEY, PEAS, CILANTRO AND CREAM. SEASON WITH SALT
AND PEPPER. DIVIDE MIXTURE AMONG PREPARED RAMEKINS.
PLACE RAMEKINS ON A RIMMED BAKING SHEET, TOP EACH
WITH PUFF PASTRY AND GENTLY CUT 4 VENTS IN EACH
CRUST. BRUSH CRUSTS WITH BEATEN EGG. BAKE FOR 20
TO 25 MINUTES OR UNTIL CRUSTS ARE GOLDEN BROWN.
LET COOL FOR 5 MINUTES BEFORE SERVING. SERVES 6.

TIP: YOU CAN THAW PUFF PASTRY OVERNIGHT IN THE
FRIDGE OR ON THE COUNTER FOR 45 TO 60 MINUTES.

MEDITERRANEAN TURKEY SPINACH MEATBALLS WITH GARLIC YOGURT SAUCE

THESE TURKEY MEATBALLS ARE TENDER AND FLAVORFUL, AND THEY'RE BAKED, SO THERE'S NO MESSY FRYING INVOLVED. SERVE WITH A SALAD AND A SIDE DISH OF RICE OR ROASTED POTATOES.

GARLIC YOGURT SAUCE

I	GARLIC CLOVE, MINCED	I
2 TSP	DRIED DILL	10 ML
I TSP	GRATED LEMON ZEST	5 ML
3/4 CUP	PLAIN GREEK YOGURT	175 ML
I TBSP	CANOLA OIL	15 ML

TURKEY SPINACH MEATBALLS

I LB	GROUND TURKEY	500 G
I	GARLIC CLOVE, MINCED	I
1/2	PACKAGE (10 OZ/300 G) FROZEN CHOPPED SPINACH, THAWED AND THOROUGHLY SQUEEZED DRY	1/2
I CUP	DRY BREAD CRUMBS	250 ML
1/2 CUP	CRUMBLED FETA CHEESE	125 ML
I TSP	ONION POWDER	5 ML
I TSP	DRIED OREGANO	5 ML
I TSP	DRIED DILL	5 ML
I TSP	BLACK PEPPER	5 ML
1/2 TSP	SALT	2 ML
I	LARGE EGG, LIGHTLY BEATEN	I

SAUCE: IN A SMALL BOWL, STIR TOGETHER ALL INGREDIENTS. COVER AND REFRIGERATE UNTIL READY TO SERVE.

MEATBALLS: LIGHTLY OIL A 13- BY 9-INCH (33 BY 23 CM) BAKING PAN. IN A LARGE BOWL, GENTLY MIX ALL INGREDIENTS UNTIL WELL COMBINED. FORM INTO 1½-INCH (4 CM) MEATBALLS AND PLACE CLOSE TOGETHER IN PREPARED PAN. REFRIGERATE FOR 15 MINUTES.

MEANWHILE, PREHEAT OVEN TO 375°F (190°C). BAKE MEATBALLS FOR 18 TO 20 MINUTES OR UNTIL NO LONGER PINK INSIDE. SERVE WITH YOGURT SAUCE. SERVES 4.

TIP: FOR THE BEST FLAVOR AND TEXTURE, CHOOSE GROUND TURKEY THAT HAS A BLEND OF WHITE AND DARK MEAT.

TIP: USING A SMALL ICE CREAM SCOOP HELPS TO FORM UNIFORM-SIZED MEATBALLS.

FOOD MAKES THE KIDS COME HOME.
COOKING MAKES THEM STAY.

CREAMY TURKEY CARROT LINGUINE

WHEN THE WHOLE FAMILY ENJOYS DINNER, IT MAKES MOM AND DAD SMILE. THIS "LINGUINE" IS MADE OF CARROTS, BUT YOU CAN COOK UP PASTA INSTEAD.

I LB	GROUND TURKEY	500 G
I TBSP	BUTTER	15 ML
2	GARLIC CLOVES, MINCED	2
I	SMALL ONION, CHOPPED	I
1/2 TSP	DRIED THYME	2 ML
1/2 TSP	DRIED SAGE	2 ML
1/2 TSP	SALT	2 ML
1/2 TSP	BLACK PEPPER	2 ML
1 1/2 CUPS	READY-TO-USE VEGETABLE OR CHICKEN BROTH	375 ML
4 OZ	CUBED BRICK-STYLE CREAM CHEESE	125 G
2 TBSP	CHOPPED FRESH PARSLEY	30 ML
1/2 TSP	GRATED LEMON ZEST	2 ML
I TBSP	LEMON JUICE	15 ML
4	LARGE CARROTS, SPIRALIZED	4

IN A LARGE NONSTICK SKILLET, COOK TURKEY OVER MEDIUM-HIGH HEAT, BREAKING IT UP WITH A SPOON, FOR ABOUT 8 MINUTES OR UNTIL NO LONGER PINK. DRAIN AND SET ASIDE. RETURN SKILLET TO MEDIUM HEAT AND MELT BUTTER. SAUTÉ GARLIC AND ONION FOR 2 MINUTES. RETURN TURKEY TO SKILLET, ALONG WITH THYME, SAGE, SALT AND PEPPER. STIR IN BROTH AND CREAM CHEESE UNTIL MELTED AND HOT. STIR IN PARSLEY, LEMON ZEST AND LEMON JUICE. ADD CARROT NOODLES AND COOK UNTIL HEATED THROUGH. SERVES 4.

FISH AND SEAFOOD

COCONUT FISH WITH MANGO SALSA

A TASTE OF FRESH MANGO BRINGS THE TROPICS HOME FOR DINNER.

MANGO SALSA

1 CUP	DICED MANGO	250 ML
2 TSP	MINCED SEEDED JALAPEÑO OR OTHER HOT CHILE PEPPER	10 ML
1/2 TSP	GRATED LIME ZEST	2 ML
1 TBSP	LIME JUICE	15 ML
	SALT TO TASTE	

COCONUT FISH

4	SMALL SKINLESS TILAPIA FILLETS (ABOUT 1 1/4 LBS/625 G TOTAL)	4
1/4 TSP	SALT	1 ML
1/4 TSP	BLACK PEPPER	1 ML
1/3 CUP	MANGO CHUTNEY	75 ML
2/3 CUP	FLAKED COCONUT	150 ML

SALSA: IN A BOWL, STIR TOGETHER ALL INGREDIENTS; SET ASIDE.

FISH: PREHEAT OVEN TO 425°F (220°C). SPRINKLE TILAPIA WITH SALT AND PEPPER. COAT BOTH SIDES WITH MANGO CHUTNEY AND PLACE ON A PARCHMENT-LINED RIMMED BAKING SHEET. SPRINKLE COCONUT EVENLY OVER TOP, PRESSING LIGHTLY TO ADHERE. BAKE FOR ABOUT 10 MINUTES OR UNTIL FISH FLAKES EASILY WHEN TESTED WITH A FORK. SERVE TOPPED WITH SALSA. SERVES 4.

TIP: FOR A SPICIER SALSA, LEAVE THE SEEDS IN THE JALAPEÑO.

Savory Baked French Toast (page 229)

Potato Pancakes with Fried Eggs (page 230)

Baked Mushroom and Herb Barley Risotto (page 234)

Quinoa-Stuffed Peppers (page 235)

CRISPY FISH FINGERS WITH MINI POTATOES

BOTH KIDS AND ADULTS WILL LOVE THE EASE OF THIS SHEET PAN DINNER — ROASTED AND READY TO SERVE.

1½ LBS	MINI POTATOES, HALVED	750 G
¼ CUP	CANOLA OIL, DIVIDED	60 ML
½ TSP	DRIED THYME	2 ML
¾ TSP	SALT, DIVIDED	3 ML
¾ TSP	BLACK PEPPER, DIVIDED	3 ML
1 LB	SKINLESS HADDOCK FILLETS	500 G
½ CUP	ITALIAN-SEASONED PANKO	125 ML
1 TBSP	GRATED PARMESAN CHEESE	15 ML

PREHEAT OVEN TO 425°F (220°C). TOSS POTATOES WITH HALF THE OIL, THYME AND ½ TSP (2 ML) EACH OF THE SALT AND PEPPER. SPREAD ON A PARCHMENT-LINED BAKING SHEET. ROAST FOR 15 MINUTES.

MEANWHILE, CUT HADDOCK FILLETS IN HALF LENGTHWISE INTO STRIPS ABOUT 1 INCH (2.5 CM) THICK AND 4 INCHES (10 CM) LONG. DRIZZLE WITH REMAINING OIL AND SPRINKLE WITH REMAINING SALT AND PEPPER. IN A SHALLOW DISH, COMBINE PANKO AND CHEESE. DREDGE FILLETS ON BOTH SIDES IN PANKO MIXTURE UNTIL WELL COATED. DISCARD ANY EXCESS PANKO MIXTURE. PUSH POTATOES TO ONE SIDE OF BAKING SHEET AND PLACE FISH ON THE OTHER SIDE, SPACING PIECES APART. BAKE FOR ABOUT 10 MINUTES OR UNTIL POTATOES ARE GOLDEN AND FISH FLAKES EASILY WHEN TESTED WITH A FORK. SERVES 4.

CHIP-CRUSTED FISH WITH AVOCADO AND TOMATO SALSA

YOU NOW HAVE A WAY TO USE UP THOSE BROKEN CHIP PIECES AND CRUMBS FOR DINNER!

AVOCADO AND TOMATO SALSA

2	PLUM (ROMA) TOMATOES, DICED	2
1	AVOCADO, DICED	1
1	SMALL JALAPEÑO PEPPER, SEEDED AND MINCED	1
1 TBSP	CHOPPED FRESH CILANTRO	15 ML
1/2 TSP	SALT	2 ML
1 TBSP	CANOLA OIL	15 ML
1 TBSP	SHERRY VINEGAR	15 ML

CHIP-CRUSTED FISH

2 CUPS	TORTILLA CHIPS (YOUR FAVORITE FLAVOR)	500 ML
1 TBSP	CHOPPED FRESH CILANTRO	15 ML
4	SKINLESS TILAPIA FILLETS (ABOUT 1 1/2 LBS/750 G TOTAL)	4
1/4 TSP	SALT	1 ML
1/4 TSP	BLACK PEPPER	1 ML
1	SMALL GARLIC CLOVE, MINCED	1
2 TBSP	BUTTER, MELTED	30 ML

SALSA: IN A BOWL, STIR TOGETHER ALL INGREDIENTS; SET ASIDE.

FISH: PREHEAT OVEN TO 425°F (220°C). PLACE TORTILLA CHIPS IN A SMALL SEALABLE PLASTIC BAG, SEAL AND CRUSH INTO FINE CRUMBS WITH YOUR HANDS OR A

ROLLING PIN. TRANSFER CRUMBS TO A SHALLOW DISH AND STIR IN CILANTRO. SPRINKLE TILAPIA WITH SALT AND PEPPER. COMBINE GARLIC AND BUTTER; BRUSH EVENLY OVER BOTH SIDES OF FISH. DREDGE FILLETS ON BOTH SIDES WITH CHIP MIXTURE AND PLACE ON A PARCHMENT-LINED BAKING SHEET. DISCARD ANY EXCESS GARLIC BUTTER AND CHIP MIXTURE. BAKE FOR ABOUT 12 MINUTES OR UNTIL FISH FLAKES EASILY WHEN TESTED WITH A FORK. SERVE WITH SALSA. SERVES 4.

VARIATION: SUBSTITUTE POTATO CHIPS FOR THE TORTILLA CHIPS.

BEING IN LOVE IS LIKE GETTING THE MAIN COURSE AND SIDE DISHES OUT AT THE SAME TIME.

COD WITH FETA AND TOMATOES OVER RICE

THIS MEDITERRANEAN-INSPIRED FISH DINNER INCLUDES FRESH FLAVORS OF LEMON AND FETA THAT MAKE YOU WANT TO SOP UP THE TOMATO-BASED SAUCE WITH SOME CRUSTY BREAD TO SAVOR EVERY BITE.

1 TBSP	CANOLA OIL	15 ML
3	GARLIC CLOVES, MINCED	3
1	ONION, DICED	1
2 TSP	DRIED OREGANO	10 ML
1	CAN (14 OZ/398 ML) CHERRY TOMATOES, WITH JUICE	1
2 TBSP	CHOPPED FRESH PARSLEY	30 ML
1/2 TSP	GRATED LEMON ZEST	2 ML
1 LB	SKINLESS COD FILLETS	500 G
1/4 TSP	SALT	1 ML
1/4 TSP	BLACK PEPPER	1 ML
2 TBSP	CRUMBLED FETA CHEESE	30 ML
1 CUP	WHITE BASMATI RICE	250 ML
2 CUPS	READY-TO-USE VEGETABLE OR CHICKEN BROTH	500 ML
1 TBSP	LEMON JUICE	15 ML

IN A LARGE NONSTICK SKILLET, HEAT OIL OVER MEDIUM HEAT. SAUTÉ GARLIC, ONION AND OREGANO FOR 4 MINUTES OR UNTIL ONION IS SOFTENED. STIR IN TOMATOES WITH JUICE, PARSLEY AND LEMON ZEST; SIMMER FOR 5 MINUTES. SPRINKLE COD WITH SALT AND PEPPER. NESTLE COD INTO TOMATO MIXTURE; REDUCE HEAT, COVER AND SIMMER GENTLY FOR ABOUT 5 MINUTES

OR UNTIL FISH FLAKES EASILY WHEN TESTED WITH A FORK. SPRINKLE WITH FETA.

MEANWHILE, IN A SMALL POT, COMBINE RICE AND BROTH; BRING TO A BOIL. REDUCE HEAT, COVER AND SIMMER FOR 15 MINUTES OR UNTIL BROTH IS ABSORBED AND RICE IS TENDER. STIR IN LEMON JUICE. SPOON RICE ONTO PLATES AND SPOON COD AND SAUCE OVER TOP. SERVES 4.

TIP: WHEN USING FROZEN FISH, BE SURE TO LET IT THAW IN THE FRIDGE OVERNIGHT FOR BEST RESULTS. IN A PINCH, IF THE PACKAGING IS WATER-TIGHT, YOU CAN THAW IT IN COLD WATER IN A BOWL.

TIP: USING A FRAGRANT RICE LIKE BASMATI ADDS A WONDERFUL HINT OF FLAVOR TO THIS DINNER DISH. IF YOU PREFER, YOU CAN SUBSTITUTE JASMINE RICE.

ROASTED RED PEPPER LEMON COD

THIS QUICK MEAL COMES TOGETHER SO EASILY.
SYLVIA LIKES TO SERVE IT OVER JASMINE RICE;
EMILY, OVER PASTA.

1 TBSP	CANOLA OIL	15 ML
3	GARLIC CLOVES, MINCED	3
PINCH	HOT PEPPER FLAKES	PINCH
3/4 CUP	DICED DRAINED ROASTED RED BELL PEPPERS	175 ML
1/4 CUP	CHOPPED FRESH PARSLEY	60 ML
1 TSP	DRAINED SMALL CAPERS	5 ML
3 TBSP	LEMON JUICE	45 ML
1 LB	SKINLESS COD FILLETS	500 G
1/4 TSP	SALT	1 ML
1/4 TSP	BLACK PEPPER	1 ML

IN A LARGE NONSTICK SKILLET, HEAT OIL OVER MEDIUM-LOW HEAT. SAUTÉ GARLIC AND HOT PEPPER FLAKES FOR 30 SECONDS. STIR IN ROASTED PEPPERS, PARSLEY, CAPERS AND LEMON JUICE. SPRINKLE COD WITH SALT AND PEPPER. NESTLE COD INTO SAUCE AND SIMMER GENTLY, TURNING ONCE, FOR ABOUT 6 MINUTES OR UNTIL FISH FLAKES EASILY WHEN TESTED WITH A FORK. SERVES 4.

SHEET PAN SALMON SUPPER

THIS EASY, LOW-FUSS MEAL IS BIG ON FLAVOR. SERVE
WITH A SIDE OF RICE OR POTATOES, AND DINNER IS DONE.

1 1/2 LB	SKINLESS SALMON FILLET	750 G
1/4 CUP	BARBECUE SAUCE	60 ML
2 TBSP	GRAINY MUSTARD	30 ML
1/2 TSP	GARLIC POWDER	2 ML
1	YELLOW OR ORANGE BELL PEPPER, SLICED	1
1	ZUCCHINI, THINLY SLICED	1
1/2	SMALL ONION, THINLY SLICED	1/2
1 CUP	CHERRY OR GRAPE TOMATOES, HALVED	250 ML
1/2 TSP	SALT	2 ML
1/2 TSP	BLACK PEPPER	2 ML
1/2 TSP	SMOKED PAPRIKA	2 ML
1 TBSP	CANOLA OIL	15 ML

PREHEAT OVEN TO 425°F (220°C). PLACE SALMON ON A
FOIL-LINED LARGE RIMMED BAKING SHEET. IN A SMALL
BOWL, COMBINE BARBECUE SAUCE, MUSTARD AND GARLIC
POWDER; SPREAD OVER SALMON. IN A MEDIUM BOWL,
COMBINE YELLOW PEPPER, ZUCCHINI, ONION, TOMATOES,
SALT, PEPPER, PAPRIKA AND OIL. SPREAD VEGETABLE
MIXTURE IN A SINGLE LAYER AROUND SALMON. BAKE FOR
15 TO 17 MINUTES OR UNTIL FISH FLAKES EASILY WHEN
TESTED WITH A FORK. SERVES 4.

TIP: YOU CAN SWAP OUT SOME OF THE VEGGIES IN THIS
RECIPE WITH ASPARAGUS, MUSHROOMS OR BROCCOLI.
JUST MAKE SURE THE PIECES ARE ALL ABOUT THE SAME
SIZE, FOR EVEN COOKING.

GRILLED SALMON, VEGETABLE AND COUSCOUS PACKETS

TINY MOROCCAN COUSCOUS COOKS VERY QUICKLY
AND ABSORBS THE FLAVOR OF THE SPICES.
THE PACKETS HAVE AN OUTER FOIL LAYER TO
PROMOTE EVEN HEATING, WHILE THE INNER LAYER
OF PARCHMENT PREVENTS STICKING.

SPICE MIXTURE

2 TSP	GRATED LEMON ZEST	10 ML
I TSP	PAPRIKA	5 ML
I TSP	SUGAR	5 ML
1/2 TSP	GROUND CUMIN	2 ML
1/2 TSP	EACH SALT AND BLACK PEPPER	2 ML
1/2 TSP	GARLIC POWDER	2 ML
1/2 TSP	GROUND CINNAMON	2 ML
2 TBSP	CANOLA OIL	30 ML

PACKETS

3/4 CUP	MOROCCAN COUSCOUS	175 ML
1/2 TSP	GARLIC POWDER	2 ML
1/2 TSP	SALT	2 ML
1/2 CUP	BOILING WATER	125 ML
I TBSP	CANOLA OIL	15 ML
I	RED BELL PEPPER, THINLY SLICED	I
I	SMALL ZUCCHINI, THINLY SLICED	I
I	TOMATO, CUT INTO 1/2-INCH (I CM) THICK SLICES	I
4	SALMON STEAKS (EACH ABOUT 6 OZ/175 G)	4
1/4 CUP	SLICED ALMONDS, TOASTED	60 ML
1/4 CUP	FINELY CHOPPED FRESH CILANTRO	60 ML
	LEMON WEDGES	

SPICE MIXTURE: IN A SMALL BOWL, COMBINE ALL INGREDIENTS. SET ASIDE.

PACKETS: PREHEAT BARBECUE GRILL TO MEDIUM-HIGH. LAY OUT FOUR 12-INCH (30 CM) LENGTHS OF HEAVY-DUTY FOIL AND PLACE A 10-INCH (25 CM) LENGTH OF PARCHMENT PAPER ON EACH. IN A MEDIUM BOWL, COMBINE COUSCOUS, GARLIC POWDER, SALT, BOILING WATER AND OIL. DIVIDE MIXTURE ONTO PARCHMENT PIECES. EVENLY TOP WITH RED PEPPER, ZUCCHINI AND TOMATO. PLACE A PIECE OF SALMON ON TOP OF EACH. SPREAD SPICE MIXTURE OVER SALMON. FOLD FOIL TO CREATE A WELL-SEALED PACKET, LEAVING A LITTLE HEADSPACE SO THE STEAM CAN CIRCULATE, FOR EVEN COOKING.

REDUCE BARBECUE HEAT TO MEDIUM, PLACE PACKETS ON GRILL, CLOSE LID AND GRILL FOR 15 MINUTES. CAREFULLY OPEN ONE PACKET TO CHECK FOR DONENESS; THE FISH SHOULD FLAKE EASILY WHEN TESTED WITH A FORK. GRILL FOR A FEW MORE MINUTES, IF NECESSARY. REMOVE PACKETS FROM GRILL AND LET REST FOR 5 MINUTES. OPEN PACKETS CAREFULLY, TO AVOID ESCAPING STEAM. SPRINKLE WITH ALMONDS AND CILANTRO. SERVE WITH LEMON WEDGES. SERVES 4.

TIP: ASSEMBLE AND REFRIGERATE THE PACKETS THE NIGHT BEFORE. ADD 5 MINUTES TO THE COOKING TIME.

OVEN VARIATION: PREHEAT OVEN TO 425°F (220°C). PLACE PACKETS ON A RIMMED BAKING SHEET AND BAKE FOR 20 MINUTES, THEN TEST FOR DONENESS AND FINISH THE DISH AS DESCRIBED ABOVE.

OVEN-ROASTED MISO SALMON WITH BOK CHOY

SYLVIA'S BROTHER IS A BIG SEAFOOD LOVER AND THIS IS ONE OF HIS FAVORITE WAYS TO COOK FISH. HE PREFERS TO USE FISH FILLETS THAT ARE 1½ INCHES (4 CM) THICK, FOR TENDER, JUICY RESULTS. SERVE WITH COOKED RICE.

¼ CUP	SUGAR	60 ML
2 TSP	GRATED FRESH GINGER	10 ML
¼ CUP	WHITE MISO PASTE	60 ML
¼ CUP	DRY SHERRY	60 ML
2 TBSP	SEASONED RICE VINEGAR	30 ML
2 TSP	SOY SAUCE	10 ML
2 TBSP	CANOLA OIL, DIVIDED	30 ML
4	SKIN-ON SALMON FILLETS (EACH ABOUT 5 OZ/150 G)	4
1 LB	BABY BOK CHOY, QUARTERED LENGTHWISE	500 G
½ TSP	SALT	2 ML
1 TBSP	TOASTED SESAME SEEDS (SEE TIP)	15 ML

IN A SEALABLE PLASTIC BAG, COMBINE SUGAR, GINGER, MISO, SHERRY, VINEGAR, SOY SAUCE AND 1 TBSP (15 ML) OIL; SEAL BAG AND SHAKE TO MIX. ADD SALMON, SEAL AND REFRIGERATE FOR AT LEAST 1 HOUR OR OVERNIGHT.

PREHEAT BROILER, WITH RACK SET IN THE HIGHEST POSITION. REMOVE SALMON FROM MARINADE, DISCARDING MARINADE, AND PLACE, SKIN SIDE DOWN, ON ONE SIDE OF A FOIL-LINED RIMMED BAKING SHEET. PLACE BOK CHOY ON THE OTHER SIDE, DRIZZLE WITH REMAINING OIL AND

SPRINKLE WITH SALT. BROIL FOR 5 MINUTES. TURN FISH SKIN SIDE UP AND TURN BOK CHOY OVER. BROIL FOR 5 MINUTES OR UNTIL SALMON SKIN IS CRISP AND LIGHTLY CHARRED AND FISH FLAKES EASILY WHEN TESTED WITH A FORK. SPRINKLE BOK CHOY WITH SESAME SEEDS. SERVES 4.

TIP: CHOOSE FISH THAT IS UNIFORM IN THICKNESS, FOR EVEN COOKING.

TIP: TOAST SESAME SEEDS IN A SMALL SKILLET OVER MEDIUM HEAT FOR ABOUT 2 MINUTES OR UNTIL GOLDEN BROWN.

TUNA RICE BOWLS WITH CUCUMBER CARROT SALAD

SIMPLE ASIAN COMFORT FOOD ON A WEEKNIGHT.

CUCUMBER CARROT SALAD

2	CARROTS, CUT INTO THIN STRIPS	2
1	LONG ENGLISH CUCUMBER, THINLY SLICED	1
2 TSP	SUGAR	10 ML
1 TSP	TOASTED SESAME SEEDS (SEE TIP, PAGE 209)	5 ML
1/4 TSP	HOT PEPPER FLAKES	1 ML
2 TBSP	SEASONED RICE VINEGAR	30 ML
1 TBSP	CANOLA OIL	15 ML
2 TSP	SOY SAUCE	10 ML
1 TSP	SESAME OIL	5 ML

TUNA RICE BOWLS

2	CANS (EACH 6 OZ/170 G) SOLID TUNA, DRAINED	2
3	GREEN ONIONS, THINLY SLICED	3
4 CUPS	HOT COOKED SHORT-GRAIN RICE	1 L
3 TBSP	TOASTED SESAME SEEDS	45 ML
3 TBSP	MAYONNAISE	45 ML
2	SHEETS TOASTED NORI (ABOUT 8 BY 7 INCHES/20 BY 18 CM), CUT INTO THIN STRIPS	2
1	AVOCADO, SLICED	1
	PICKLED GINGER	

SALAD: IN A MEDIUM BOWL, COMBINE ALL INGREDIENTS. COVER AND REFRIGERATE UNTIL READY TO SERVE.

TUNA RICE BOWLS: IN ANOTHER MEDIUM BOWL, BREAK TUNA INTO CHUNKS. ADD GREEN ONIONS, RICE, SESAME SEEDS AND MAYONNAISE, GENTLY MIXING TO COMBINE. DIVIDE MIXTURE INTO BOWLS AND TOP WITH NORI, AVOCADO AND GINGER. SERVE WITH CUCUMBER CARROT SALAD. SERVES 4.

TIP: NORI IS JAPANESE SEAWEED AND CAN BE FOUND IN THE ASIAN FOODS SECTION OF MOST GROCERY STORES. MINI PACKETS OF SNACK NORI CAN BE USED INSTEAD OF THE LARGE SHEETS.

CRAB CAKES WITH GREENS AND LEMON GARLIC MAYONNAISE

THESE REFRESHING CRAB CAKES ARE FULL OF FLAVOR AND PERFECT SERVED ATOP A BED OF MIXED GREENS.

LEMON GARLIC MAYONNAISE

1	GARLIC CLOVE, GRATED	1
1/3 CUP	MAYONNAISE	75 ML
1 TSP	GRATED LEMON ZEST	5 ML
1 TBSP	LEMON JUICE	15 ML
PINCH	SALT	PINCH

CRAB CAKES

2	CANS (EACH 4 OZ/120 G) CRABMEAT, DRAINED	2
1/4 CUP	FINELY DICED RED BELL PEPPER	60 ML
2 TBSP	CHOPPED FRESH PARSLEY	30 ML
1 TBSP	MINCED ONION	15 ML
1/4 TSP	OLD BAY SEASONING (OPTIONAL)	1 ML
3 TBSP	TARTAR SAUCE	45 ML
1 TBSP	LEMON JUICE	15 ML
3/4 CUP	PANKO	175 ML
1 TBSP	CANOLA OIL	15 ML
6 CUPS	MIXED GREENS	1.5 L
2 TBSP	BALSAMIC SALAD DRESSING	30 ML

MAYONNAISE: IN A BOWL, WHISK TOGETHER ALL INGREDIENTS; SET ASIDE.

CRAB CAKES: IN A LARGE BOWL, STIR TOGETHER CRAB, RED PEPPER, PARSLEY, ONION, OLD BAY SEASONING (IF USING), TARTAR SAUCE AND LEMON JUICE. ADD PANKO AND STIR

UNTIL MIXTURE COMES TOGETHER. SHAPE INTO FOUR 1-INCH (2.5 CM) THICK PATTIES. IN A LARGE NONSTICK SKILLET, HEAT OIL OVER MEDIUM-HIGH HEAT. COOK CRAB CAKES, TURNING ONCE, FOR ABOUT 8 MINUTES OR UNTIL BROWNED ON BOTH SIDES. TRANSFER TO A PLATE.

TOSS GREENS WITH DRESSING AND DIVIDE AMONG PLATES. TOP EACH WITH A CRAB CAKE. DOLLOP CRAB CAKES WITH LEMON GARLIC MAYONNAISE. SERVES 4.

TIP: THESE MAKE GREAT APPETIZERS FOR A PARTY! MAKE 12 SMALLER PATTIES AND COOK THEM IN BATCHES FOR ABOUT 5 MINUTES. SERVE THEM ON THEIR OWN, WITH THE MAYONNAISE DOLLOPED ON TOP.

CRAB IS TOO MUCH WORK, SO I EAT IT OUT OF A CAN.

MUSSELS IN A
COCONUT CURRY BROTH

MARY HALPEN IS ONE OF THE ORIGINAL BEST OF BRIDGE FAMILY MEMBERS, AND THIS RECIPE IS ONE OF HER FAVORITES THAT SHE'S BEEN MAKING FOR YEARS. RECENTLY, WITH A LITTLE RESEARCH, IT WAS DISCOVERED THAT THE RECIPE WAS ADAPTED FROM ONE OF JULIE VAN ROSENDAAL'S (ALSO WITH TEAM BEST OF BRIDGE). TALK ABOUT FULL CIRCLE!

1 TBSP	CANOLA OIL	15 ML
2	GARLIC CLOVES, CRUSHED	2
1	ONION, SLICED	1
1	RED BELL PEPPER, CHOPPED	1
2 CUPS	CAULIFLOWER FLORETS	500 ML
1 TBSP	GRATED FRESH GINGER	15 ML
2 TSP	HOT CURRY PASTE	10 ML
1	CAN (14 OZ/400 ML) COCONUT MILK	1
2 LBS	MUSSELS, SCRUBBED AND DEBEARDED (SEE TIP)	1 KG
2 CUPS	COARSELY CHOPPED SPINACH LEAVES	500 ML
	SALT AND BLACK PEPPER TO TASTE	
	HOT COOKED RICE	
1 CUP	CHOPPED FRESH CILANTRO (OPTIONAL)	250 ML
1/2 CUP	CHOPPED ROASTED PEANUTS (OPTIONAL)	125 ML

IN A LARGE HEAVY SKILLET, HEAT OIL OVER MEDIUM-HIGH HEAT. SAUTÉ GARLIC AND ONION FOR 5 MINUTES. ADD RED PEPPER, CAULIFLOWER, GINGER AND CURRY PASTE; SAUTÉ FOR 4 MINUTES. STIR IN COCONUT MILK AND BRING TO A SIMMER. ADD MUSSELS, COVER AND BOIL GENTLY FOR

5 MINUTES OR UNTIL MUSSELS HAVE OPENED. DISCARD ANY MUSSELS THAT DON'T OPEN. PLACE SPINACH ON TOP (DO NOT STIR IT IN) AND COOK FOR 1 MINUTE OR UNTIL WILTED. SERVE OVER RICE, GARNISHED WITH CILANTRO AND PEANUTS, IF DESIRED. SERVES 4.

TIP: MUSSELS SHOULD BE TIGHTLY CLOSED; DISCARD ANY WITH CRACKED SHELLS. IF THE SHELL IS OPEN, TAP THE MUSSEL FIRMLY AGAINST THE COUNTER OR ANOTHER MUSSEL; IF THE SHELL DOESN'T CLOSE IN A FEW MINUTES, DISCARD IT. DEBEARDING THE MUSSEL SIMPLY MEANS REMOVING THE SHORT FIBROUS TUFTS COMING OUT OF THE MUSSEL.

THOSE WHO WORK, EAT.
THOSE WHO DON'T WORK, EAT, DRINK AND SLEEP!

SHRIMP, PROSCIUTTO AND PEAS ON PASTA

THE SALTY, CRISP PROSCIUTTO AND SUCCULENT SHRIMP CREATE THE PERFECT BALANCE IN THIS QUICK AND SIMPLE PASTA DISH.

I LB	DRIED THIN PASTA (SPAGHETTINI, SPAGHETTI, LINGUINE)	500 G
I TBSP	CANOLA OIL	15 ML
8 OZ	PROSCIUTTO, CHOPPED	250 G
4	GARLIC CLOVES, MINCED	4
1/2 TSP	SALT	2 ML
1/2 TSP	HOT PEPPER FLAKES	2 ML
1/2 TSP	BLACK PEPPER	2 ML
1/2 TSP	DRIED ROSEMARY, CRUMBLED	2 ML
I LB	LARGE SHRIMP, PEELED AND DEVEINED	500 G
1 1/2 CUPS	FROZEN GREEN PEAS, THAWED	375 ML
1/4 CUP	CHOPPED FRESH PARSLEY	60 ML
2 TBSP	LEMON JUICE	30 ML
	GRATED PARMESAN CHEESE	

IN A LARGE POT OF BOILING SALTED WATER, COOK PASTA ACCORDING TO PACKAGE DIRECTIONS UNTIL AL DENTE. DRAIN PASTA, RESERVING I CUP (250 ML) PASTA WATER.

MEANWHILE, IN A LARGE SKILLET, HEAT OIL OVER MEDIUM-HIGH HEAT. COOK PROSCIUTTO, STIRRING, FOR ABOUT 2 MINUTES OR UNTIL CRISP. USING A SLOTTED SPOON, TRANSFER PROSCIUTTO TO A PLATE. ADD GARLIC, SALT, HOT PEPPER FLAKES, BLACK PEPPER AND ROSEMARY TO SKILLET, STIRRING UNTIL COMBINED; COOK FOR 30 SECONDS. ADD SHRIMP AND COOK, STIRRING, FOR

2 MINUTES OR UNTIL PINK, FIRM AND OPAQUE. STIR IN PROSCIUTTO, PEAS, PARSLEY AND LEMON JUICE. ADD PASTA AND TOSS TO COMBINE. ADD JUST ENOUGH RESERVED PASTA WATER TO CREATE A BIT OF SAUCE. SERVE SPRINKLED WITH PARMESAN. SERVES 6.

TIP: THIN PASTA, LIKE SPAGHETTINI, COOKS UP A LITTLE FASTER THAN A THICKER PASTA SUCH AS SPAGHETTI OR LINGUINE.

TIP: SHRIMP ARE SOLD BY COUNT PER POUND. THE HIGHER THE NUMBER, THE SMALLER THE SHRIMP. LARGE SHRIMP IS LABELED 31/35, MEANING THERE ARE 31 TO 35 SHRIMP IN EACH POUND.

IF NOTHING IS GOING WELL, CALL YOUR GRANDMOTHER.
— ITALIAN PROVERB

THAI SHRIMP STIR-FRY

HOT, SWEET AND SOUR FLAVORS ARE CAPTURED IN
THIS QUICK STIR-FRY. SERVE WITH HOT COOKED RICE.

1 LB	LARGE SHRIMP, PEELED AND DEVEINED	500 G
1/4 TSP	SALT	1 ML
1/4 TSP	BLACK PEPPER	1 ML
2 TBSP	PACKED BROWN SUGAR	30 ML
1 TBSP	CORNSTARCH	15 ML
1 CUP	COCONUT MILK	250 ML
1/4 CUP	WATER	60 ML
2 TBSP	LIME JUICE	30 ML
1 TBSP	FISH SAUCE	15 ML
1 TBSP	SOY SAUCE	15 ML
2 TSP	THAI RED CURRY PASTE	10 ML
2 TBSP	CANOLA OIL	30 ML
2 CUPS	SNOW PEAS, TRIMMED	500 ML
4	GARLIC CLOVES, MINCED	4
2 TSP	GRATED FRESH GINGER	10 ML
1	GREEN ONION, SLICED	1
3 TBSP	COARSELY CHOPPED FRESH BASIL	45 ML
1/4 CUP	CHOPPED FRESH CILANTRO	60 ML

PAT SHRIMP DRY AND SEASON WITH SALT AND PEPPER;
SET ASIDE. IN A SMALL BOWL, COMBINE BROWN SUGAR,
CORNSTARCH, COCONUT MILK, WATER, LIME JUICE, FISH
SAUCE, SOY SAUCE AND CURRY PASTE; SET ASIDE. IN
A LARGE SKILLET, HEAT OIL OVER MEDIUM-HIGH HEAT.
STIR-FRY SNOW PEAS FOR 1 MINUTE. ADD SHRIMP, GARLIC
AND GINGER; STIR-FRY FOR 1 MINUTE OR UNTIL SHRIMP
ARE JUST PINK. TRANSFER SHRIMP MIXTURE TO A PLATE.

IN THE SAME SKILLET, COOK COCONUT MILK MIXTURE OVER MEDIUM HEAT FOR 2 MINUTES OR UNTIL STARTING TO THICKEN. RETURN SHRIMP MIXTURE TO SKILLET, ALONG WITH GREEN ONION AND BASIL, STIRRING TO COMBINE; COOK, STIRRING, FOR ABOUT 1 MINUTE OR UNTIL JUST HEATED THROUGH AND SHRIMP ARE JUST OPAQUE (DO NOT OVERCOOK SHRIMP). SERVE GARNISHED WITH CILANTRO. SERVES 4 TO 5.

TIP: USE BOTH THE LEAVES AND THE STEMS OF CILANTRO FOR FLAVOR AND A CRUNCHY TEXTURE.

LIVE, LOVE, COOK!

MRS. STAGG'S SKILLET TOMATO AND SHRIMP

SYLVIA'S FRIEND SANDRA SHARED A FAMILY RECIPE THAT THEY FIRST RECEIVED FROM MRS. STAGG, A NEIGHBOR, OVER 50 YEARS AGO.

3 TBSP	OLIVE OIL, DIVIDED	45 ML
I LB	LARGE SHRIMP, PEELED AND DEVEINED	500 G
I	ONION, THINLY SLICED	I
I TSP	DRIED BASIL	5 ML
1/4 TSP	HOT PEPPER FLAKES	I ML
2	GARLIC CLOVES, FINELY CHOPPED	2
1/2 CUP	DRY WHITE WINE	125 ML
I CUP	CHOPPED PLUM (ROMA) TOMATOES OR HALVED CHERRY TOMATOES	250 ML
1/4 CUP	CHOPPED DRAINED OIL-PACKED SUN-DRIED TOMATOES (OPTIONAL)	60 ML
	SALT AND BLACK PEPPER TO TASTE	

IN A LARGE SKILLET, HEAT I TBSP (15 ML) OIL OVER MEDIUM-HIGH HEAT. COOK SHRIMP FOR 30 SECONDS PER SIDE OR UNTIL JUST PINK. TRANSFER SHRIMP TO A PLATE. ADD REMAINING OIL, ONION, BASIL AND HOT PEPPER FLAKES TO SKILLET; COOK, STIRRING OCCASIONALLY, FOR 7 MINUTES. ADD GARLIC AND COOK, STIRRING, FOR I MINUTE. ADD WINE AND DEGLAZE SKILLET. STIR IN PLUM TOMATOES AND SUN-DRIED TOMATOES (IF USING); BRING TO A BOIL. BOIL FOR 2 MINUTES. RETURN SHRIMP TO SKILLET AND COOK, STIRRING, FOR ABOUT I MINUTE OR UNTIL JUST HEATED THROUGH AND SHRIMP ARE JUST OPAQUE (DO NOT OVERCOOK SHRIMP). SEASON WITH SALT AND PEPPER. SERVES 4.

VEGETARIAN SUPPERS

JARED'S FAVORITE MUSHROOM AND GRUYÈRE PHYLLO PIE

SYLVIA'S SON JARED LOVES THIS PIE. THE CRISP, GOLDEN PASTRY IS A PERFECT CONTRAST WITH THE CREAMY FILLING.

6 TBSP	CANOLA OIL, DIVIDED	90 ML
1	ONION, FINELY CHOPPED	1
3	GARLIC CLOVES, MINCED	3
6 CUPS	SLICED ASSORTED MUSHROOMS (ABOUT 1 LB/500 G)	1.5 L
1½ TSP	DRIED THYME	7 ML
1 TSP	SALT	5 ML
1 TSP	BLACK PEPPER	5 ML
2 TSP	DIJON MUSTARD	10 ML
2 CUPS	SHREDDED GRUYÈRE CHEESE	500 ML
6	LARGE EGGS, BEATEN	6
8	SHEETS PHYLLO PASTRY, THAWED	8

PREHEAT OVEN TO 400°F (200°C). IN A LARGE OVENPROOF SKILLET, HEAT 2 TBSP (30 ML) OIL OVER MEDIUM-HIGH HEAT. SAUTÉ ONION FOR 5 MINUTES. ADD GARLIC, MUSHROOMS, THYME, SALT, PEPPER AND MUSTARD; COOK, STIRRING OCCASIONALLY, FOR 15 MINUTES OR UNTIL MOST OF THE MOISTURE HAS EVAPORATED. TRANSFER ONION MIXTURE TO A LARGE BOWL (SETTING SKILLET ASIDE FOR BAKING PIE) AND LET COOL FOR A FEW MINUTES, THEN STIR IN CHEESE AND EGGS.

STACK 2 SHEETS OF PHYLLO ON A WORK SURFACE AND BRUSH LIGHTLY WITH OIL, INCLUDING EDGES. LAYER ANOTHER 2 SHEETS OF PHYLLO ON TOP AND BRUSH WITH

OIL. CONTINUE WITH REMAINING PHYLLO AND OIL. PLACE LAYERED PHYLLO IN SKILLET AND GENTLY PRESS DOWN TO FIT PAN, LEAVING AN OVERHANG DRAPING OVER THE EDGE. POUR MUSHROOM MIXTURE INTO CRUST. GENTLY FOLD PASTRY OVERHANG OVER EDGES OF FILLING, LEAVING CENTER OF PIE EXPOSED. BAKE FOR 20 TO 25 MINUTES OR UNTIL FILLING IS SET. LET COOL FOR 5 MINUTES BEFORE SERVING. SERVES 6 TO 8.

TIP: FOR A TIME SAVER, THE MUSHROOMS, ONIONS AND GARLIC CAN BE COOKED THE NIGHT BEFORE AND STORED IN THE REFRIGERATOR UNTIL READY TO USE.

TIP: ANY UNUSED PHYLLO CAN BE REFROZEN. WRAP TIGHTLY IN PLASTIC WRAP, THEN IN FOIL. IT KEEPS FOR UP TO 9 MONTHS IN THE FREEZER.

WHEN YOU EAT WITH THE ONES YOU LOVE,
YOU HAVE EVERYTHING.

SAUTÉED VEGETABLE PIE

THIS QUICHE-LIKE PIE IS QUICK TO PUT TOGETHER FOR DINNER WHEN YOU HAVE PIE SHELLS IN THE FREEZER. JUST ADD A SIMPLE SALAD AND DINNER IS DONE!

2 TBSP	CANOLA OIL	30 ML
8 OZ	CREMINI MUSHROOMS, QUARTERED	250 G
3	GARLIC CLOVES, MINCED	3
1	LEEK (WHITE AND LIGHT GREEN PARTS ONLY), THINLY SLICED	1
1	RED BELL PEPPER, CHOPPED	1
1 TSP	DRIED ITALIAN SEASONING	5 ML
1/2 TSP	SALT	2 ML
1/2 TSP	BLACK PEPPER	2 ML
1/4 CUP	CHOPPED FRESH PARSLEY	60 ML
3	LARGE EGGS	3
1/2 CUP	CRUMBLED FETA CHEESE	125 ML
1/2 CUP	RICOTTA CHEESE	125 ML
2	9-INCH (23 CM) FROZEN PIE SHELLS, THAWED SLIGHTLY	2

PREHEAT OVEN TO 400°F (200°C), WITH RACK PLACED IN BOTTOM THIRD. IN A LARGE NONSTICK SKILLET, HEAT OIL OVER MEDIUM-HIGH HEAT. SAUTÉ MUSHROOMS, GARLIC, LEEK AND RED PEPPER FOR 5 MINUTES OR UNTIL STARTING TO TURN GOLDEN. STIR IN ITALIAN SEASONING, SALT AND PEPPER; SAUTÉ FOR ABOUT 3 MINUTES OR UNTIL VEGETABLES ARE SOFTENED AND GOLDEN. REMOVE FROM HEAT. IN A LARGE BOWL, WHISK TOGETHER PARSLEY, EGGS, FETA AND RICOTTA. STIR IN VEGETABLE MIXTURE. SCRAPE INTO ONE OF THE PIE SHELLS. WET A

FINGER WITH WATER AND RUN AROUND EDGE OF PIE SHELL. TOP WITH OTHER PIE SHELL AND REMOVE TOP PIE TIN. PRESS AROUND EDGES TO SEAL. MAKE 3 SMALL SLITS IN TOP CRUST. BAKE FOR ABOUT 35 MINUTES OR UNTIL PASTRY IS GOLDEN. LET COOL SLIGHTLY BEFORE CUTTING INTO WEDGES. SERVES 6.

TIP: CHANGE UP THIS VEGETABLE PIE BY USING DIFFERENT MUSHROOMS AND VEGGIES. OYSTER, SHIITAKE AND BUTTON MUSHROOMS ARE GREAT OPTIONS, AND ONION AND ZUCCHINI WOULD BE GREAT SUBSTITUTES FOR THE LEEK AND BELL PEPPER.

THE KITCHEN IS SEASONED WITH LOVE,
AND MAYBE SOME CRUMBS, TOO.

ZUCCHINI PARMESAN PATTIES

CHICKEN PARMESAN FANS LIKE EMILY AND SYLVIA ENJOY THIS VEGGIE SWAP-OUT TO SERVE ON MEATLESS MONDAYS.

4	LARGE ZUCCHINI (ABOUT 1 1/2 LBS/750 G TOTAL), TRIMMED AND QUARTERED LENGTHWISE	4
1 TBSP	CANOLA OIL	15 ML
1/4 TSP	SALT	1 ML
1/4 TSP	BLACK PEPPER	1 ML
1/2 CUP	UNSALTED DRY-ROASTED CASHEWS, BLANCHED ALMONDS OR PEANUTS	125 ML
1	GARLIC CLOVE, GRATED	1
1 CUP	PANKO	250 ML
1/3 CUP	GRATED PARMESAN CHEESE	75 ML
1 TBSP	ALL-PURPOSE FLOUR	15 ML
1/2 TSP	DRIED OREGANO	2 ML
1	LARGE EGG YOLK	1
6 TBSP	MARINARA SAUCE	90 ML
1 CUP	SHREDDED MOZZARELLA CHEESE	250 ML

PREHEAT OVEN TO 400°F (200°C). IN A LARGE BOWL, TOSS ZUCCHINI WITH OIL, SALT AND PEPPER. SPREAD IN A SINGLE LAYER ON A PARCHMENT-LINED BAKING SHEET. ROAST FOR 30 MINUTES. LET COOL FOR 10 MINUTES. RESERVE LINED BAKING SHEET TO BAKE PATTIES.

IN A FOOD PROCESSOR, PULSE CASHEWS UNTIL COARSELY CHOPPED. ADD ZUCCHINI, GARLIC, PANKO, PARMESAN, FLOUR, OREGANO AND EGG YOLK; PULSE UNTIL UNIFORM BUT NOT PURÉED. MOUND ZUCCHINI MIXTURE INTO A GREASED 1/3-CUP (75 ML) MEASURE, TAP ONTO

THE LINED BAKING SHEET AND RESHAPE AS NEEDED INTO A ¾-INCH (2 CM) THICK PATTY. (MIXTURE IS LOOSE BUT SETS UP ONCE BAKED.) REPEAT TO MAKE 6 PATTIES. BAKE FOR 15 MINUTES. TURN PATTIES OVER AND TOP WITH MARINARA SAUCE AND CHEESE, DIVIDING EVENLY. BAKE FOR 10 MINUTES OR UNTIL HOT IN THE CENTER. SERVES 6.

TIP: ONCE FORMED ON THE BAKING SHEET, THE PATTIES CAN BE LOOSELY COVERED WITH PLASTIC WRAP AND REFRIGERATED FOR UP TO 1 DAY. ADD 5 MINUTES TO THE BAKING TIME.

COOKING IS ANOTHER WAY TO SHOW LOVE.

SPINACH AND PANEER

PANEER IS AN INDIAN CHEESE. FIRM TOFU CAN BE USED INSTEAD, IF YOU PREFER. SERVE OVER HOT COOKED RICE.

3 TBSP	CANOLA OIL, DIVIDED	45 ML
1	PACKAGE (14 OZ/400 G) PANEER, CUT INTO 3/4-INCH (2 CM) CUBES	1
1/2 TSP	CUMIN SEEDS	2 ML
4	GARLIC CLOVES, MINCED	4
1	ONION, FINELY CHOPPED	1
1 TBSP	GRATED FRESH GINGER	15 ML
1 TBSP	GARAM MASALA	15 ML
1 TSP	SALT	5 ML
1/2 TSP	CAYENNE PEPPER	2 ML
1/2 TSP	GROUND TURMERIC	2 ML
2	PLUM (ROMA) TOMATOES, FINELY CHOPPED	2
8 CUPS	LIGHTLY PACKED SPINACH LEAVES (ABOUT 8 OZ/250 G), SHREDDED	2 L
3/4 CUP	HALF-AND-HALF (10%) CREAM	175 ML

IN A LARGE SKILLET, HEAT 2 TBSP (30 ML) OIL OVER MEDIUM-HIGH HEAT. FRY PANEER, STIRRING OCCASIONALLY, FOR ABOUT 4 MINUTES OR UNTIL GOLDEN ON ALL SIDES. TRANSFER PANEER TO A PLATE. ADD REMAINING OIL AND CUMIN SEEDS TO SKILLET; COOK FOR 30 SECONDS. ADD GARLIC, ONION, GINGER, GARAM MASALA, SALT, CAYENNE AND TURMERIC; SAUTÉ FOR 5 MINUTES OR UNTIL ONION IS SOFTENED. STIR IN TOMATOES AND SPINACH; COOK, STIRRING, FOR 4 MINUTES OR UNTIL SPINACH IS TENDER. STIR IN CREAM. RETURN PANEER TO SKILLET, REDUCE HEAT TO MEDIUM AND HEAT THROUGH. SERVES 6.

SAVORY BAKED FRENCH TOAST

FRENCH TOAST IS TRADITIONALLY SWEET,
BUT THIS VERSION HAS A TASTY SAVORY TWIST.
THIS RECIPE IS PERFECT FOR USING UP DAY-OLD ITALIAN
OR FRENCH BREAD. SERVE WITH A SIDE SALAD.

6 TBSP	BASIL PESTO	90 ML
8	LARGE OVAL SLICES BREAD (ABOUT 6 INCHES/15 CM WIDE)	8
8	SLICES DELI HAM	8
3	PLUM (ROMA) TOMATOES, SLICED	3
8	LARGE EGGS	8
1/2 CUP	HALF-AND-HALF (10%) CREAM	125 ML
1 1/2 CUPS	SHREDDED MOZZARELLA CHEESE	375 ML

GREASE AN 11- BY 7-INCH (28 BY 18 CM) BAKING DISH.
SPREAD PESTO OVER ONE SIDE OF EACH BREAD SLICE,
THEN LAYER A SLICE OF HAM AND TOMATO SLICES ON
TOP. CAREFULLY LIFT EACH STACK INTO PREPARED DISH,
OVERLAPPING TO FIT. IN A MEDIUM BOWL, COMBINE EGGS
AND CREAM; POUR EVENLY OVER BREAD. COVER AND
REFRIGERATE FOR 30 MINUTES.

PREHEAT OVEN TO 350°F (180°C). BAKE CASSEROLE FOR
40 MINUTES OR UNTIL GOLDEN AND PUFFED. REMOVE
FROM OVEN AND PREHEAT BROILER. SPRINKLE CHEESE
OVER CASSEROLE. BROIL FOR 2 TO 3 MINUTES OR UNTIL
CHEESE IS MELTED AND LIGHTLY BROWNED. LET STAND
FOR 10 MINUTES BEFORE SERVING. SERVES 6 TO 8.

POTATO PANCAKES WITH FRIED EGGS

MOST OF US HAVE A CARTON OF EGGS IN THE FRIDGE, SO WHY NOT SHAKE THINGS UP WITH THIS BRINNER (BREAKFAST-FOR-DINNER) RECIPE. IF YOU DON'T HAPPEN TO HAVE LEFTOVER MASHED POTATOES, JUST MAKE A FRESH BATCH THE NIGHT BEFORE. SERVE THE PANCAKES AND EGGS WITH A SIDE SALAD.

POTATO PANCAKES

3/4 CUP	PANKO	175 ML
4 CUPS	CHILLED LEFTOVER MASHED POTATOES	1 L
1 CUP	SHREDDED CHEDDAR CHEESE	250 ML
1 CUP	SHREDDED MOZZARELLA CHEESE	250 ML
1/2 CUP	SLICED GREEN ONIONS	125 ML
1/4 CUP	ALL-PURPOSE FLOUR (APPROX.)	60 ML
1 TSP	GARLIC POWDER	5 ML
1/2 TSP	BLACK PEPPER	2 ML
1 OR 2	LARGE EGGS, LIGHTLY BEATEN	1 OR 2
	CANOLA OIL	

FRIED EGGS

2 TBSP	BUTTER	30 ML
8	LARGE EGGS	8
	SALT AND BLACK PEPPER TO TASTE	

PANCAKES: PLACE PANKO IN A SHALLOW DISH. IN A LARGE BOWL, USING A POTATO MASHER, MASH TOGETHER POTATOES, CHEDDAR, MOZZARELLA, GREEN ONIONS, FLOUR, GARLIC POWDER, PEPPER AND 1 EGG. IF MIXTURE IS TOO DRY TO HOLD A PANCAKE SHAPE, ADD MORE EGG; IF IT'S TOO MOIST, ADD A BIT MORE FLOUR. SHAPE INTO 8

PANCAKES, ABOUT $\frac{1}{2}$ INCH (1 CM) THICK. COAT PANCAKES IN PANKO. ADD ENOUGH OIL TO A LARGE NONSTICK SKILLET TO COVER THE BOTTOM AND HEAT OVER MEDIUM-HIGH HEAT. IN BATCHES, FRY PANCAKES FOR 3 TO 4 MINUTES PER SIDE OR UNTIL GOLDEN BROWN AND CRISP. DO NOT OVERCROWD PAN, AND ADD MORE OIL AS NEEDED BETWEEN BATCHES. TRANSFER PANCAKES TO A PLATE AND LOOSELY TENT WITH FOIL TO KEEP WARM.

FRIED EGGS: MEANWHILE, IN ANOTHER LARGE NONSTICK SKILLET, MELT BUTTER OVER MEDIUM-HIGH HEAT. BREAK EGGS INTO PAN, REDUCE HEAT TO MEDIUM AND COOK TO DESIRED DONENESS. SEASON WITH SALT AND PEPPER. SERVE WITH POTATO PANCAKES. SERVES 4.

TIP: USING A COOKIE SCOOP OR ICE CREAM SCOOP HELPS TO PORTION OUT EVEN-SIZED PANCAKES.

ROASTED RED PEPPER AND FETA FRITTATA

EGGS FOR DINNER? OF COURSE! EMILY GREW UP EATING A VARIETY OF FRITTATAS FOR DINNER AND CONTINUES TO MAKE THEM OFTEN FOR HER FAMILY. WITH A FEW STAPLES OF EGGS, ONIONS, POTATOES AND CHEESE, YOU WILL ALWAYS HAVE A WHOLESOME DINNER THAT IS FAST AND TASTY!

2 TBSP	CANOLA OIL	30 ML
3	RED-SKINNED POTATOES, CUBED	3
6	GREEN ONIONS, CHOPPED	6
3	GARLIC CLOVES, MINCED	3
1 TSP	DRIED OREGANO	5 ML
1/2 TSP	SALT	2 ML
1/2 TSP	BLACK PEPPER	2 ML
1	JAR (12 OZ/340 ML) ROASTED RED BELL PEPPERS, DRAINED AND CHOPPED	1
8	LARGE EGGS	8
2 TBSP	CHOPPED FRESH PARSLEY	30 ML
1/2 CUP	CRUMBLED FETA CHEESE	125 ML
1/4 CUP	SLICED PITTED DRAINED KALAMATA OLIVES	60 ML

PREHEAT BROILER. IN A 9-INCH (23 CM) NONSTICK OVENPROOF SKILLET, HEAT OIL OVER MEDIUM HEAT. ADD POTATOES, COVER AND COOK, STIRRING OCCASIONALLY, FOR ABOUT 10 MINUTES OR UNTIL TENDER BUT FIRM. ADD GREEN ONIONS, GARLIC, OREGANO, SALT AND PEPPER; COOK, UNCOVERED, STIRRING, FOR ABOUT 8 MINUTES OR UNTIL POTATOES ARE GOLDEN. STIR IN ROASTED PEPPERS. IN A BOWL, USING A FORK, BEAT

TOGETHER EGGS AND PARSLEY. POUR OVER POTATO MIXTURE, LIFTING AND STIRRING EGGS IN WITH A SPATULA. COVER AND COOK FOR ABOUT 8 MINUTES OR UNTIL EDGES ARE SET AND PUFFED. SPRINKLE WITH FETA AND OLIVES. BROIL FOR ABOUT 2 MINUTES OR UNTIL A KNIFE INSERTED IN THE CENTER COMES OUT CLEAN. SERVES 4 TO 6.

TIP: IF THE HANDLE OF YOUR NONSTICK SKILLET IS NOT OVENPROOF, WRAP THE HANDLE COMPLETELY WITH FOIL BEFORE USE. THIS WILL PROTECT THE HANDLE WHEN THE FRITTATA GOES INTO THE OVEN.

TIP: FOR AN ADDED KICK, ADD $\frac{1}{2}$ TSP (2 ML) HOT PEPPER FLAKES WITH THE OREGANO.

YOU CAN'T HAVE A FULL WINE BARREL AND A DRUNK WIFE.

BAKED MUSHROOM AND HERB BARLEY RISOTTO

BARLEY OFFERS UP A DELICIOUS AND RICH-TASTING ALTERNATIVE TO RICE IN A RISOTTO. WITH ITS SLIGHTLY FIRM TEXTURE AND EASE OF PREPARATION, THIS CREAMY RISOTTO IS A BREEZE BECAUSE THERE IS NO CONTINUOUS STIRRING INVOLVED.

2 TSP	CANOLA OIL	10 ML
8 OZ	MUSHROOMS, SLICED	250 G
4	GARLIC CLOVES, MINCED	4
1	ONION, FINELY CHOPPED	1
1 TSP	DRIED ITALIAN SEASONING	5 ML
1 CUP	POT BARLEY	250 ML
1/2 CUP	ROASTED OR DRAINED OIL-PACKED SUN-DRIED TOMATOES, CHOPPED	125 ML
4 CUPS	READY-TO-USE VEGETABLE BROTH	1 L
1/4 CUP	HERBED CREAM CHEESE	60 ML

PREHEAT OVEN TO 400°F (200°C). IN AN OVENPROOF DUTCH OVEN, HEAT OIL OVER MEDIUM-HIGH HEAT. SAUTÉ MUSHROOMS, GARLIC, ONION AND ITALIAN SEASONING FOR ABOUT 10 MINUTES OR UNTIL NO LIQUID REMAINS. STIR IN BARLEY UNTIL COATED. STIR IN ROASTED TOMATOES AND BROTH; BRING TO BOIL. COVER, TRANSFER TO OVEN AND BAKE FOR 30 MINUTES OR UNTIL BARLEY IS TENDER BUT FIRM. REMOVE FROM OVEN AND STIR IN CREAM CHEESE UNTIL MELTED AND CREAMY. SERVES 4 TO 6.

TIP: FOR ADDED PROTEIN, STIR IN A 19-OZ (540 ML) CAN OF CHICKPEAS, RINSED AND DRAINED (2 CUPS/500 ML), WITH THE ROASTED TOMATOES.

White Chocolate Gingersnap Cookies (page 254), Lime Sparkle Cookies (page 258)
and No-Bake Chocolate Oat Squares (page 261)

Apple Cranberry Pie Squares (page 262)

Emily's Favorite
Chocolate Cupcakes (page 274)

QUINOA-STUFFED PEPPERS

THESE COME TOGETHER EASILY AND ARE EVEN BETTER FOR LUNCH THE NEXT DAY.

1/2 CUP	QUINOA, RINSED	125 ML
1 CUP	READY-TO-USE VEGETABLE BROTH	250 ML
4	LARGE BELL PEPPERS (ANY COLOR)	4
1 TBSP	CANOLA OIL	15 ML
8 OZ	MUSHROOMS, CHOPPED	250 G
4	GARLIC CLOVES, MINCED	4
1	RED ONION, DICED	1
1/2 TSP	SALT	2 ML
1/2 TSP	HOT PEPPER FLAKES	2 ML
2 CUPS	CHOPPED BABY ARUGULA	500 ML
1/3 CUP	CRUMBLED FETA CHEESE	75 ML

IN A SAUCEPAN, COMBINE QUINOA AND BROTH; BRING TO A BOIL. REDUCE HEAT, COVER AND SIMMER FOR 15 MINUTES OR UNTIL QUINOA IS TENDER. FLUFF WITH A FORK.

PREHEAT OVEN TO 400°F (200°C). CUT STEM END OFF BELL PEPPERS AND REMOVE SEEDS. TRIM BOTTOM OF PEPPERS TO STAND FLAT IN A SMALL BAKING DISH. REMOVE STEM AND DICE PEPPER TOPS. IN A LARGE NONSTICK SKILLET, HEAT OIL OVER MEDIUM-HIGH HEAT. SAUTÉ DICED PEPPER TOPS, MUSHROOMS, GARLIC, ONION, SALT AND HOT PEPPER FLAKES FOR 10 MINUTES OR UNTIL VEGETABLES ARE GOLDEN AND LIQUID HAS EVAPORATED. REMOVE FROM HEAT AND STIR IN COOKED QUINOA AND ARUGULA. SPOON FILLING INTO PEPPERS AND SPRINKLE WITH FETA. BAKE FOR ABOUT 20 MINUTES OR UNTIL PEPPERS ARE SOFTENED AND FILLING IS HOT. SERVES 4.

MEAL IN A MUFFIN

THESE SAVORY MUFFINS ARE PERFECT FOR A GRAB-AND-GO MEAL (OR FOR SCHOOL LUNCHES).

1/2 CUP	QUINOA, RINSED	125 ML
1 CUP	WATER	250 ML
2	GREEN ONIONS, SLICED	2
1	PACKAGE (10 OZ/300 G) FROZEN CHOPPED SPINACH, THAWED AND SQUEEZED DRY	1
1 CUP	SHREDDED MONTEREY JACK CHEESE	250 ML
1/4 CUP	FINELY CHOPPED DRAINED OIL-PACKED SUN-DRIED TOMATOES	60 ML
1 TSP	DRIED DILL	5 ML
1/2 TSP	EACH SALT AND BLACK PEPPER	2 ML
6	LARGE EGGS	6
1/2 CUP	CRUMBLED FETA CHEESE	125 ML

IN A MEDIUM POT, COMBINE QUINOA AND WATER. BRING TO A BOIL OVER MEDIUM-HIGH HEAT. REDUCE HEAT, COVER AND SIMMER FOR 15 MINUTES OR UNTIL WATER IS ABSORBED AND QUINOA IS TENDER. REMOVE FROM HEAT AND LET STAND, COVERED, FOR 5 MINUTES. UNCOVER AND LET COOL.

PREHEAT OVEN TO 375°F (190°C) AND PLACE LINERS IN A 12-CUP MUFFIN TIN. IN A LARGE BOWL, COMBINE COOLED QUINOA, GREEN ONIONS, SPINACH, MONTEREY JACK, SUN-DRIED TOMATOES, DILL, SALT, PEPPER AND EGGS. DIVIDE MIXTURE INTO MUFFIN CUPS AND SPRINKLE FETA OVER TOP. BAKE FOR 20 TO 25 MINUTES OR UNTIL FIRM AND LIGHTLY BROWNED ON TOP. LET COOL FOR 5 MINUTES BEFORE SERVING. SERVES 6.

— EGG AND TOFU FRIED RICE —

*COOK THE RICE THE DAY BEFORE FOR THIS TASTY
ASIAN CLASSIC. FEEL FREE TO ADD UP TO 2 CUPS
(500 ML) LEFTOVER COOKED VEGGIES TO THIS DISH.*

3 TBSP	CANOLA OIL, DIVIDED	45 ML
3	LARGE EGGS, LIGHTLY BEATEN	3
12 OZ	FIRM TOFU, DRAINED AND CUT INTO SMALL CUBES	375 G
1	LARGE CARROT, GRATED	1
2	GARLIC CLOVES, MINCED	2
3	GREEN ONIONS, SLICED	3
4 CUPS	COOKED RICE, COOLED	1 L
1 CUP	FROZEN GREEN PEAS, THAWED	250 ML
3 TBSP	SOY SAUCE	45 ML
1 TBSP	OYSTER SAUCE	15 ML
1 TSP	SESAME OIL	5 ML

IN A LARGE NONSTICK SKILLET, HEAT 1 TBSP (15 ML) OIL
OVER MEDIUM-HIGH HEAT. COOK EGGS FOR 20 SECONDS.
GENTLY STIR EGGS, CREATING LARGE CURDS, AND
COOK FOR 1 MINUTE. TRANSFER EGGS TO A PLATE.
ADD REMAINING OIL TO SKILLET AND HEAT OVER MEDIUM-
HIGH HEAT. COOK TOFU, STIRRING OCCASIONALLY, UNTIL
LIGHTLY BROWNED. ADD CARROT AND COOK, STIRRING, FOR
1 MINUTE. ADD GARLIC AND COOK FOR 20 SECONDS. STIR
IN GREEN ONIONS, RICE, PEAS, SOY SAUCE, OYSTER SAUCE
AND SESAME OIL; COOK, STIRRING CONSTANTLY, FOR
ABOUT 5 MINUTES OR UNTIL HEATED THROUGH. RETURN
EGGS TO SKILLET AND COOK FOR 1 MINUTE OR UNTIL
HEATED THROUGH. SERVES 4.

SHORTCUT BIRYANI

PURCHASED BIRYANI PASTE SPEEDS UP THE
PREPARATION OF THIS DISH. BIRYANI IS OFTEN
SERVED WITH POPADAMS (DRIED LENTIL CRACKERS).

RAITA

1/2 CUP	FINELY CHOPPED CUCUMBER	125 ML
2 TBSP	CHOPPED FRESH CILANTRO	30 ML
2 TBSP	CHOPPED FRESH MINT (OR 2 TSP/10 ML DRIED)	30 ML
1/2 TSP	BLACK PEPPER	2 ML
1/2 TSP	GROUND CUMIN	2 ML
1/4 TSP	SALT	1 ML
1/2 CUP	PLAIN YOGURT	125 ML

BIRYANI

3 TBSP	CANOLA OIL	45 ML
2	CARROTS, GRATED	2
1	ONION, FINELY CHOPPED	1
2 CUPS	FINELY CHOPPED CAULIFLOWER	500 ML
1 CUP	WHITE BASMATI RICE	250 ML
2 TBSP	RAISINS OR CURRANTS	30 ML
2 CUPS	WATER	500 ML
2 TBSP	BIRYANI CURRY PASTE	30 ML
1 CUP	FROZEN GREEN PEAS, THAWED	250 ML
1/4 CUP	TOASTED SLICED ALMONDS	60 ML
3 TBSP	TOASTED SHREDDED COCONUT	45 ML
1 CUP	COARSELY CHOPPED FRESH CILANTRO	250 ML

RAITA: IN A SMALL BOWL, COMBINE ALL INGREDIENTS;
COVER AND REFRIGERATE UNTIL READY TO SERVE.

BIRYANI: IN A LARGE SAUCEPAN, HEAT OIL OVER MEDIUM HEAT. COOK CARROTS, ONION AND CAULIFLOWER, STIRRING OCCASIONALLY, FOR 5 MINUTES. STIR IN RICE, RAISINS, WATER AND CURRY PASTE; COVER AND BRING TO A BOIL. REDUCE HEAT AND SIMMER FOR 20 MINUTES. STIR IN PEAS, COVER AND SIMMER FOR 5 MINUTES OR UNTIL RICE IS TENDER AND LIQUID IS ABSORBED. REMOVE FROM HEAT AND STIR IN ALMONDS, COCONUT AND CILANTRO. SERVE WITH RAITA ON THE SIDE. SERVES 4 TO 5.

TIP: JARS OF BIRYANI CURRY PASTE AND POPADAMS CAN BE FOUND IN THE INTERNATIONAL FOODS SECTION OF MANY GROCERY STORES.

I PREFER MY KALE WITH A SILENT "K."

SPICY TOFU AND BOK CHOY

HERE'S A GREAT VEGETARIAN DISH FOR A SMALL HOUSEHOLD! THIS DISH IS TASTY ON ITS OWN OR SERVED OVER A BED OF RICE OR NOODLES.

6 OZ	EXTRA-FIRM TOFU	175 G
2 TBSP	ALL-PURPOSE FLOUR	30 ML
2 TSP	SESAME SEEDS	10 ML
1 TBSP	SESAME OIL, DIVIDED	15 ML
2 TBSP	CANOLA OIL	30 ML
3	BABY BOK CHOY, CUT IN HALF LENGTHWISE	3
2	GARLIC CLOVES, MINCED	2
1 TBSP	MINCED FRESH GINGER	15 ML
1/2 TSP	ASIAN GARLIC CHILI PASTE OR HOT PEPPER SAUCE	2 ML
1/2 CUP	WATER	125 ML
2 TBSP	REDUCED-SODIUM SOY SAUCE	30 ML
2 TBSP	UNSEASONED RICE VINEGAR	30 ML
3 TBSP	SMOOTH PEANUT BUTTER	45 ML
3 TBSP	CHOPPED SALTED ROASTED PEANUTS (OPTIONAL)	45 ML

CUT TOFU IN HALF LENGTHWISE AND CUT EACH HALF INTO TRIANGLES. PAT DRY WITH A PAPER TOWEL. IN A SHALLOW DISH, COMBINE FLOUR AND SESAME SEEDS. BRUSH TOFU WITH SOME OF THE SESAME OIL AND COAT IN FLOUR MIXTURE. IN A NONSTICK SKILLET, HEAT VEGETABLE OIL OVER MEDIUM-HIGH HEAT. FRY TOFU, TURNING ONCE, FOR 6 TO 8 MINUTES OR UNTIL GOLDEN BROWN. REMOVE TO A PLATE LINED WITH PAPER TOWEL. WIPE OUT SKILLET AND RETURN TO MEDIUM HEAT. ADD REMAINING SESAME

OIL, THEN ADD BOK CHOY, GARLIC, GINGER AND CHILI PASTE; COOK, STIRRING GENTLY, FOR 2 MINUTES. COVER AND STEAM FOR ABOUT 3 MINUTES OR UNTIL TENDER-CRISP. TRANSFER BOK CHOY TO PLATE WITH TOFU. ADD WATER, SOY SAUCE AND VINEGAR TO SKILLET AND BRING TO A BOIL. REDUCE HEAT TO LOW AND WHISK IN PEANUT BUTTER UNTIL SMOOTH. RETURN BOK CHOY AND TOFU TO SAUCE AND STIR GENTLY TO COAT. SERVE SPRINKLED WITH PEANUTS, IF DESIRED. SERVES 2.

TIP: MINCE EXTRA GINGER AS A TIME-SAVER FOR OTHER DINNER RECIPES. FREEZE IT IN 1-TBSP (15 ML) AMOUNTS, WRAPPED IN PLASTIC WRAP AND PLACED ON A SMALL PLATE IN THE FREEZER. ONCE THEY ARE SOLID, REMOVE THEM FROM THE PLATE AND TUCK THEM INTO A SMALL SEALABLE PLASTIC BAG. STORE THEM IN THE FREEZER AND PULL ONE WHENEVER YOU NEED SOME MINCED GINGER.

I NEVER REALIZED HOW FUNNY I WAS UNTIL I STARTED TALKING TO MYSELF.

COURTNEY'S TRIPLE-BEAN SLOW COOKER CHILI

SYLVIA'S FRIEND COURTNEY MAKES A BIG POT
OF THIS CHILI ALMOST EVERY WEEKEND SO SHE
CAN ENJOY IT THROUGHOUT THE WEEK.
IT'S A DELICIOUS DINNER TO COME HOME TO
AND PERFECT FOR TAKE-TO-WORK LUNCHES.

5 TSP	CANOLA OIL	25 ML
4	GARLIC CLOVES, MINCED	4
1	ONION, DICED	1
1 CUP	CHOPPED CELERY	250 ML
1	RED BELL PEPPER, CHOPPED	1
1	YELLOW BELL PEPPER, CHOPPED	1
1	CAN (19 OZ/540 ML) RED KIDNEY BEANS, RINSED AND DRAINED (2 CUPS/500 ML)	1
1	CAN (19 OZ/540 ML) PINTO BEANS, RINSED AND DRAINED (2 CUPS/500 ML)	1
1	CAN (19 OZ/540 ML) BLACK BEANS, RINSED AND DRAINED (2 CUPS/500 ML)	1
1	CAN (28 OZ/796 ML) DICED TOMATOES, WITH JUICE	1
1	CAN (5½ OZ/156 ML) TOMATO PASTE	1
1 CUP	READY-TO-USE VEGETABLE BROTH	250 ML
2 TBSP	CHILI POWDER	30 ML
1 TBSP	GROUND CUMIN	15 ML
2 TSP	SMOKED PAPRIKA	10 ML
1 TSP	DRIED OREGANO	5 ML
	SALT TO TASTE	
	CHOPPED GREEN ONION, CHOPPED FRESH CILANTRO, SHREDDED CHEESE, CHOPPED AVOCADO, TORTILLA CHIPS, HOT PEPPER SAUCE (OPTIONAL)	

IN A LARGE SKILLET, HEAT OIL OVER MEDIUM HEAT. SAUTÉ GARLIC AND ONION FOR 5 MINUTES. ADD CELERY, RED PEPPER AND YELLOW PEPPER; SAUTÉ FOR 5 MINUTES. TRANSFER TO A 4- TO 6-QUART SLOW COOKER AND ADD KIDNEY, PINTO AND BLACK BEANS, TOMATOES WITH JUICE, TOMATO PASTE, BROTH, CHILI POWDER, CUMIN, PAPRIKA AND OREGANO. COVER AND COOK ON LOW FOR 6 TO 8 HOURS OR ON HIGH FOR 3 TO 4 HOURS, UNTIL VEGETABLES ARE TENDER AND CHILI IS THICKENED. SEASON WITH SALT. SERVE WITH TOPPINGS AS DESIRED. SERVES 8.

STOVETOP VARIATION: SAUTÉ THE VEGETABLES AS DESCRIBED, BUT IN A LARGE POT, THEN STIR IN THE REMAINING CHILI INGREDIENTS AND BRING TO A BOIL. REDUCE HEAT, COVER AND SIMMER FOR 20 TO 25 MINUTES. SEASON WITH SALT.

BUFFET: FRENCH FOR "GET IT YOURSELF."

BEAN TAMALE MINI PIES

IN THESE YUMMY MINI TAMALES, A HEARTY FILLING IS TOPPED WITH A GOLDEN, VELVETY CORNMEAL LAYER.

2 TBSP	CANOLA OIL	30 ML
1	ONION, FINELY CHOPPED	1
2	GARLIC CLOVES, MINCED	2
1	RED OR GREEN BELL PEPPER, CHOPPED	1
1	CAN (19 OZ/540 ML) BLACK BEANS, RINSED AND DRAINED (2 CUPS/500 ML)	1
1	CAN (19 OZ/540 ML) PINTO BEANS, RINSED AND DRAINED (2 CUPS/500 ML)	1
2 CUPS	DICED TOMATOES	500 ML
1 CUP	CORN KERNELS (THAWED IF FROZEN)	250 ML
1/2 CUP	SLICED PITTED DRAINED OLIVES	125 ML
1 TBSP	CHILI POWDER	15 ML
1 TSP	GROUND CUMIN	5 ML
1 TSP	DRIED OREGANO	5 ML
1/2 TSP	HOT PEPPER FLAKES	2 ML
1 1/2 CUPS	SHREDDED MEXICAN-BLEND CHEESE	375 ML
	SOUR CREAM (OPTIONAL)	

TAMALE TOPPING

1 1/2 CUPS	WATER	375 ML
2 TBSP	CANOLA OIL	30 ML
1/2 TSP	SALT	2 ML
1/2 CUP	CORNMEAL	125 ML
1 CUP	SHREDDED CHEDDAR CHEESE	250 ML
2	LARGE EGGS, LIGHTLY BEATEN	2

PREHEAT OVEN TO 425°F (220°C). LIGHTLY GREASE SIX
2-CUP (500 ML) OVENPROOF BOWLS OR MINI FOIL LOAF

PANS AND PLACE ON A RIMMED BAKING SHEET. IN A LARGE SKILLET, HEAT OIL OVER MEDIUM-HIGH HEAT. SAUTÉ ONION FOR 5 MINUTES. ADD GARLIC, RED PEPPER, BLACK BEANS, PINTO BEANS, TOMATOES, CORN, OLIVES, CHILI POWDER, CUMIN, OREGANO AND HOT PEPPER FLAKES; COOK, STIRRING OCCASIONALLY, FOR 15 MINUTES. DIVIDE MIXTURE INTO PREPARED BOWLS AND SPRINKLE CHEESE OVER TOP.

TOPPING: IN A MEDIUM SAUCEPAN, HEAT WATER, OIL AND SALT OVER MEDIUM HEAT UNTIL HOT. GRADUALLY STIR IN CORNMEAL AND COOK, STIRRING VIGOROUSLY, UNTIL THICKENED. REMOVE FROM HEAT AND LET COOL SLIGHTLY, THEN STIR IN CHEESE AND EGGS UNTIL COMBINED.

GENTLY SPREAD TOPPING OVER EACH BOWL TO FORM A TOP CRUST. BAKE FOR 20 MINUTES OR UNTIL TOPPING IS LIGHTLY BROWNED. SERVE WITH SOUR CREAM ON THE SIDE, IF DESIRED. SERVES 6.

TIP: THIS RECIPE CAN ALSO BE COOKED AS A SINGLE LARGER PIE IN A 10-INCH (25 CM) CAST-IRON SKILLET OR AN 11- BY 7-INCH (28 BY 18 CM) CASSEROLE DISH.

CURRIED CHICKPEA AND LENTIL STUFFED SWEET POTATOES

*THIS SPICY AND CREAMY TOPPING IS PERFECT
OVER SILKY BAKED SWEET POTATOES.*

4	SMALL SWEET POTATOES	4
2 TBSP	CANOLA OIL	30 ML
I	ONION, FINELY CHOPPED	I
2	GARLIC CLOVES, MINCED	2
2 TSP	GRATED FRESH GINGER	10 ML
2 TSP	GARAM MASALA	10 ML
I TSP	SALT	5 ML
I TSP	CURRY POWDER	5 ML
1/4 TSP	GROUND CINNAMON	I ML
2 CUPS	CHOPPED TOMATOES	500 ML
1/4 CUP	DRIED RED LENTILS, SORTED AND RINSED	60 ML
I	CAN (19 OZ/540 ML) CHICKPEAS, RINSED AND DRAINED (2 CUPS/500 ML)	I
I	CAN (14 OZ/400 ML) COCONUT MILK	I
I CUP	COARSELY CHOPPED FRESH CILANTRO (OPTIONAL)	250 ML

SCRUB SWEET POTATOES, THEN PRICK ALL OVER WITH A FORK. PLACE ON A MICROWAVE-SAFE PLATE AND MICROWAVE ON HIGH, TURNING HALFWAY THROUGH, FOR 10 TO 12 MINUTES OR UNTIL TENDER. LET COOL SLIGHTLY. USING A KNIFE, CUT AN X IN EACH SWEET POTATO AND GENTLY SQUEEZE TO SPLIT OPEN. KEEP WARM.

MEANWHILE, IN A LARGE SKILLET, HEAT OIL OVER MEDIUM-HIGH HEAT. SAUTÉ ONION FOR 5 MINUTES.

ADD GARLIC, GINGER, GARAM MASALA, SALT, CURRY POWDER AND CINNAMON; SAUTÉ FOR 1 MINUTE. STIR IN TOMATOES, LENTILS, CHICKPEAS AND COCONUT MILK; BRING TO A BOIL. REDUCE HEAT TO MEDIUM, COVER AND BOIL GENTLY, STIRRING OCCASIONALLY, FOR 15 TO 20 MINUTES OR UNTIL LENTILS ARE TENDER. TOP EACH SWEET POTATO WITH CHICKPEA MIXTURE, THEN SPRINKLE WITH CILANTRO, IF DESIRED. SERVES 4.

TIP: THE SWEET POTATOES CAN ALSO BE PREPARED IN THE OVEN. SCRUB SWEET POTATOES, THEN PRICK ALL OVER WITH A FORK. PLACE ON A FOIL-LINED BAKING SHEET AND BAKE IN A PREHEATED 400°F (200°C) OVEN FOR 45 TO 55 MINUTES OR UNTIL TENDER.

WHERE DID THE VEGETABLES GO FOR A FEW DRINKS?
THE SALAD BAR!

OVEN MEATLESS MEATBALLS

SYLVIA'S VEGAN FRIEND SHARED HER FAVORITE "MEATBALL" RECIPE. SHE ENJOYS THEM ON TOP OF GLUTEN-FREE PASTA, ALONG WITH TOMATO SAUCE AND SAUTÉED PEPPERS. TO SWITCH THINGS UP, YOU CAN ALSO SERVE THEM AS AN APPETIZER, WITH A TOMATO SAUCE DIP.

2 TBSP	GROUND FLAX SEEDS (FLAXSEED MEAL)	30 ML
6 TBSP	WATER	90 ML
I TBSP	CANOLA OIL	15 ML
6	GARLIC CLOVES, MINCED	6
I	ONION, FINELY CHOPPED	I
2	CANS (EACH 19 OZ/540 ML) CHICKPEAS, DRAINED AND RINSED (4 CUPS/I L), LIQUID RESERVED	2
3/4 CUP	DRY BREAD CRUMBS (APPROX.)	175 ML
I TSP	DRIED PARSLEY	5 ML
I TSP	DRIED BASIL	5 ML
1/2 TSP	SALT	2 ML
1/4 TSP	BLACK PEPPER	I ML

IN A SMALL BOWL, COMBINE FLAX SEEDS AND WATER; LET STAND FOR 10 TO 15 MINUTES OR UNTIL THICKENED.

PREHEAT OVEN TO 375°F (190°C). IN A LARGE SKILLET, HEAT OIL OVER MEDIUM HEAT. SAUTÉ GARLIC AND ONION FOR 5 MINUTES. IN A FOOD PROCESSOR, PROCESS CHICKPEAS UNTIL FINELY GROUND. ADD ONION MIXTURE, FLAX MIXTURE, BREAD CRUMBS, PARSLEY, BASIL, SALT AND PEPPER; PROCESS UNTIL MIXTURE FORMS A DOUGH-LIKE TEXTURE. IF MIXTURE IS TOO MOIST, ADD MORE BREAD

CRUMBS, 1 TBSP (15 ML) AT A TIME; IF MIXTURE IS TOO DRY, ADD A LITTLE RESERVED CHICKPEA LIQUID UNTIL MIXTURE HOLDS TOGETHER WHEN SQUEEZED. WORKING WITH 2 TBSP (30 ML) CHICKPEA MIXTURE AT A TIME, ROLL INTO 15 OR 16 BALLS AND PLACE ON A LIGHTLY GREASED OR PARCHMENT-LINED RIMMED BAKING SHEET. BAKE FOR 15 MINUTES. TURN BALLS OVER AND BAKE FOR 10 MINUTES OR UNTIL LIGHTLY BROWNED. SERVES 4 TO 5.

TIP: IF YOU ARE NOT VEGAN, YOU CAN USE A LARGE EGG IN PLACE OF THE FLAXSEED EGG SUBSTITUTE.

I MAY NOT BE A WAITRESS,
BUT I WILL BRING THE FOOD TO THE TABLE.

CHICKPEA EGGPLANT CURRY

THE EGGPLANT ABSORBS THE ZESTY, AROMATIC THAI FLAVORS OF THIS RICH CURRY. SERVE WITH RICE OR QUINOA, WITH LIME WEDGES ON THE SIDE.

2 TBSP	CANOLA OIL	30 ML
1	ONION, SLICED	1
4	GARLIC CLOVES, MINCED	4
1 TSP	GRATED FRESH GINGER	5 ML
1 TBSP	GREEN CURRY PASTE	15 ML
2	ASIAN EGGPLANTS, SLICED	2
1	RED BELL PEPPER, CHOPPED	1
1	CAN (19 OZ/540 ML) CHICKPEAS, RINSED AND DRAINED (2 CUPS/500 ML)	1
1 TBSP	PACKED BROWN SUGAR	15 ML
1	CAN (14 OZ/400 ML) COCONUT MILK	1
2 TBSP	FISH SAUCE	30 ML
1/2 CUP	FRESH BASIL LEAVES, SLICED	125 ML
1 TBSP	LIME JUICE	15 ML

IN A SKILLET, HEAT OIL OVER MEDIUM-HIGH HEAT. SAUTÉ ONION FOR 3 MINUTES. ADD GARLIC, GINGER AND CURRY PASTE; SAUTÉ FOR 30 SECONDS. ADD EGGPLANTS, RED PEPPER, CHICKPEAS, BROWN SUGAR, COCONUT MILK AND FISH SAUCE; BRING TO A BOIL. REDUCE HEAT AND SIMMER, STIRRING OCCASIONALLY, FOR 10 MINUTES OR UNTIL VEGETABLES ARE TENDER. REMOVE FROM HEAT AND STIR IN BASIL AND LIME JUICE. SERVES 5 TO 6.

TIP: ASIAN EGGPLANTS ARE LIGHT PURPLE TO PURPLE-BLACK, LONG AND SLENDER.

QUICK-AND-EASY SWEET STUFF

ALMOND BUTTER CRUNCH COOKIES

WE LOVE NUT BUTTERS! WITH A CRUNCHY BITE, THESE COOKIES MAKE A NICE CHANGE FROM CLASSIC PEANUT BUTTER.

1/2 CUP	CRUNCHY ALMOND BUTTER	125 ML
1/3 CUP	BUTTER, SOFTENED	75 ML
1/2 CUP	PACKED LIGHT BROWN (GOLDEN YELLOW) SUGAR	125 ML
1/2 TSP	BAKING SODA	2 ML
1/2 TSP	BAKING POWDER	2 ML
PINCH	SALT	PINCH
1	LARGE EGG	1
2 TSP	VANILLA	10 ML
3/4 CUP	ALL-PURPOSE FLOUR	175 ML
3/4 CUP	CRUSHED BRAN FLAKES CEREAL	175 ML
1/2 CUP	SLIVERED ALMONDS	125 ML
	GRANULATED SUGAR	

PREHEAT OVEN TO 350°F (180°C). IN A LARGE BOWL, USING AN ELECTRIC MIXER, BEAT ALMOND BUTTER AND BUTTER UNTIL CREAMY. BEAT IN BROWN SUGAR, BAKING SODA, BAKING POWDER, SALT, EGG AND VANILLA UNTIL STICKY. STIR IN FLOUR, CEREAL AND ALMONDS UNTIL COMBINED. USING A LEVEL SMALL ICE CREAM SCOOP OR TABLESPOON (15 ML), SCOOP UP DOUGH AND ROLL INTO BALLS. PLACE BALLS ABOUT 2 INCHES (5 CM) APART ON PARCHMENT-LINED BAKING SHEETS. DIP A FORK IN GRANULATED SUGAR AND FLATTEN COOKIES SLIGHTLY WITH TINES. BAKE, ONE SHEET AT A TIME, FOR ABOUT 10 MINUTES OR UNTIL LIGHT BROWN ON BOTTOM. LET COOL ON PAN ON A WIRE RACK

FOR 2 MINUTES, THEN TRANSFER COOKIES TO RACK TO COOL COMPLETELY. MAKES ABOUT 38 COOKIES.

TIP: YOU WILL NEED TO CRUSH ABOUT 2 CUPS (500 ML) BRAN FLAKES CEREAL FOR THIS RECIPE.

TIP: STORE COOLED COOKIES IN AN AIRTIGHT CONTAINER, BETWEEN LAYERS OF WAXED OR PARCHMENT PAPER, AT ROOM TEMPERATURE FOR UP TO 3 DAYS OR IN THE FREEZER FOR UP TO 2 WEEKS.

I STEPPED ON A CHEERIO. NOW I'M A CEREAL KILLER.

WHITE CHOCOLATE GINGERSNAP COOKIES

EMILY'S FRIEND DONNA IS A WONDERFUL BAKER, AND EVERY YEAR SHE CHANGES UP THE COOKIES SHE BRINGS TO EMILY'S COOKIE EXCHANGE. ONE YEAR IT WAS THESE CLASSIC GINGERSNAPS THAT GET A LIFT FROM WHITE CHOCOLATE. IF YOU'RE A SEMISWEET CHOCOLATE LOVER, NO WORRIES — THAT WORKS TOO!

2 CUPS	ALL-PURPOSE FLOUR	500 ML
1 TSP	BAKING SODA	5 ML
1 1/2 TSP	GROUND GINGER	7 ML
3/4 TSP	GROUND CINNAMON	3 ML
1/2 TSP	GROUND CLOVES	2 ML
1/4 TSP	SALT	1 ML
PINCH	GROUND NUTMEG	PINCH
3/4 CUP	GRANULATED SUGAR	175 ML
1/2 CUP	BUTTER, SOFTENED	125 ML
1	LARGE EGG	1
1/4 CUP	LIGHT (FANCY) MOLASSES	60 ML
1 TSP	VANILLA	5 ML
3/4 CUP	CHOPPED WHITE CHOCOLATE	175 ML
	ADDITIONAL GRANULATED SUGAR	

PREHEAT OVEN TO 350°F (180°C). IN A MEDIUM BOWL, WHISK TOGETHER FLOUR, BAKING SODA, GINGER, CINNAMON, CLOVES, SALT AND NUTMEG. IN A LARGE BOWL, USING AN ELECTRIC MIXER, CREAM SUGAR AND BUTTER UNTIL FLUFFY. BEAT IN EGG, MOLASSES AND VANILLA UNTIL SMOOTH. STIR FLOUR MIXTURE INTO EGG MIXTURE UNTIL COMBINED. STIR IN CHOCOLATE. USING A

LEVEL SMALL ICE CREAM SCOOP OR TABLESPOON (15 ML), SCOOP UP DOUGH AND ROLL INTO BALLS. ROLL BALLS IN SUGAR AND PLACE ABOUT 2 INCHES (5 CM) APART ON PARCHMENT-LINED BAKING SHEETS. BAKE, ONE SHEET AT A TIME, FOR ABOUT 12 MINUTES OR UNTIL EDGES ARE SET AND CENTER IS SOFT. LET COOL COMPLETELY ON PAN ON A WIRE RACK. MAKES ABOUT 35 COOKIES.

TIP: USE A SHALLOW BOWL TO ROLL THE COOKIES IN SUGAR; IT'S EASIER TO MOVE THEM AROUND AND COAT THEM EVENLY THAN WHEN USING A PLATE.

TIP: STORE COOLED COOKIES IN AN AIRTIGHT CONTAINER AT ROOM TEMPERATURE FOR UP TO 5 DAYS OR IN THE FREEZER FOR UP TO 1 MONTH.

I'M COOKING LOVE FOR DINNER TONIGHT.
WHAT'S FOR DESSERT?

PUMPKIN CHOCOLATE CARAMEL COOKIES

HERE, PUMPKIN PIE SPICES ARE MIXED WITH CHOCOLATE AND CARAMEL FOR A SPECIAL TREAT FIT FOR ANY DAY OF THE WEEK. VERY MOIST, CAKE-LIKE COOKIES AND GOOEY CARAMEL ARE THE IDEAL COMBO.

3 CUPS	ALL-PURPOSE FLOUR	750 ML
I TSP	BAKING POWDER	5 ML
I TSP	GROUND CINNAMON	5 ML
1/2 TSP	BAKING SODA	2 ML
1/2 TSP	GROUND NUTMEG	2 ML
PINCH	SALT	PINCH
I CUP	PACKED BROWN SUGAR	250 ML
1/2 CUP	GRANULATED SUGAR	125 ML
I CUP	BUTTER, SOFTENED	250 ML
2	LARGE EGGS	2
I CUP	PUMPKIN PURÉE (NOT PIE FILLING)	250 ML
2 TSP	VANILLA	10 ML
I	BAG (7 OZ/203 G) MINI CHOCOLATE CARAMEL CANDIES (SUCH AS MINI ROLOS)	I
I CUP	CHOPPED PECANS, TOASTED	250 ML
3 OZ	SEMISWEET CHOCOLATE, MELTED AND SLIGHTLY COOLED	90 G

PREHEAT OVEN TO 350°F (180°C). IN A LARGE BOWL, WHISK TOGETHER FLOUR, BAKING POWDER, CINNAMON, BAKING SODA, NUTMEG AND SALT. IN ANOTHER LARGE BOWL, USING AN ELECTRIC MIXER, CREAM BROWN SUGAR, GRANULATED SUGAR AND BUTTER UNTIL FLUFFY. ADD EGGS, ONE AT A TIME, BEATING WELL AFTER EACH. BEAT IN PUMPKIN AND VANILLA UNTIL COMBINED. STIR

IN FLOUR MIXTURE UNTIL WELL COMBINED. FOLD IN CANDIES AND PECANS. USING A LEVEL SMALL ICE CREAM SCOOP OR A HEAPING TABLESPOON (15 ML), DROP BATTER ONTO PARCHMENT-LINED BAKING SHEETS, SPACING COOKIES 2 INCHES (5 CM) APART. BAKE, ONE SHEET AT A TIME, FOR ABOUT 13 MINUTES OR UNTIL GOLDEN AND FIRM TO THE TOUCH. LET COOL ON PAN ON A WIRE RACK FOR 5 MINUTES TO LET CARAMEL SET. USING A SMALL SPATULA, TRANSFER COOKIES TO RACK TO COOL COMPLETELY. DRIZZLE WITH MELTED CHOCOLATE BEFORE SERVING. MAKES ABOUT 4 DOZEN COOKIES.

TIP: TO MELT SMALLER AMOUNTS OF CHOCOLATE, PLACE IT IN A MICROWAVE-SAFE BOWL AND MICROWAVE ON HIGH, IN 30-SECOND INTERVALS, STIRRING IN BETWEEN, UNTIL ALMOST ALL THE CHOCOLATE IS MELTED, THEN STIR UNTIL MELTED AND SMOOTH.

TIP: BEFORE STORING, BE SURE CHOCOLATE IS SET ON COOKIES. STORE IN AIRTIGHT CONTAINERS, BETWEEN LAYERS OF WAXED OR PARCHMENT PAPER, AT ROOM TEMPERATURE FOR UP TO 5 DAYS OR IN THE FREEZER FOR UP TO 2 WEEKS.

LIME SPARKLE COOKIES

THESE CITRUSY COOKIES HAVE
A SPARKLY CRACKLED TOP.

2¼ CUPS	ALL-PURPOSE FLOUR	550 ML
¾ CUP	CORNSTARCH	175 ML
I TSP	BAKING SODA	5 ML
½ TSP	SALT	2 ML
½ CUP	UNSWEETENED SHREDDED COCONUT	125 ML
1½ CUPS	GRANULATED SUGAR	375 ML
I CUP	BUTTER, SOFTENED	250 ML
I	LARGE EGG	I
I TBSP	GRATED LIME ZEST	15 ML
2 TBSP	LIME JUICE	30 ML
½ TSP	VANILLA	2 ML
½ CUP	COARSE SANDING SUGAR	125 ML

IN A MEDIUM BOWL, SIFT TOGETHER FLOUR, CORNSTARCH, BAKING SODA AND SALT. STIR IN COCONUT. IN A LARGE BOWL, USING AN ELECTRIC MIXER, CREAM GRANULATED SUGAR AND BUTTER UNTIL FLUFFY. BEAT IN EGG, LIME ZEST, LIME JUICE AND VANILLA UNTIL WELL COMBINED. STIR FLOUR MIXTURE INTO EGG MIXTURE UNTIL COMBINED. COVER AND REFRIGERATE FOR 20 MINUTES.

MEANWHILE, PREHEAT OVEN TO 375°F (190°C). USING A LEVEL SMALL ICE CREAM SCOOP OR TABLESPOON (15 ML), SCOOP UP DOUGH AND ROLL INTO BALLS. ROLL BALLS IN SANDING SUGAR AND PLACE ABOUT 2 INCHES (5 CM) APART ON 2 PARCHMENT-LINED OR LIGHTLY GREASED BAKING SHEETS. BAKE FOR 8 TO 10 MINUTES, SWAPPING PANS' POSITIONS ON RACKS HALFWAY THROUGH, UNTIL EDGES

ARE LIGHTLY BROWNED. LET COOL ON PANS ON WIRE RACKS FOR 5 MINUTES, THEN TRANSFER COOKIES TO RACKS TO COOL. MAKES ABOUT 5 DOZEN COOKIES.

TIP: YOU CAN DIVIDE THE DOUGH IN HALF — HALF TO BAKE RIGHT AWAY AND HALF TO FREEZE FOR A FUTURE SUGAR FIX. COOKIE DOUGH CAN BE FROZEN FOR UP TO 6 MONTHS.

TIP: STORE COOLED COOKIES IN AIRTIGHT CONTAINERS, BETWEEN LAYERS OF WAXED OR PARCHMENT PAPER, AT ROOM TEMPERATURE FOR UP TO 4 DAYS OR IN THE FREEZER FOR UP TO 1 MONTH.

LEMON COOKIES

THESE LITTLE LEMONY BITES ARE PERFECT TO ENJOY WITH TEA OR TUCKED INTO A LUNCH BOX.

1/3 CUP	GRANULATED SUGAR	75 ML
1	LARGE EGG	1
1/3 CUP	MILK	75 ML
1/4 CUP	CANOLA OIL	60 ML
2 TSP	GRATED LEMON ZEST	10 ML
1 1/2 CUPS	ALL-PURPOSE FLOUR	375 ML
2 TSP	BAKING POWDER	10 ML
3 TBSP	POWDERED (ICING) SUGAR	45 ML

PREHEAT OVEN TO 350°F (180°C). IN A LARGE BOWL, WHISK TOGETHER GRANULATED SUGAR, EGG, MILK AND OIL UNTIL FROTHY. WHISK IN LEMON ZEST. STIR IN FLOUR AND BAKING POWDER UNTIL A DOUGH FORMS. USING A LEVEL SMALL ICE CREAM SCOOP OR TABLESPOON (15 ML), SCOOP UP DOUGH AND ROLL INTO BALLS. ROLL BALLS IN POWDERED SUGAR AND PLACE ABOUT 2 INCHES (5 CM) APART ON PARCHMENT-LINED BAKING SHEETS. BAKE, ONE SHEET AT A TIME, FOR ABOUT 10 MINUTES OR UNTIL SET. LET COOL SLIGHTLY ON PAN BEFORE ENJOYING. MAKES ABOUT 30 COOKIES.

TIP: ONCE COMPLETELY COOLED, STORE COOKIES IN AN AIRTIGHT CONTAINER AT ROOM TEMPERATURE FOR UP TO 5 DAYS OR IN THE FREEZER FOR UP TO 1 MONTH.

NO-BAKE CHOCOLATE OAT SQUARES

THESE CLASSIC NO-BAKE SQUARES ARE LOVED BY ALL.

3/4 CUP	BUTTER	175 ML
1/2 CUP	PACKED BROWN SUGAR	125 ML
1 TSP	GROUND CINNAMON	5 ML
1 TSP	VANILLA	5 ML
3 CUPS	QUICK-COOKING ROLLED OATS	750 ML
1 CUP	SEMISWEET CHOCOLATE CHIPS	250 ML
3/4 CUP	SMOOTH PEANUT BUTTER	175 ML

LINE AN 8-INCH (20 CM) SQUARE BAKING PAN WITH PARCHMENT PAPER. IN A MEDIUM SAUCEPAN, MELT BUTTER OVER MEDIUM HEAT. STIR IN BROWN SUGAR, CINNAMON AND VANILLA. STIR IN OATS, REDUCE HEAT TO LOW AND COOK, STIRRING CONSTANTLY, FOR 4 MINUTES. PRESS HALF THE OAT MIXTURE INTO BOTTOM OF PREPARED PAN; TRANSFER REMAINING OAT MIXTURE TO A SMALL BOWL. IN THE SAME SAUCEPAN, OVER LOW HEAT, MELT CHOCOLATE CHIPS AND PEANUT BUTTER, STIRRING UNTIL SMOOTH; RESERVE 1/4 CUP (60 ML) FOR DRIZZLING. SPREAD REMAINING CHOCOLATE MIXTURE EVENLY OVER CRUST IN PAN. SPRINKLE RESERVED OAT MIXTURE OVER CHOCOLATE LAYER AND GENTLY PRESS IT IN. DRIZZLE RESERVED CHOCOLATE MIXTURE OVER TOP. COVER AND REFRIGERATE FOR 3 HOURS, THEN LET COME TO ROOM TEMPERATURE FOR 15 MINUTES BEFORE CUTTING INTO SQUARES. MAKES 16 SQUARES.

TIP: SQUARES WILL BECOME A LITTLE SOFT IF LEFT AT ROOM TEMPERATURE FOR MORE THAN 1 HOUR.

APPLE CRANBERRY PIE SQUARES

SHORTBREAD MEETS APPLE CRANBERRY PIE —
A PERFECTLY DELICIOUS COMBINATION.

CRUST

1 CUP	GRANULATED SUGAR	250 ML
3/4 CUP	BUTTER, SOFTENED	175 ML
1 TSP	VANILLA	5 ML
2 CUPS	ALL-PURPOSE FLOUR	500 ML
1/2 TSP	SALT	2 ML

FILLING

2	BAKING APPLES, PEELED AND CUT INTO 1/2-INCH (1 CM) CUBES	2
1/2 CUP	COARSELY CHOPPED FRESH OR FROZEN CRANBERRIES	125 ML
3 TBSP	GRANULATED SUGAR	45 ML
2 TSP	ALL-PURPOSE FLOUR	10 ML
1/2 TSP	GROUND CINNAMON	2 ML
1/4 TSP	FRESHLY GRATED NUTMEG (SEE TIP)	1 ML
1 TSP	LEMON JUICE	5 ML

PREHEAT OVEN TO 375°F (190°C) AND LINE AN 8-INCH (20 CM) SQUARE BAKING PAN WITH PARCHMENT PAPER.

CRUST: IN A LARGE BOWL, USING AN ELECTRIC MIXER, CREAM SUGAR, BUTTER AND VANILLA FOR 3 TO 5 MINUTES OR UNTIL LIGHT AND FLUFFY. ADD FLOUR AND SALT; MIX UNTIL JUST COMBINED (DOUGH WILL BE CRUMBLY). PRESS TWO-THIRDS OF THE DOUGH INTO THE BOTTOM AND ABOUT 1/2 INCH (1 CM) UP THE SIDES OF PREPARED PAN. SET REMAINING DOUGH ASIDE.

FILLING: IN A MEDIUM BOWL, COMBINE APPLES, CRANBERRIES, SUGAR, FLOUR, CINNAMON, NUTMEG AND LEMON JUICE, TOSSING TO COAT. SPREAD EVENLY OVER CRUST. CRUMBLE REMAINING DOUGH OVER TOP. BAKE FOR 45 TO 50 MINUTES OR UNTIL OUTER CRUST IS GOLDEN. LET COOL COMPLETELY IN PAN ON A WIRE RACK BEFORE CUTTING INTO SQUARES. MAKES 16 SQUARES.

TIP: FOR THE APPLES, TRY VARIETIES THAT HOLD THEIR SHAPE WHEN BAKING, SUCH AS GRANNY SMITH, PINK LADY, GALA, BRAEBURN, HONEYCRISP OR CORTLAND.

TIP: USE A NUTMEG GRATER OR RASP TO GRATE WHOLE NUTMEG. FRESHLY GRATED NUTMEG HAS A DELICATE, SWEET FLAVOR THAT IS A WONDERFUL ADDITION TO BAKED GOODS. COMMERCIALLY GROUND NUTMEG CAN SOMETIMES HAVE A SPICIER HEAT THAT COMES ACROSS IN BAKING.

TIP: STORE THESE SQUARES IN AN AIRTIGHT CONTAINER IN THE REFRIGERATOR FOR UP TO 3 DAYS.

COFFEE AND WHITE CHOCOLATE BLONDIES

CREAMY WHITE CHOCOLATE GOES SO WELL WITH COFFEE-FLAVORED BROWNIES, SAYS BRIDGE AUTHOR JULIE VAN ROSENDAAL ABOUT THESE SQUARES.

1 CUP	PACKED LIGHT BROWN (GOLDEN YELLOW) SUGAR	250 ML
2 TSP	INSTANT COFFEE OR ESPRESSO GRANULES	10 ML
1/3 CUP	BUTTER	75 ML
1	LARGE EGG, LIGHTLY BEATEN	1
1 TSP	VANILLA	5 ML
1 CUP	ALL-PURPOSE FLOUR	250 ML
1 TSP	BAKING POWDER	5 ML
1/4 TSP	SALT	1 ML
1/2 CUP	WHITE CHOCOLATE CHIPS OR CHUNKS	125 ML

PREHEAT OVEN TO 350°F (180°C) AND LINE AN 8-INCH (20 CM) SQUARE BAKING PAN WITH PARCHMENT PAPER. IN A SMALL SAUCEPAN OVER MEDIUM HEAT, COMBINE BROWN SUGAR, COFFEE AND BUTTER; COOK, STIRRING OFTEN, UNTIL MELTED AND SMOOTH. TRANSFER TO A LARGE BOWL AND LET COOL SLIGHTLY, THEN STIR IN EGG AND VANILLA UNTIL WELL BLENDED AND SMOOTH. ADD FLOUR, BAKING POWDER AND SALT, STIRRING UNTIL ALMOST COMBINED. STIR IN WHITE CHOCOLATE JUST UNTIL BLENDED. SPREAD BATTER IN PREPARED PAN. BAKE FOR 22 TO 28 MINUTES OR UNTIL EDGES ARE PALE GOLDEN AND JUST STARTING TO PULL AWAY FROM THE SIDES OF THE PAN. LET COOL COMPLETELY IN PAN ON A WIRE RACK BEFORE CUTTING INTO SQUARES. MAKES 16 BLONDIES.

TIP: WHEN IN DOUBT, UNDERBAKE YOUR BLONDIES RATHER THAN OVERBAKE THEM.

TIP: STORE BLONDIE SQUARES IN AIRTIGHT CONTAINERS, BETWEEN LAYERS OF WAXED OR PARCHMENT PAPER, AT ROOM TEMPERATURE FOR UP TO 3 DAYS OR IN THE FREEZER FOR UP TO 2 WEEKS. FOR LONGER FREEZER STORAGE (UP TO I MONTH), CUT THE BLONDIE CAKE INTO QUARTERS AND WRAP IN WAXED PAPER, THEN IN FOIL, BEFORE FREEZING. LET THAW SLIGHTLY, THEN CUT EACH QUARTER INTO 4 SQUARES.

IF THE RECIPE LACKS QUALITY,
IT WILL BE MADE UP IN BUTTER.

SNICKERDOODLE BARS

THESE TENDER BAR COOKIES WILL FILL YOUR HOME WITH THE DELICIOUS AROMA OF CINNAMON.

2 CUPS	GRANULATED SUGAR, DIVIDED	500 ML
1 CUP	BUTTER, SOFTENED	250 ML
2	LARGE EGGS	2
1 TSP	VANILLA	5 ML
3 CUPS	ALL-PURPOSE FLOUR	750 ML
1 1/2 TSP	CREAM OF TARTAR	7 ML
1 TSP	BAKING SODA	5 ML
1/2 TSP	SALT	2 ML
2 1/2 TSP	GROUND CINNAMON, DIVIDED	12 ML
1/4 TSP	GROUND NUTMEG	1 ML

PREHEAT OVEN TO 375°F (190°C) AND LIGHTLY OIL A 13- BY 9-INCH (33 BY 23 CM) PAN. IN A LARGE BOWL, USING AN ELECTRIC MIXER, CREAM 1 3/4 CUPS (425 ML) SUGAR AND BUTTER UNTIL FLUFFY. ADD EGGS, ONE AT A TIME, BEATING WELL AFTER EACH. BEAT IN VANILLA. ADD FLOUR, CREAM OF TARTAR, BAKING SODA, SALT, 1/2 TSP (2 ML) CINNAMON AND NUTMEG, STIRRING UNTIL JUST COMBINED. SCRAPE DOUGH INTO PREPARED PAN AND PRESS GENTLY TO SMOOTH SURFACE. IN A SMALL BOWL, COMBINE REMAINING SUGAR AND CINNAMON; SPRINKLE EVENLY OVER DOUGH. BAKE FOR 25 TO 30 MINUTES OR UNTIL LIGHT GOLDEN BROWN. LET COOL COMPLETELY IN PAN ON A WIRE RACK BEFORE CUTTING INTO BARS. MAKES 20 BARS.

TIP: STORE THESE BARS IN AN AIRTIGHT CONTAINER AT ROOM TEMPERATURE FOR UP TO 1 WEEK OR IN THE FREEZER FOR UP TO 6 MONTHS.

BANANA TOFFEE SNACK CAKE

THIS SNACKING CAKE GIVES YOU A WAY TO USE UP THOSE MUSHY BANANAS.

1¾ CUPS	ALL-PURPOSE FLOUR	425 ML
1 TSP	BAKING SODA	5 ML
½ TSP	BAKING POWDER	2 ML
¼ TSP	SALT	1 ML
¾ CUP	PACKED BROWN SUGAR	175 ML
½ CUP	BUTTER, SOFTENED	125 ML
2	LARGE EGGS	2
2 TSP	VANILLA	10 ML
2	VERY RIPE BANANAS, MASHED	2
¾ CUP	VANILLA-FLAVORED YOGURT	175 ML
½ CUP	TOFFEE CHIPS	125 ML

PREHEAT OVEN TO 350°F (180°C) AND LINE AN 8- OR 9-INCH (20 OR 23 CM) SQUARE BAKING PAN WITH PARCHMENT PAPER. IN A MEDIUM BOWL, WHISK TOGETHER FLOUR, BAKING SODA, BAKING POWDER AND SALT. IN A LARGE BOWL, USING AN ELECTRIC MIXER, CREAM BROWN SUGAR AND BUTTER UNTIL FLUFFY. ADD EGGS, ONE AT A TIME, BEATING WELL AFTER EACH. BEAT IN VANILLA. STIR IN BANANAS AND YOGURT. ADD FLOUR MIXTURE TO BANANA MIXTURE AND STIR TO MOISTEN. FOLD IN TOFFEE CHIPS. SCRAPE BATTER INTO PREPARED PAN. BAKE FOR ABOUT 35 MINUTES OR UNTIL A TESTER INSERTED IN THE CENTER COMES OUT CLEAN. LET COOL IN PAN ON A WIRE RACK. SERVES 16.

TIP: STORE CAKE IN PAN, WRAPPED WITH PLASTIC WRAP, IN THE REFRIGERATOR FOR UP TO 5 DAYS.

POUND CAKE POPS

THE PERFECT WAY TO SURPRISE THE KIDS AFTER DINNER, MAKING WEDNESDAY FEEL LIKE THE WEEKEND!

CREAM CHEESE MAPLE FROSTING

1/4 CUP	BRICK-STYLE CREAM CHEESE	60 ML
1 TBSP	PURE MAPLE SYRUP	15 ML
1 TSP	VANILLA	5 ML
2/3 CUP	POWDERED (ICING) SUGAR	150 ML

CAKE POPS

1	STORE-BOUGHT POUND CAKE (ABOUT 12 OZ/340 G)	1
2 1/2 CUPS	COLORED OR CHOCOLATE CANDY COATING WAFERS	625 ML
	CAKE POP OR LOLLIPOP STICKS	
	SPRINKLES	

FROSTING: IN A BOWL, USING AN ELECTRIC MIXER, BEAT TOGETHER CREAM CHEESE, MAPLE SYRUP AND VANILLA. GRADUALLY ADD POWDERED SUGAR AND BEAT UNTIL FLUFFY AND SMOOTH.

CAKE POPS: BREAK CAKE INTO LARGE PIECES AND PLACE IN A LARGE BOWL. KEEP BREAKING CAKE INTO SMALLER PIECES UNTIL YOU HAVE AN EVEN CRUMB-LIKE TEXTURE (ABOUT 3 CUPS/750 ML). STIR IN FROSTING AND USE YOUR HANDS TO BLEND THOROUGHLY. USING A MINI ICE CREAM SCOOP OR A HEAPING TABLESPOON (15 ML), SCOOP UP CAKE MIXTURE AND ROLL FIRMLY INTO BALLS. PLACE ON A BAKING SHEET AND REFRIGERATE FOR ABOUT 1 HOUR OR UNTIL FIRM.

MEANWHILE, PLACE CANDY WAFERS IN A HEATPROOF BOWL SET OVER HOT (NOT BOILING) WATER AND STIR UNTIL MELTED AND SMOOTH. GENTLY PUSH A CAKE POP STICK ABOUT HALFWAY INTO EACH CAKE POP AND DIP IN MELTED CANDY, TURNING TO COAT EVENLY. DIP IN SPRINKLES AND PLACE ON A PARCHMENT-LINED BAKING SHEET. REFRIGERATE FOR AT LEAST 2 HOURS OR UNTIL SET. MAKES 14 CAKE POPS.

TIP: FOR PERFECTLY ROUND CAKE POPS, SIMPLY PUSH THE STICKS INTO A PIECE OF STYROFOAM AND LET THEM SET STANDING UP.

TIP: STORE CAKE POPS COVERED LIGHTLY WITH PLASTIC WRAP IN THE REFRIGERATOR FOR UP TO 1 WEEK.

THERE IS NOTHING FUN ABOUT FUN-SIZE CANDY BARS.

MOCHA PUDDING CAKE

THIS DESSERT GIVES YOU CAKE ON TOP AND PUDDING ON THE BOTTOM. IT'S DELICIOUS ON ITS OWN, OR YOU CAN DRESS IT UP WITH A DUSTING OF COCOA POWDER AND A SCOOP OF ICE CREAM OR WHIPPED CREAM.

1 CUP	ALL-PURPOSE FLOUR	250 ML
1/4 CUP	UNSWEETENED COCOA POWDER	60 ML
2 TSP	BAKING POWDER	10 ML
1/2 CUP	ALMOND OR HAZELNUT FLOUR	125 ML
1/2 CUP	PACKED BROWN SUGAR	125 ML
1/4 TSP	SALT	1 ML
2	LARGE EGGS, LIGHTLY BEATEN	2
1 CUP	MILK	250 ML
1/4 CUP	CANOLA OIL	60 ML
1 TSP	VANILLA	5 ML

TOPPING

3/4 CUP	PACKED BROWN SUGAR	175 ML
3 TBSP	UNSWEETENED COCOA POWDER	45 ML
3 TBSP	INSTANT COFFEE GRANULES	45 ML
1 1/4 CUPS	HOT WATER	300 ML

PREHEAT OVEN TO 350°F (180°C) AND BUTTER A 9-INCH (23 CM) SQUARE BAKING PAN. IN A LARGE BOWL, SIFT TOGETHER ALL-PURPOSE FLOUR, COCOA AND BAKING POWDER. STIR IN ALMOND FLOUR, BROWN SUGAR AND SALT UNTIL WELL COMBINED. ADD EGGS, MILK, OIL AND VANILLA, STIRRING UNTIL COMBINED. POUR BATTER INTO PREPARED PAN AND PLACE ON A BAKING SHEET.

TOPPING: IN THE SAME BOWL, COMBINE BROWN SUGAR, COCOA, COFFEE AND WATER, STIRRING UNTIL SUGAR IS

DISSOLVED. GENTLY POUR OVER CAKE BATTER; DO NOT STIR. BAKE FOR 30 TO 35 MINUTES OR UNTIL CAKE IS SPRINGY TO THE TOUCH. LET COOL FOR 5 TO 10 MINUTES BEFORE SERVING. SERVES 6 TO 8.

TIP: THE COFFEE GRANULES AND HOT WATER CAN BE REPLACED WITH 1$\frac{1}{4}$ CUPS (300 ML) HOT STRONGLY BREWED COFFEE.

TIP: WRAP AND REFRIGERATE ANY LEFTOVERS FOR UP TO 2 DAYS.

I HATE WHEN I BUY ORGANIC VEGETABLES AND, WHEN I GET HOME, I DISCOVER THEY'RE JUST REGULAR DONUTS.

JULIE'S CHOCOLATE ZUCCHINI SNACK CAKE

BRIDGE AUTHOR JULIE VAN ROSENDAAL LIKES TO USE UP HER SURPLUS OF ZUCCHINI EVERY SUMMER TO MAKE THIS SNACK CAKE TO SHARE WITH NEIGHBORS AND FRIENDS.

2 CUPS	ALL-PURPOSE FLOUR	500 ML
1 1/2 CUPS	GRANULATED SUGAR	375 ML
1/2 CUP	UNSWEETENED COCOA POWDER	125 ML
1 TSP	BAKING POWDER	5 ML
1 TSP	BAKING SODA	5 ML
1/2 TSP	SALT	2 ML
2	LARGE EGGS	2
1 CUP	PLAIN YOGURT OR SOUR CREAM	250 ML
1/4 CUP	CANOLA OIL	60 ML
2 TSP	VANILLA	10 ML
2 CUPS	COARSELY GRATED ZUCCHINI (UNPEELED)	500 ML
1/2 CUP	SEMISWEET CHOCOLATE CHIPS	125 ML

PREHEAT OVEN TO 350°F (180°C) AND LINE A 13- BY 9-INCH (33 BY 23 CM) BAKING PAN WITH PARCHMENT PAPER (OR GREASE IT). IN A LARGE BOWL, WHISK TOGETHER FLOUR, SUGAR, COCOA, BAKING POWDER, BAKING SODA AND SALT. IN A MEDIUM BOWL, WHISK TOGETHER EGGS, YOGURT, OIL AND VANILLA. ADD EGG MIXTURE AND ZUCCHINI TO FLOUR MIXTURE, STIRRING JUST UNTIL INCORPORATED AND THERE ARE NO STREAKS OF FLOUR. FOLD IN CHOCOLATE CHIPS. SCRAPE BATTER INTO PREPARED BAKING PAN. BAKE FOR 30 MINUTES OR UNTIL SPRINGY TO THE TOUCH.

LET COOL COMPLETELY IN PAN ON A WIRE RACK. SERVES 12 TO 16.

TIP: THE BATTER CAN ALSO BE USED TO MAKE 16 CUPCAKES. USE TWO 12-CUP MUFFIN PANS, WITH 16 CUPS LINED WITH PAPER LINERS, AND DIVIDE THE BATTER EVENLY AMONG THE PREPARED MUFFIN CUPS. BAKE FOR 15 TO 20 MINUTES OR UNTIL A TESTER INSERTED IN THE CENTER COMES OUT CLEAN.

TIP: STORE CAKE IN PAN, WRAPPED WITH PLASTIC WRAP, AT ROOM TEMPERATURE FOR UP TO 2 DAYS OR IN THE REFRIGERATOR FOR UP TO 5 DAYS.

I EXERCISE TO STAY HEALTHY.
I BRING CHOCOLATE TO KEEP IT REAL.

EMILY'S FAVORITE CHOCOLATE CUPCAKES

EMILY'S GODSON OSCAR HAS MANY ALLERGIES, AND THESE CUPCAKES HAVE BECOME THE FAMILY GO-TO FOR GET-TOGETHERS AND BIRTHDAY CELEBRATIONS. SPRINKLE WITH COLORED SPRINKLES OR CANDIES AS DESIRED.

I TBSP	GROUND FLAX SEEDS (FLAXSEED MEAL)	15 ML
3 TBSP	COLD WATER	45 ML
I CUP	ALL-PURPOSE FLOUR OR GLUTEN-FREE FLOUR MIX	250 ML
I CUP	GRANULATED SUGAR	250 ML
1/2 CUP	UNSWEETENED COCOA POWDER	125 ML
1/2 TSP	BAKING SODA	2 ML
PINCH	SALT	PINCH
3/4 CUP	HOT WATER	175 ML
1/3 CUP	CANOLA OIL	75 ML
2 TSP	VANILLA	10 ML

VANILLA BUTTER ICING

2 CUPS	POWDERED (ICING) SUGAR	500 ML
1/2 CUP	BUTTER, SOFTENED	125 ML
I TBSP	HEAVY OR WHIPPING (35%) CREAM (APPROX.)	15 ML
I TSP	VANILLA	5 ML

PREHEAT OVEN TO 375°F (190°C) AND PLACE PAPER LINERS IN A 12-CUP MUFFIN PAN. IN A SMALL BOWL, STIR TOGETHER FLAX SEEDS AND COLD WATER; LET STAND FOR 5 MINUTES OR UNTIL THICKENED. IN A LARGE BOWL, WHISK TOGETHER FLOUR, SUGAR, COCOA, BAKING SODA AND SALT. WHISK IN FLAXSEED MIXTURE, HOT

WATER, OIL AND VANILLA UNTIL WELL COMBINED. DIVIDE BATTER EVENLY AMONG MUFFIN CUPS. BAKE FOR ABOUT 15 MINUTES OR UNTIL A TESTER INSERTED IN THE CENTER OF A CUPCAKE COMES OUT CLEAN. LET COOL COMPLETELY IN PAN ON A WIRE RACK BEFORE ICING.

ICING: IN A BOWL, USING AN ELECTRIC MIXER, BEAT POWDERED SUGAR, BUTTER, CREAM AND VANILLA, ADDING MORE CREAM AS NECESSARY AND BEATING UNTIL CREAMY AND SMOOTH. SPREAD OVER CUPCAKES. MAKES 12 CUPCAKES.

TIP: STORE CUPCAKES (WITHOUT ICING) IN A LARGE, STURDY AIRTIGHT CONTAINER AT ROOM TEMPERATURE FOR UP TO 1 WEEK. STORE ICED CUPCAKES LIGHTLY COVERED WITH PLASTIC WRAP IN THE REFRIGERATOR FOR UP TO 2 DAYS.

DAIRY-FREE ICING VARIATION: REPLACE THE BUTTER WITH VEGAN BUTTER SUBSTITUTE AND SUBSTITUTE ALMOND MILK FOR THE CREAM.

BANANA BLUEBERRY MUFFINS

THESE DELICIOUS MUFFINS ARE EXTRA-LARGE, SO BE
SURE TO USE THE LARGEST PAPER LINERS YOU CAN
FIND, TO PREVENT THE BATTER FROM OVERFLOWING.
WE'VE INCLUDED A TIP ON MAKING YOUR OWN
TULIP-SHAPED LINERS OUT OF PARCHMENT PAPER!

I CUP	ALL-PURPOSE FLOUR	250 ML
I CUP	WHOLE WHEAT FLOUR	250 ML
I TSP	BAKING POWDER	5 ML
1/2 TSP	BAKING SODA	2 ML
1/2 TSP	SALT	2 ML
1/2 TSP	GROUND CINNAMON	2 ML
3/4 CUP	PACKED BROWN SUGAR	175 ML
2	LARGE EGGS	2
1 1/2 CUPS	MASHED BANANAS (ABOUT 3 MEDIUM)	375 ML
1/2 CUP	PLAIN YOGURT	125 ML
1/3 CUP	CANOLA OIL	75 ML
I CUP	FRESH OR FROZEN BLUEBERRIES	250 ML

PREHEAT OVEN TO 375°F (190°C) AND PLACE PAPER LINERS
IN A 12-CUP MUFFIN PAN. IN A LARGE BOWL, COMBINE
ALL-PURPOSE FLOUR, WHOLE WHEAT FLOUR, BAKING
POWDER, BAKING SODA, SALT AND CINNAMON. IN A
MEDIUM BOWL, BEAT BROWN SUGAR, EGGS, BANANAS,
YOGURT AND OIL UNTIL WELL COMBINED. ADD BANANA
MIXTURE TO FLOUR MIXTURE AND STIR JUST UNTIL
COMBINED. GENTLY FOLD IN BLUEBERRIES. DIVIDE
BATTER EVENLY AMONG MUFFIN CUPS. BAKE FOR 20
TO 25 MINUTES OR UNTIL A TESTER INSERTED IN THE
CENTER OF A MUFFIN COMES OUT CLEAN. LET COOL IN

PAN ON A WIRE RACK FOR 5 MINUTES, THEN TRANSFER MUFFINS TO RACK TO COOL. MAKES 12 MUFFINS.

TIP: TO MAKE TULIP-SHAPED PARCHMENT LINERS, CUT TWELVE 6-INCH (15 CM) SQUARES OF PARCHMENT PAPER. MOLD EACH SQUARE OVER A TOMATO-PASTE-SIZE CAN OR A DRINKING GLASS THAT IS ABOUT THE SAME SIZE AS A MUFFIN CUP.

TIP: AN ICE CREAM SCOOP IS HELPFUL IN PORTIONING THE BATTER INTO EACH LINER.

TIP: STORE COOLED MUFFINS IN AN AIRTIGHT CONTAINER AT ROOM TEMPERATURE FOR UP TO 1 DAY OR WRAP EACH MUFFIN IN PLASTIC WRAP AND FREEZE IN AN AIRTIGHT CONTAINER FOR UP TO 2 WEEKS.

MARK'S FAVORITE QUICK CINNAMON ROLLS

IF YEASTED CINNAMON ROLLS AND BAKING POWDER BISCUITS HAD A CHILD, THIS WOULD BE THE RESULT, AND SYLVIA'S NEIGHBOR MARK SAYS THEY ARE SOME OF THE BEST CINNAMON ROLLS HE'S EVER HAD. THESE SWEET TREATS TASTE BEST WARM.

FILLING

1/4 CUP	GRANULATED SUGAR	60 ML
1/4 CUP	PACKED BROWN SUGAR	60 ML
2 TSP	GROUND CINNAMON	10 ML
1/4 TSP	GROUND NUTMEG	1 ML
PINCH	SALT	PINCH
1/4 CUP	MELTED BUTTER	60 ML

ROLLS

3 CUPS	ALL-PURPOSE FLOUR	750 ML
2 TBSP	GRANULATED SUGAR	30 ML
1 TBSP	BAKING POWDER	15 ML
1/4 TSP	SALT	1 ML
3/4 CUP	COLD BUTTER, CUBED	175 ML
1	LARGE EGG	1
3/4 CUP	MILK	175 ML

ICING

8 OZ	BRICK-STYLE CREAM CHEESE, SOFTENED	250 G
2 TBSP	BUTTER, SOFTENED	30 ML
1/2 TSP	VANILLA	2 ML
1 CUP	POWDERED (ICING) SUGAR (APPROX.)	250 ML

FILLING: IN A MEDIUM BOWL, COMBINE ALL INGREDIENTS; SET ASIDE.

ROLLS: PREHEAT OVEN TO 425°F (220°C) AND LIGHTLY OIL A 9-INCH (23 CM) SQUARE BAKING PAN OR DEEP-DISH PIE PLATE. IN A LARGE BOWL, COMBINE FLOUR, SUGAR, BAKING POWDER AND SALT. USING A PASTRY CUTTER OR TWO KNIVES, CUT IN BUTTER UNTIL IT RESEMBLES COARSE CRUMBS. IN A SMALL BOWL, WHISK TOGETHER EGG AND MILK; POUR OVER FLOUR MIXTURE AND STIR GENTLY UNTIL JUST COMBINED. TURN DOUGH OUT ONTO A LIGHTLY FLOURED SURFACE, PRESS AND FOLD A FEW TIMES, THEN ROLL OUT INTO A 14- BY 12-INCH (35 BY 30 CM) RECTANGLE. SPREAD FILLING OVER DOUGH, THEN ROLL TIGHTLY INTO A LOG. PINCH THE EDGE OF THE ROLL TO SEAL. CUT CROSSWISE INTO 9 EQUAL PIECES AND PLACE IN PREPARED PAN. BAKE FOR 20 TO 25 MINUTES OR UNTIL GOLDEN BROWN.

ICING: MEANWHILE, IN A LARGE BOWL, CREAM TOGETHER CREAM CHEESE, BUTTER AND VANILLA. GRADUALLY BEAT IN SUGAR UNTIL SMOOTH AND SPREADABLE, ADDING MORE SUGAR IF ICING IS TOO THIN. SPREAD OVER WARM BUNS. MAKES 9 ROLLS.

TIP: THESE CINNAMON ROLLS ARE BEST THE DAY THEY ARE BAKED.

MAPLE GRANOLA APPLE CRISP

*WE ALL LOVE APPLE CRISP, AND MAPLE SYRUP
ADDS ANOTHER LAYER OF DELICIOUS FLAVOR.
SERVE WARM WITH ICE CREAM OR WHIPPED CREAM.*

1 TBSP	CORNSTARCH	15 ML
1 TSP	GROUND CINNAMON	5 ML
1/4 TSP	GROUND NUTMEG	1 ML
PINCH	SALT	PINCH
3	TART APPLES (SUCH AS GRANNY SMITH, JONATHAN OR MCINTOSH), PEELED AND SLICED	3
2	SWEET APPLES (SUCH AS GALA, AMBROSIA OR FUJI), PEELED AND SLICED	2
1/2 CUP	PURE MAPLE SYRUP	125 ML
3/4 CUP	LARGE-FLAKE (OLD-FASHIONED) ROLLED OATS	175 ML
1/2 CUP	ALL-PURPOSE FLOUR	125 ML
1/4 CUP	GRANULATED MAPLE SUGAR OR PACKED BROWN SUGAR	60 ML
1/4 CUP	CHOPPED WALNUTS OR PECANS	60 ML
1/2 CUP	CANOLA OIL	125 ML

PREHEAT OVEN TO 375°F (190°C). IN A LARGE BOWL, COMBINE CORNSTARCH, CINNAMON, NUTMEG AND SALT. ADD TART AND SWEET APPLES, TOSSING TO COAT. DRIZZLE WITH MAPLE SYRUP AND STIR TO COMBINE. ARRANGE APPLES IN A 9-INCH (23 CM) DEEP-DISH PIE PLATE OR SQUARE BAKING DISH. IN A MEDIUM BOWL, STIR TOGETHER OATS, FLOUR, SUGAR, NUTS AND OIL; SPRINKLE OVER APPLES. BAKE FOR 45 TO 50 MINUTES OR UNTIL TOP IS GOLDEN AND FRUIT IS TENDER. LET COOL SLIGHTLY ON A WIRE RACK BEFORE SERVING. SERVES 6 TO 8.

QUICK CARAMEL TARTS

THIS SPEEDY DESSERT IS SO SIMPLE, AND YOU CAN KEEP THE INGREDIENTS ON HAND TO WHIP UP ANYTIME!

18	FROZEN MINI TART SHELLS	18
1/4 CUP	CURRANTS, RAISINS OR CHOPPED PECANS	60 ML
1	LARGE EGG	1
1 CUP	CARAMEL OR BUTTERSCOTCH SAUCE	250 ML

PREHEAT OVEN TO 450°F (230°C). PLACE TART SHELLS ON A BAKING SHEET AND SPRINKLE CURRANTS INTO BOTTOMS OF SHELLS. IN A BOWL, WHISK EGG UNTIL FROTHY. WHISK IN CARAMEL SAUCE UNTIL SMOOTH AND WELL COMBINED. SPOON INTO TART SHELLS. BAKE FOR ABOUT 10 MINUTES OR UNTIL PASTRY IS LIGHT GOLDEN. LET COOL COMPLETELY ON PAN ON A WIRE RACK BEFORE SERVING. MAKES 18 MINI TARTS.

TIP: STORE TARTS IN AN AIRTIGHT CONTAINER AT ROOM TEMPERATURE FOR UP TO 3 DAYS.

VARIATION: OMIT THE CURRANTS AND CARAMEL SAUCE. USING AN ELECTRIC MIXER, BEAT EGG WITH 1/2 CUP (125 ML) EACH MASCARPONE CHEESE AND CHOCOLATE HAZELNUT SPREAD (SUCH AS NUTELLA). FILL SHELLS AND BAKE AT 400°F (200°C) FOR ABOUT 12 MINUTES.

INDEX

Library and Archives Canada Cataloguing in Publication

Best of Bridge weekday suppers : all-new easy everyday recipes.

Includes index.
"Text copyright ©2018 Sylvia Kong and Emily Richards."—Title page verso.
ISBN 978-0-7788-0610-3 (spiral bound)

 1. Suppers. 2. Cookbooks. I. Kong, Sylvia, 1963-, author
II. Richards, Emily, author III. Title: Weekday suppers.

TX738.B49 2018   641.5'3   C2018-903467-X